Ancient Judaism in its Hellenistic Context

Supplements

to the

Journal for the Study of Judaism

Editor

John J. Collins
The Divinity School, Yale University

Associate Editor

Florentino García Martínez
Qumran Institute, University of Groningen

Advisory Board

J. DUHAIME — A. HILHORST — P.W. VAN DER HORST

A. KLOSTERGAARD PETERSEN — M.A. KNIBB — J.T.A.G.M. VAN RUITEN

J. SIEVERS — G. STEMBERGER — E.J.C. TIGCHELAAR — J. TROMP

VOLUME 95

Ancient Judaism in its Hellenistic Context

Edited by

Carol Bakhos

BRILL

LEIDEN • BOSTON

2005

This book is printed on acid-free paper.

Library of Congress Cataloging-in-Publication Data

Detailed Library of Congress Cataloging-in-Publication
data are available on the Internet at http:catalog.loc.gov.
LC Control Number: 2004058524

DS
121.7
.A53
2004

ISSN 1384–2161
ISBN 90 04 138714

CONTENTS

ACKNOWLEDGEMENTS

We would like to thank the UCLA Center for Jewish Studies for organizing the conference, especially Ken Reinhard and his staff, Susan Spitzer and Vivian Holenbeck. We would also like to extend our gratitude to the conference participants: John Collins, Eric Gruen, Martin Goodman, Martha Himmelfarb, Hava Tirosh-Samuelson, Norbert Samuelson, Menachem Lorberbaum, Gregory Sterling, Claudia Setzer, Leora Batnitzky, Peter Gordon and Samuel Moyn. Their stimulating presentations and camaraderie during the course of the conference made for a most rewarding experience. And finally, many thanks to Maccabee Avishur and Elliot Martin for their help in editing this volume.

INTRODUCTION

> I will bend Judah as I bend my bow and fill it
> with Ephraim. I will rouse your sons, O Zion,
> against your sons, O Greece, and make you like a
> warrior's sword.
>
> Zechariah 9:13

> Are we Greeks? Are we Jews? We live in the
> difference between the Jew and the Greek, which
> is perhaps the unity of what is called history.
>
> Jacques Derrida,
Violence and Metaphysics

The encounter of Judaism and Hellenism has engaged the minds of
some of the finest scholars of the ancient world over the last century. The names of Elias Bickerman, Victor Tcherikover and Martin
Hengel come to mind.[1] In recent years there has again been an upsurge of interest in this encounter, focusing especially on the issue of
Jewish identity in the Hellenistic world.[2] The problems that confronted
Judaism in antiquity are hauntingly similar to those that confront it

---

[1] Elias Bickerman, *Der Gott der Makkabäer: Untersuchungen über Sinn und Ursprung der makkäischen Erhebung* (Berlin: Schocken, 1937); English trans. by H. R. Moehring, *The God of the Maccabees: Studies on the Meaning and Origin of the Maccabean Revolt* (Leiden: E.J. Brill, 1979); Victor Tcherikover, *Hellenistic Civilization and the Jews* (reprinted ed. Peabody, Mass.: Hendrickson Publishers, 1999) and M. Hengel, *Judentum und Hellenismus: Studien zu ihrer Begegnung unter besonderer Berücksichtigung Palästinas bis zur Mitte des 2 Jh.s. v.Chr.* (Tübingen: Mohr / Siebeck, 1973); English trans. by J. Bowden, *Judaism and Hellenism: Studies in their Encounter in Palestine during the Early Hellenistic Period* (one vol. ed. Philadelphia: Fortress Press, 1981).

[2] See, for example, Eric Gruen, *Heritage and Hellenism: The Reinvention of Jewish Tradition* (Berkeley: University of California Press, 1998), John J. Collins, *Between Athens and Jerusalem: Jewish Identity in the Hellenistic Diaspora*, (revised ed. Grand Rapids: Eerdmans, 2000), John J. Collins, and Greg E. Sterling, eds., *Hellenism in the Land of Israel*, (Notre Dame: University of Notre Dame Press, 2001), John M. G. Barclay, *Jews in the Mediterranean Diaspora from Alexander to Trajan (323 B.C.E.–117 C.E.)* (Edinburgh: Clark, 1996), Lee I. Levine, *Judaism and Hellenism in Antiquity: Conflict or Confluence* (Seattle, Wash: University of Washington, 1998), James L. Kugel, ed., *Shem in the Tents of Japhet*: Essays on the Encounter of Judaism and Hellenism (Leiden: E.J. Brill, 2002).

in modern culture[3] or, for that matter, to those that confront any minority religion absorbed in a greater society that is at once attractive and alien. Scholars today more than ever have noted the "irreducible complexities"[4] that both Judaism and Hellenism present in the ancient world, and have thus demonstrated the need to abandon the image of Judaism standing over against Hellenism, an image that misconceives of the process by which to varying degrees Judaism adapted to cultural, social and political hegemony. Rather than starkly casting the issue as a dilemma between resistance to Hellenism, resulting in an unadulterated adherence to Jewish tradition, or a binge imbibition of Hellenistic ways, leading to a diluted, inauthentic Judaism, we should embrace an image of a minority people encountering an imperial power whose forces extend beyond governance and into the realm of social and cultural intercourse. This encounter led not to a conscious struggle with alien forces but rather in many instances to an active re-tailoring and re-shaping of tradition in light of their material, ideological and philosophical surroundings. That is to say, the Jews maintained their identity by adapting the trappings, again to varying degrees, of their *milieu*. As Erich Gruen writes:

> Numerous studies have traced the impact of Greek institutions, language, literature, philosophy, historiography, art, material culture, and even religion upon Judaism. The registering of such influences, however, can leave the impression of a somewhat passive receptivity or compliant adjustment on the part of Jewish thinkers to Hellenic culture. . . . Jews engaged actively with the traditions of Hellas, adapting genres and transforming legends to articulate their own legacy in modes congenial to a Hellenistic setting. At the same time they recreated their past, retold stories in different shapes, and amplified the scriptural corpus itself through the medium of the Greek language and Greek literary forms. In a world where Hellenic culture held an ascendant position, Jews strained to develop their own cultural self-definition, one that would give them a place within the broader Mediterranean world and would also establish their distinctiveness. Those twin objectives operated conjointly.[5]

---

[3] Jacob Shavit, *Athens in Jerusalem: Classical Antiquity and Hellenism in the Making of the Modern Secular Jew*, C. Naor and N. Werner, trans. (London: Mitchell, 1997).

[4] Dale B. Martin, "Paul and the Judaism/Hellenism Dichotomy: Toward a Social History of the Question," in *Paul Beyond the Judaism/Hellenism Divide*, ed. T. Engberg-Pedersen (Louisville: Westminster John Knox Press, 2001) 30.

[5] *Heritage and Hellenism*, xv.

The essays of this collection attempt to explore the ways in which Jews lived within the Hellenistic and Greco-Roman contexts, and how they negotiated their religious and social boundaries in their own distinctive manner. The volume had its origins in a conference, "Jewish Civilization between Athens and Jerusalem," held at the University of California, Los Angeles in June 2003. With the support of the National Endowment for the Humanities, the UCLA Center for Jewish Studies sponsored the three-day conference, the second of a three-year colloquium on Jewish Civilization and Its Discontents, which was convened by the then director of the Center, Ken Reinhard, William Schneidewind, Chair of Near Eastern Languages and Cultures, and myself. Of the articles in this volume, the following were presented at the conference: Eric Gruen, "Greeks and Jews: Mutual Misperceptions," Martha Himmelfarb, "The Torah Between Athens and Jerusalem," Gregory Sterling, " 'The Jewish Philosophy': The Presence of Hellenistic Philosophy in Jewish Exegesis in the Second Temple Period," and Claudia Setzer, " 'Talking Their Way into Empire': Jews, Christians, and Pagans Debate Resurrection of the Body."[6] John Collins gave the keynote address, "Hellenistic Judaism in Recent Scholarship."[7] The other papers were as follows: Hava Tirosh-Samuelson, "Happiness in Medieval Jewish Philosophy: Between Athens and Jerusalem," Norbert Samuelson, "Maimonides' Intellectual Integrity: A Critical Study of Ralbag's and Leo Strauss' Criticism of the Guide in the Comparative Light of Rabad's Exalted Faith," Menahem Loberbaum, "Basic Paradigms of Medieval Jewish Thought," Leora Batnitzky, "Leo Strauss Between Athens and Jerusalem," Peter Gordon, "Ataraxia and Utopia: Franz Rosenzweig Between Judaism and Stoicism," and Samuel Moyn, " 'If there is a God, We will Describe Him': Strauss, Levinas, Athens, and Jerusalem."

By bringing together major scholars in the fields of ancient, medieval and modern Judaism, the conference examined both historical and theoretical accounts of the relationship between "Athens" and "Jerusalem," between Reason and Faith, philosophy and prophecy, *logos and nomos*.

---

[6] Richard Kalmin was scheduled to present his paper, "Between Rome and Mesopotamia: Sadducees in Sasanian Persia" but due to unforeseen circumstances, he was unable to attend the conference.

[7] Collins' address will be published in A. J. Avery-Peck, W. S. Green and J. Neusner, eds., Encyclopaedia of Judaism, Supplement 2 (Leiden: Brill).

The articles in this volume, although devoted solely to the ancient period, nonetheless reflect many of the fundamental issues that emerge when we study the development of several aspects of Judaism through the ages in light of broad cultural, social, political and philosophical phenomena. Again, the question is no longer whether or not, but rather how non-Jewish stimuli affected Judaism internally, and in turn how Judaism participated in the intricacies of its intellectual, religious and social surroundings.

The collection, which distinctively includes articles on the late antique period, begins with an essay, "Anti-Semitism in Antiquity? The Case of Alexandria,"[8] by John Collins who discusses the Alexandrian riots of 38 C.E. as a test case for whether we can speak of anti-Semitism in antiquity. Collins argues that these riots must be understood in the very specific context of Egypt under Roman rule. While they bear unfortunate analogies to later pogroms, it is not helpful to posit an ahistorical virus of anti-Semitism that is always and ever the same.

In the second essay, contrary to the generally held view that Josephus' *Contra Apionem* is a rich repository of information of Hellenistic attitudes toward Jews, Erich Gruen contends that it is a fabricated clash between Athens and Jerusalem. That is to say, it is a creative attempt on the part of Josephus to respond to personal attacks for his previously published works. Josephus, according to Gruen, delved into his treasure trove of texts in search of the most ludicrous claims against Jews, in order to build straw men to rebut with aplomb. Gruen therefore calls into question the reading of *Contra Apionem* for its value in understanding attitudes of learned Hellenes toward Jews, and provides a nuanced perspective, not only of the work itself, but also of the relationship between Judaism and Hellenism.

The third essay by Seth Schwartz, which was not presented at the conference, changes the focus to the land of Israel, and is a study of the social history of Hebrew language in antiquity. Drawing primarily on his basic approach in "Language, Power and Identity in Ancient Palestine,"[9] he argues that there were four stages in the social history of Hebrew. Schwartz outlines and to some extent details the four stages, but his paper concentrates on the first two, high-

---

[8] The essay was originally presented at a conference at Ohio State University on "Persecution and Conflict in Ancient Mediterranean Religions" in October 2003.

[9] "Language, Power and Identity in Ancient Palestine," in *Past and Present* 148 (1995).

lighting the complexity of the connections between the use of Hebrew in late antiquity and social, cultural and political history. In the first stage, lasting until c. 300 B.C.E., Hebrew was commonly spoken by Israelites/Jews in Palestine. This fact, however, played a minor role in the construction of their group identity, a role unlike the essential role Greek played in maintaining corporate identity certainly by the fifth century B.C.E. Even though in the second stage (300 B.C.E. to 70 C.E.) Aramaic became the commonly spoken language, Hebrew nonetheless played an important role as the language of the Jerusalem temple and of the Torah. The third stage is marked by a decline in practical importance of Hebrew, although it retained at least in some circles its symbolic power. Finally in the fourth stage, the middle of the fourth century to the seventh, Hebrew experienced a revival as a result of the limited religious autonomy of the Jews.

Brent Nongbri's essay, also not presented at the conference, offers a fresh approach to understanding the motivations of the Maccabees who are often depicted as a pious family fighting to preserve the laws of their ancestors. The Maccabees were like others who struggled to gain authority in Jerusalem by means of political alliances as well as by the power of rhetoric, that is, by evoking the need to preserve ancestral traditions, similar to the appeals to the *patrios politeia* evoked in Athens in 411 and 404 B.C.E. In his attempt to shed light on the Maccabean motivations, Nongbri discards the fallacious dichotomy between political and religious, thus putting in bold relief the interplay between these seemingly separate realms.

In "Torah Between Athens and Jerusalem: Jewish Difference," Martha Himmelfarb takes Bickerman's view as her starting point, namely that the Jews, like the Romans succeeded in sustaining a sense of identity despite their encounter with Hellenism. She attributes Judaism's unusual success to its possession of a single document, the Torah, which enabled the Jews to adapt Greek culture in a variety of ways unlike other people of the ancient near east. The Torah qua document, including an elaborate account of Israel's formation and its liberation from Egyptian bondage, is a full-scale narrative replete with law that thus reinforces its authority as a vital institution of the Hellenistic period. That *Jubilees* and the *Temple Scroll* unabashedly improve on the version of the Torah, Himmelfarb argues, is recognition of its special status. The possession of the Torah furthermore enables Philo of Alexandria and Josephus to adapt Greek ideas and values in the service of a new, yet distinctively Jewish, understanding. The Torah therefore is that which makes Judaism's encounter with Hellenism unique, for it both provides a means for stability and adaptability, continuity and change.

In the sixth essay of the volume, Gregory Sterling illustrates the many ways in which Hellenistic philosophy and Jewish thought shared overlapping interests in the areas of theology, creation and ethics. His elaborate examination of some of the exegetical traditions of Second Temple Jewish literature, such as the works of Philo, Josephus, *4 Maccabees* and *2 Enoch*, for example, lead him to conclude that Hellenistic philosophy influenced Jewish ethics more than it did speculations about God or creation, and that this influence which had wide circulation should be taken seriously.

In the next essay, Claudia Setzer draws our attention to the ways in which both Jews and early Christians use belief in the resurrection in order to maintain group identity. The two groups, however, employ different rhetorical strategies. The rabbis exploit difference in their attempt to distinguish themselves from Epicureans, whereas in an effort to dilute difference, Christian apologists exploit sameness. In both cases, belief in resurrection is essential to both arguments, but this belief is used differently in order to maintain group boundaries, however fixed or flexible those boundaries may have been. In pointing to the ways discourse is used to both attenuate and reinforce difference, Setzer's essay underscores the ways in which Hellenistic philosophy is woven into both rabbinic and early Christian thought.

In "Jews and Judaism in the Mediterranean Diaspora in the Late-Roman Period: The Limitations of Evidence,"[10] Martin Goodman argues for the importance of studying diaspora Judaism of this period separately from religion of Jews in the land of Israel. Despite factors such as geographical and economic constraints on all Jewish communities, and the common role Torah played in the lives of all Mediterranean Jews, factors that allow for continuity, the Jews' religious geography, the center of which is the Holy of Holies in the Jerusalem Temple, must give way to significant differences between the religious outlook of those in the homeland and of those in the diaspora. In evaluating the archeological and literary evidence before us, Goodman's article explores the relationship between the two com-

---

[10] First published in the *Journal of Meidterranean Studies* 4 (1994) 208–24. Reprinted here with the author's additional comments.

munities and especially highlights the ways such evidence sheds light on the Jewry of the diaspora in the late Roman period. Moreover, Goodman's article draws our attention to the interplay between practice and belief, and notions of insider and outsider in trying to make sense of Jewish identity in late antiquity.

In its examination of the Sadducees in both the rabbinic and Josephan traditions, "Between Rome and Mesopotamia: Sadducees in Sasanian Persia," by Richard Kalmin, this final essay of the collection draws our attention to the cultural ties between Rome and Mesopotamia, which should be considered in addition to the relationship between Athens and Jerusalem. Marshalling several examples of parallels between Josephus or Josephan traditions, Kalmin argues for the possibility of the introduction into Babylonia of these traditions during the mid-fourth century, for it was during this period, namely the fourth Amoraic generation, that the Josephan characterization of the Sadducees achieved currency in Babylonia. Kalmin's work is highly suggestive of the need to look at ways in which the rabbis of the "west," that is Palestinian traditions made their way to Babylonia.

Carol Bakhos
Los Angeles, California 2004

ANTI-SEMITISM IN ANTIQUITY?
THE CASE OF ALEXANDRIA

JOHN J. COLLINS*

I. THE RIOTS IN ALEXANDRIA

In 38 C.E., an incident occurred in Alexandria that is often described as the first pogrom.[1] When Agrippa, the grandson of King Herod who had just been given the rank of king by Caligula,[2] stopped in Alexandria on his way back from Rome, an Alexandrian mob staged a mime in the gymnasium mocking him, and proceeded to call for the installation of images in the synagogues. The demand was accepted and implemented by the governor Flaccus. A few days later, Flaccus issued a proclamation in which the Jews were declared to be foreigners and aliens. Then, according to Philo, who is our only source for these events, he permitted the mob "to pillage the Jews as at the sacking of a city," (*Flacc.* 54). Whereas Jews had previously occupied two of the city's five districts, and some also lived in the others, they were now herded into a very small part of one. Their houses and places of business were ransacked. Those who ventured outside this ghetto were attacked, beaten and murdered. Some were burnt to death in the middle of the city. Others were dragged and trampled. Relatives who tried to intervene were arrested and tortured, and in some cases crucified. Then Flaccus arrested 39 members of the Jewish gerousia, and had them flogged in the theater, so that some of them died. To add insult to injury, they were beaten with the kind of whip usually used on Egyptians, rather than with the flat blade used on Alexandrians. Flaccus then had his soldiers search

---

* Yale University.

[1] The details are supplied by Philo in his treatise *In Flaccum*. See now Pieter W. van der Horst, *Philo's Flaccus. The First Pogrom. Introduction, Translation and Commentary* (Leiden: Brill, 2003).

[2] On Agrippa, see Emil Schürer, *The History of the Jewish People in the Time of Jesus Christ* (revised and edited by Geza Vermes and Fergus Millar; Edinburgh: Clark, 1973) 1.442–54; Daniel R. Schwartz, *Agrippa* I: *The Last King of Judaea* (Tübingen: Mohr-Siebeck, 1990).

the houses of the Jews for arms. The violence was finally interrupted when Flaccus was arrested and taken off to Rome. There, we are told, the leaders of the Alexandrian mob, the very people Flaccus had sought to conciliate, appeared to accuse him before the emperor.

At this point the focus shifted to Rome. Both Jews and Alexandrians sent delegations to Caligula, but neither got much satisfaction. The Jewish delegation was led by the philosopher Philo, who has left us an account in his *Legatio ad Gaium*.[3] According to Josephus, the Alexandrian delegation included the grammarian and Homeric scholar Apion (*Ant.* 18.257). The emperor did not even give them his attention. At one point he asked the Jewish delegation about their civic rights but then did not allow them to answer (*Leg.* 363). The Jews were relieved when he finally dismissed them as "unfortunate rather than wicked" and foolish for refusing to believe in his divinity (Leg. 367). They must have been further relieved when Caligula was assassinated. At this point, Josephus tells us that the Jews in Alexandria took heart again and at once armed themselves (Ant. 19.278). The new emperor, Claudius, however, took the matter in hand. He instructed the prefect of Egypt to restore order, and ruled on the issues in dispute in a letter to the Alexandrians.[4]

As Erich Gruen has recently emphasized, this calamitous incident lacked all precedent.[5] There had been a substantial Jewish community in Alexandria for more than 300 years, and they had never been subjected to attack like this. There are to be sure literary works that describe threats of violence to Diaspora Jews. The oldest of these, the Book of Esther, comes from the eastern Diaspora, but in

---

[3] For commentary see E. Mary Smallwood, *Philonis Alexandrini Legatio ad Gaium* (Leiden: Brill, 1961).

[4] The letter is preserved on papyrus (CPJ 153). The edict preserved by Josephus in Ant. 19.280–85 is quite different from the authentic letter found on papyrus. See Miriam Pucci ben Zeev, *Jewish Rights in the Roman World* (Tübingen: Mohr-Siebeck, 1998) 295–327. Pucci ben Zeev defends the authenticity of the edict, arguing that it was issued before the renewal of hostilities. The resumption then provoked the letter, which was less sympathetic to the Jews. But as Tcherikover remarked, every attempt to defend the authenticity of the edict in Ant. 19.280–85 "encounters numerous difficulties." (*Hellenistic Civilization and the Jews* [Peabody, MA: Hendrickson, 1999, reprint of 1959 edition by the Jewish Publication Society] 414). It is not apparent why the Jews should have renewed hostilities if Claudius had already issued a favorable edict.

[5] Erich Gruen, *Diaspora: Jews amidst Greeks and Romans* (Cambridge, MA: Harvard, 2002) 67.

one recension of the Greek translation Haman is called a Macedonian.[6] 3 Maccabees recounts a threat to the Jewish community in the time of Ptolemy IV Philopator, allegedly arising from the King's promotion of the cult of Dionysus. Josephus has a very similar story, but sets it in the time of Ptolemy VIII Physcon (*C. Ap.* 2.49–56). The story is evidently legendary, and no historical reconstruction can be based on it.[7] Stories such as Esther and 3 Maccabees are significant insofar as they reflect the fears of Jewish communities in the Gentile world, but even in these stories the calamity is always averted.

There were also precedents for actual attacks on Jews by Gentiles. In Egypt, we have the case of the Jewish community at Elephantine, whose temple was destroyed by the local Egyptians at the end of the fifth century.[8] This incident, in fact, bears some similarity to the one in Alexandria. A local mob prevailed on the governor to allow them to demolish the Jewish temple. The governor was subsequently removed. In this case the Jewish practice of sacrificing lambs was most probably offensive to the local priests of the ram-god Khnum. There was also resentment on the part of Egyptian nationalists towards the Jews, because of their loyalty to the Persians. But while the situation in Elephantine is analogous to that in Alexandria to some degree, there was no real continuity between the two events. There were also significant differences in the situations. The attacks in Alexandria were directed much more broadly against a larger Jewish population, and the specific issues were different. The anomaly of the events in Alexandria remains.

It is unfortunate that we have only one account of the actual events, Philo's treatise against Flaccus, and it makes no pretence of objectivity. Philo treats the life of Flaccus as a moral fable: Flaccus

---

[6] Addition A 17, at Esth 3:1. Carey A. Moore, *Daniel, Esther and Jeremiah. The Additions* (AB 44; New York: Doubleday, 1977) 174.

[7] See further John J. Collins, *Between Athens and Jerusalem: Jewish Identity in the Hellenistic Diaspora* (Grand Rapids: Eerdmans, 2000) 122–31; Erich Gruen, *Heritage and Hellenism* (Berkeley: University of California, 1998) 222–36; John M. G. Barclay, *Jews in the Mediterranean Diaspora from Alexander to Trajan (323 B.C.E.–117 C.E.)* (Edinburgh: Clark, 1996) 192–203.

[8] Pierre Briant, *From Cyrus to Alexander: A History of the Persian Empire* (Winona Lake, IN: Eisenbrauns, 2002) 603–7; "Une curieuse affaire à Éléphantine en 410 av. n. è.: Widranga, le sanctuaire de Khnûm et le temple de Yahweh," *Méditerranées* 6 (1996) 115–35; Joseph Mélèze Modrzejewski, *The Jews of Egypt from Rameses II to Emperor Hadrian* (Princeton: Princeton University Press, 1995) 21–44.

himself supposedly recognizes that his eventual downfall is punishment from the Most High for his crimes against the Jews (*Flacc.*
170–75). It is difficult to believe that the Jews were as passive as
Philo portrays them. The arrest of their leaders, and the search for
arms in the Jewish community, strongly suggests that there was resistance, and Josephus refers explicitly to Jewish arms when the violence was resumed after the death of Caligula. The action that
precipitated the violence was the installation of images in the synagogues. Jewish sensitivity to pagan images was well known to all
involved. It was a measure that was sure to please the emperor, who
promoted the idea of his own divinity, and who, almost contempo-
raneously, ordered that his statue be installed in the temple in
Jerusalem, precipitating a crisis that was only resolved by his assas-
sination (*Ant.* 18.261–309).

The emperor, however, was not the prime mover in the conflict
in Alexandria. This point is amply shown by his cavalier disregard
for the envoys when they came to him in Rome. It is also clear that
the governor Flaccus was not motivated by personal hostility towards
the Jews, but was attempting to save his own skin by placating the
Alexandrians. On Philo's account, Flaccus was a good governor while
the emperor Tiberius lived. But he lost his friends at court when
Caligula came to power. He had opposed the claims of Caligula,
and was one of those who had accused Caligula's mother, who had
been executed by Tiberius. He had good reason to fear if any accusation were brought against him before Caligula. His early relations
with the Alexandrian leaders had been strained. He had dissolved
the drinking clubs that were the power base of such people as Isidorus,
who had to flee from Alexandria to avoid arrest (*Flacc.* 145). Flaccus'
attempt to appease the Alexandrian leaders was futile. They eventually came to Rome to accuse him before the emperor. But it seems
clear that his actions against the Jews arose from fear of the
Alexandrians rather than from any Roman agenda.[9]

Philo vacillates in his description of the antagonists of the Jews in
Alexandria. He often refers to them as "Alexandrians" and mentions

---

[9] Sandra Gambetti, "The Alexandrian Riots of 38 C.E. and the Persecution of
the Jews: A Historical Assessment," (Diss. Berkeley, 2003) argues that Flaccus was
only implementing a mandate from Rome, restricting the rights of the Jews to those
that could be documented. In that case, however, the involvement of the Alexandrian
mob is difficult to explain. I am grateful to Ms. Gambetti for making her dissertation available to me.

some Alexandrian leaders, Dionysius, Isidorus and Lampo, by name (*Flacc.* 20). Yet much of his invective is specifically anti-Egyptian. The Egyptians, we are told, have "we might say innate hostility to the Jews" (29). They are prone to sedition (17). In the context of the setting up of images in the synagogues, he refers to "those who deified dogs and wolves and lions and crocodiles and many other wild animals on the land" (*Leg.* 139). The disposition of Caligula was due, in part, to the influence of his servants: "The majority of these were Egyptians, a seedbed of evil in whose souls both the venom and the temper of the native crocodiles and asps were reproduced" (*Leg.* 166). He makes much of the influence of Helicon, an Egyptian slave (*Leg.* 66–77). We must bear in mind that it was easier to pour invective on Egyptians, who were universally reviled, than on Greeks. Moreover, in the matter of civic status Philo and his like wanted desperately to be associated with the Greeks and distinguished from Egyptians.[10] To refer to Alexandrians as Egyptians was to insult them. Roman polemicists referred to Cleopatra as a *"mulier Aegyptia"*.[11] Josephus is at pains to insist that Apion was of Egyptian origin. He further argues:

> The real promoters of sedition, as anyone can discover, have been citizens of Alexandria of the type of Apion. The Greeks and Macedonians, so long as the citizenship was confined to them, never rose against us, but left us free to enjoy our ancient worship. But when, owing to the prevailing disorders, their numbers were swelled by a host of Egyptians, sedition became chronic (*C. Ap.* 2.69).

The implication of Josephus' tirade seems to be that the principal agitators were people of Egyptian origin who had infiltrated the ranks of the Greeks in Alexandria, and become citizens.[12] Besides Apion, Chaeremon, another member of the delegation to Claudius, is variously described as a Stoic philosopher and an Egyptian priest.[13]

---

[10] Philo's attitudes towards Greeks and their culture were complex. In the words of Maren Niehoff, "more than half of Philo's references to things Greek . . . lack a sense the Greek as Other," although he could assume a sense of superiority towards Greek writers and philosophers. See Maren Niehoff, *Philo on Jewish Identity and Culture* (Tübingen: Mohr Siebeck, 2001) 137–58. The quotation is from p. 139.

[11] Dio Cassius XLVIII.24.2; L.3.5; 6:1; 24:3 etc.

[12] Compare K. Goudriaan, "Ethnical Strategies in Greco-Roman Egypt," in Per Bilde, ed., *Ethnicity in Hellenistic Egypt* (Aarhus: Aarhus University Press, 1992) 86–93.

[13] See Pieter Willem van der Horst, *Chaeremon: Egyptian Priest and Stoic Philosopher* (Leiden: Brill, 1984).

These Greco-Egyptians were presumably a very small element in the Egyptian population. The Egyptian rank and file was still sharply distinguished from the Alexandrian citizens, as can be seen from the episode of the different kinds of whips in *Flacc.* 78. But by the Roman era there were enough Alexandrian citizens with Egyptian blood to warrant the use of anti-Egyptian rhetoric on the part of Philo and Josephus, even if the adversaries were Alexandrians.[14] In any case, the conflict presented to the Roman emperors was one between Alexandrians and Jews. Regardless of who did the actual pillaging, the ringleaders of the pogrom were clearly Alexandrian citizens, not common Egyptians. The Alexandrian delegates who pleaded their case in Rome included people of Egyptian extraction, such as Apion and Chaeremon, but they were respected Alexandrian intellectuals, just as Philo was on the Jewish side.[15]

II. The issues in dispute

The explanations given for the anti-Jewish outburst in Alexandria are basically of two kinds. Some scholars argue that the hostility arose from social and political circumstances peculiar to the situation in Alexandria in the early Roman era. Others posit widespread and deep-rooted anti-Jewish sentiment on the part of both Greeks and Egyptians, dating back to the beginning of the Hellenistic era. These explanations, of course, are not mutually exclusive and can be viewed as complementary, but the emphasis placed on one or the other can reflect different views of the conflict.

The evidence that pertains most directly to the conflict of 38 C.E. and its aftermath suggests that the status of the Jews was a major issue in the conflict. Philo expresses outrage that Flaccus declared the Jews to be "foreigners and aliens" (*Flacc.* 54) and treated the members of the gerousia who were flogged in the theater as if they were

---

[14] On the rising prominence of Jews and Egyptians from the middle of the second century B.C.E., and the growth of a class of Greco-Egyptians, see P. M. Fraser, *Ptolemaic Alexandria* (Oxford: Clarendon, 1972) 1.88–92. Fraser remarks that "the Egyptian strain, though present racially, had little social significance any longer for this group" (91). See also now Gambetti, "The Alexandrian Riots," 118–28.

[15] On Apion's scholarly credentials see now Pieter W. van der Horst, "Who Was Apion?" in idem, *Japheth in the Tents of Shem: Studies on Jewish Hellenism in Antiquity* (Leuven: Peeters, 2002) 207–221.

Egyptians (*Flacc.* 78). Caligula asks the Jewish delegates about their politeia, but does not give them a chance to respond (*Leg.* 363). We may infer that their politeia was one of the subjects at issue. Even the placing of statues in the synagogues, which ignited the conflict, must be seen in light of Apion's famous question: "why, then, if they are citizens, do they not worship the same gods as the Alexandrians?" (*C. Ap.* 2.65). The question implies that the Jews claimed to be citizens, and that Apion disputed the claim. The Letter of Claudius warns the Jews "not to aim at more than they have previously had," and reminds them that they enjoy an abundance of good things "in a city which is not their own."[16] The latter phrase recalls the ruling of Flaccus that the Jews were foreigners and aliens; it indicates clearly that the Jews as a body were not citizens of Alexandria. It is clear that the Jews were agitating for something. "Under the circumstances," suggests Gruen, "the Jewish delegates most likely sought guarantees of security, perhaps a pronouncement that would deter future prefects of Egypt from stripping them of civic privileges as Flaccus had done."[17] But this would be merely a reaffirmation of what they already had. Claudius clearly implies that they were aiming at higher status. Of course the difference here is a matter of different perspectives. From their own point of view the Jews may have only been arguing for the restoration of the privileges stripped by Flaccus. The issue was whether Flaccus had ruled correctly that the Jews were aliens. Claudius ruled that he had, and so that the Jews were agitating for privileges to which they were not entitled.

The understanding of the situation that has been most widely accepted over the last half century was articulated by Victor Tcherikover. Ptolemaic Alexandria had allowed for a range of classes, some of which enjoyed privileges even though they were not full citizens.[18] The Romans drew a sharper line between citizen and non-citizen. The difference was underlined by the *laographia*, or poll-tax, from which Greek citizens of Alexandria were exempt, but which was levied on Egyptians and other non-citizens.[19] Ever since the work

---

[16] CPJ 153. Trans. Modrzejewski, *The Jews of Egypt*, 182.

[17] Gruen, Diaspora, 80.

[18] For example, "Alexandrians" were apparently distinct from, and inferior to, demesmen, or full citizens. See P. M. Fraser, *Ptolemaic Alexandria* (Oxford: Clarendon, 1972) 1.38–92, especially 49.

[19] Tcherikover-Fuks, CPJ 1.59–62; E. Mary Smallwood, *The Jews under Roman Rule* (Leiden: Brill, 1976) 231–2; Modrzejewski, *The Jews of Egypt*, 161–3; Barclay,

of Tcherikover,[20] it has been assumed that the *laographia* entailed a loss in status for the Jews of Alexandria. In the words of Modrzejewski, "they had been 'Hellenes;' now, they had suddenly become 'Egyptians'."[21] This led to increased efforts on their part to obtain citizenship. One way of doing this was by infiltrating the gymnasium and becoming ephebes.

Gruen disputes the assumption that Jews were subject to the *laographia*.[22] The basis for this widely held assumption is two-fold. Since Jews, as a group, were evidently not citizens of Alexandria, there is no apparent reason why they should be exempt, and there is no reliable evidence that they were.[23] Second, a papyrus preserves the petition of one Helenos son of Tryphon, whose exempt status had apparently been denied by an administrator.[24] Helenos began by calling himself an "Alexandrian," but the word is crossed out and replaced with "a Jew from Alexandria." Helenos claimed that his father was an Alexandrian and that he himself had received the appropriate education as far as his father's means allowed. It is a reasonable inference that the petitioner thought that his case would be stronger if he were "an Alexandrian" rather than "a Jew from Alexandria." We do not know whether the correction was made by the petitioner or by an official who denied his claim to the status of Alexandrian.

The issue of the poll-tax is also raised in the *Acts of the Pagan Martyrs*, fictional compositions, dramatizing the fate of Alexandrian leaders at the hands of the Roman emperors, which are presumably indicative of popular Alexandrian sentiments.[25] In one passage, Isidorus

---

Jews in the Mediterranean Diaspora, 49–50. Citizens of Naucratis and Ptolemais were also exempt. There was also a third class, of Greeks outside the cities, which paid at a reduced rate. A special class was created in 4/5 C.E., for people who were graduates of the gymnasium, descendents of military settlers or inhabitants of the chief towns (*metropolitai*).

[20] *Hellenistic Civilization*, 311–12; CPJ 1.59–62.

[21] Modrzejewski, *The Jews of Egypt*, 163.

[22] Gruen, *Diaspora*, 75–77.

[23] Gambetti, "The Alexandrian Riots," 47, claims that the Jews living in Alexandria were exempt. The basis for this claim is a statement attributed to King Agrippa in the Acts of Isidorus: "[N]o one has levied taxes on the Jews," (Herbert A. Musurillo, ed., *The Acts of the Pagan Martyrs* [Oxford: Clarendon, 1954] 26). The historical value of the Acts, however, is very questionable, and in any case the passage could be taken to mean that there was no precedent before the Roman era for imposing such a tax on the Jews. The passage is discussed further below.

[24] CPJ 151. See Modrzejewski, *The Jews of Egypt*, 164; Tcherikover, Hellenistic Civilization, 312.

[25] For a lively account of the Acts, see Modrzejewski, *The Jews of Egypt*, 173–83.

engages in a dispute with Agrippa about the Jews: "I accuse them of wanting to stir up the entire world . . . They are not of the same temperament as the Alexandrians, but live rather after the fashion of the Egyptians. Are they not on a level with those who pay the poll-tax?" Agrippa retorts that "the Egyptians have had taxes levied on them by their rulers . . . But no one has levied taxes on the Jews."[26] Gruen infers, ". . . it follows that Jews are *not* subject to it."[27] A safer conclusion would be that their liability was in dispute. Isidorus argues that the Jews are akin to the Egyptians. If this argument were accepted, Jews should presumably be subject to the tax. Agrippa argues to the contrary that there was no precedent for such a tax on the Jews. (It should be remembered that the whole dialogue is fictional in any case.) The issue of the poll-tax is not as clearcut as scholars after Tcherikover have supposed, but it is very likely to have been an issue nonetheless.[28] In any case it is clear that some reduction in the civic status that the Jews had enjoyed under the Ptolemies was at issue in the disputes of 38–41 C.E.

The actual aspirations of the Jews of Alexandria are likely to remain controversial. Some individual Jews certainly became citizens of Alexandria. Philo's nephew, Tiberius Julius Alexander, went on to become prefect of Egypt and crushed Jewish resistance in Alexandria in 66 C.E., at the time of the outbreak of the rebellion in Judea. Full citizenship, however, would have been difficult to maintain without participating in the pagan cults. Some individuals may have been able to finesse this issue; Philo may well have been a citizen and Paul was a Roman citizen. But presumably it would have been more difficult for a whole community to avoid the civic cults.[29] Philo may have articulated the aspirations of many when he wrote, in the Life of Moses, that "strangers, in my judgment, must be regarded as suppliants of those who receive them, and not only suppliants but settlers and friends, who are anxious to obtain equal rights with the citizens, and are near to being citizens because they differ little from the original inhabitants."[30] Josephus' formulation of the Edict of

---

[26] Musurillo, *The Acts of the Pagan Martyrs*, 26; *CPJ* 156.

[27] *Diaspora*, 77.

[28] So also van der Horst, *Philo's Flaccus*, 21–22.

[29] The argument that Jews did not seek Alexandrian citizenship is made especially by Ayreh Kasher, *The Jews in Hellenistic and Roman Egypt: The Struggle for Equal Rights* (Tübingen: J. C. B. Mohr, 1985).

[30] *De Vita Mos.* 1.34–36.

Claudius has the emperor acknowledge that "the Jews in Alexandria, called Alexandrians, were fellow colonizers from the very earliest times jointly with the Alexandrians and received equal civic rights (ἰσῆς πολιτείας) from the kings," (*Ant.* 19.281). Such terms as "Alexandrians" and even "citizens" admitted of an imprecise, non-technical sense, and Philo and Josephus exploited the ambiguity. What they wanted were privileges similar to those of the citizens, without having to participate in the civic cults. Access to gymnasium education and exemption from the poll-tax are examples of the kind of privileges that were at issue.[31] Jews saw no reason why they should not continue to enjoy the status of quasi-Hellenes, as they had under the Ptolemies. But distinctions were more sharply drawn under the Romans. Apion and his fellow-Alexandrians were infuriated by the Jewish claim, of privilege without full participation in the life of the city. The prominence of gymnasiarchs in the conflict lends some support to the view that access to the gymnasium was one of the points at issue.

The situation was also colored by the reduced status of the Alexandrians under Roman rule. They were a conquered people, ruled by foreigners. While the Jews had their own ethnarch, at least for a time, and a senate or gerousia thereafter, the Greeks were not allowed to have a city council—hence their resentment and mockery of the Jewish king, Agrippa, and Flaccus' humiliation of the Jewish senate in his efforts to appease them. From the Alexandrian perspective, the Jews were still over-privileged, and Jewish professions of loyalty to the Romans did nothing to endear them to the Greeks or Egyptians. The Greeks knew better than to rebel against Rome, but they could at least get some satisfaction from asserting their superiority over the Jews.

In light of this situation, it is apparent that the violence against the Jews did not arise spontaneously from innate hatred on the part of the Greeks, or even of the Egyptians. It was a product of very specific circumstances in the pressure-cooker that Alexandria became under Roman rule, where status and privilege were scarce commodities, and one party's gain was viewed by the other as loss.

---

[31] It should be noted that a gymnasium education, and completion of the ephebeia, did not automatically qualify people as citizens. See Diana Delia, *Alexandrian Citizenship* (Atlanta, Scholars Press, 1991) 88.

III. A TRADITION OF HOSTILITY

This is not to suggest that there was no hostility towards the Jews in Egypt before the Romans came. A papyrus from the first century B.C.E. contains a request for lodgings in Memphis for a priest (who is presumably Jewish) because "they" (the people of Memphis) "loathe the Jews."[32] We should not assume that the Jews were exceptional in this regard. There was plenty of racial animosity to go around in Hellenistic Egypt.

The argument for widespread anti-semitism in the Hellenistic world depends on the dossier of evidence presented by Josephus in his treatise *Against Apion*. Josephus seems to have collected every reference to the Jews that he could find, both positive and negative. Part of his agenda was to show that Judaism was of great interest to Greek writers.[33] The material is taken out of context, however, and often gives an exaggerated impression of the interest of a given author in the Jews.

Much of Josephus' energy is devoted to refuting distorted accounts of Jewish origins.[34] The earliest of these are attributed to the Greek ethnographer, Hecataeus of Abdera, and the Egyptian priest Manetho, both of whom wrote at the beginning of the Ptolemaic era.[35] Both of these associate the settlers of Judea with people who were expelled from Egypt because of pestilence, which is specified as leprosy by Manetho. Manetho's account is more complex, as the initial settlers of Judea are identified with the Hyksos, who had been driven out of Egypt, but these later invaded and pillaged Egypt again at the invitation of the lepers. The lepers had settled for a time in Avaris,

---

[32] *CPJ* 141. Modrzejewski, *The Jews of Egypt*, 154–5.

[33] On the character of the treatise see Louis H. Feldman and John R. Levison, eds., *Josephus' Contra Apionem: Studies in its Character and Context* (Leiden: Brill, 1996). Cf. Erich Gruen's essay, "Greeks and Jews: Mutual Misperceptions in Josephus' Contra Apionem," next chapter.

[34] These accounts have often been reviewed. See John G. Gager, *Moses in Greco-Roman Paganism* (SBLMS 16; Nashville: Abingdon, 1972); Claude Aziza, "L'Utilisation polémique du récit de l'Exode chez les écrivains alexandrins (IVème siècle av. J.-C.–Ier siècle ap. J.-C.)," *ANRW* II.20.1 (Berlin: de Gruyter, 1987) 41–65; Gruen, Heritage and Hellenism, 41–72 ("The Use and Abuse of the Exodus Story"); Peter Schäfer, *Judeophobia: Attitudes towards the Jews in the Ancient World* (Princeton: Princeton University Press, 1997) 15–33.

[35] For Hecataeus, see Menahem Stern, *Greek and Latin Authors on Jews and Judaism* (Jerusalem: The Israel Academy of Sciences and Humanities, 1976) 1.20–44; Manetho, ibid., 1.62–86.

the deserted city of the Shepherds, which was also associated with Seth-Typhon. Their leader, Osarseph, established a law that they should neither worship the gods nor refrain from eating the sacred animals. The passage concludes: "It is said that the priest who framed their constitution and their laws was a native of Heliopolis, named Osarseph after the god Osiris . . . but when he joined this people he changed his name and was called Moses," (C. Ap. 1.228–52.).[36]

Hecataus's account is not anti-Jewish. The foreigners driven from Egypt settle in Greece as well as in Judea, even if the more outstanding among them go to Greece. He goes on to give a remarkably positive account of Moses' legislation, including the prohibition of images. He notes, however, that "as a result of their own expulsion from Egypt, he introduced "a somewhat unsocial and inhospitable mode of life" (ἀπάνθρωπόν τινα καὶ μισόξενον βίον).[37] The word *misoxenon* is often translated as "intolerant" or "hostile to strangers." As Katell Berthelot has shown, however, it should be understood as the opposite of *philoxenos*, hospitable.[38] The basis of the remark is the common refusal of Jews to participate in table fellowship, which was often in the context of sacrifice. Even this behavior, which seemed strange to Hecataeus as a Greek, is excused in part by the experience of Moses and his followers in Egypt. It does not imply that the Jews hated humankind. But while Hecataeus himself cannot be accused of bias against Jews, his characterization of their mode of life would lend itself to a more hostile interpretation by later authors.

The attitude of Manetho towards the Jews is more controversial. The account of the Hyksos is based on old Egyptian tradition, which originally was not concerned with the Jews at all. Some scholars have thought that the reference to settlement in Jerusalem was added secondarily.[39] The story that Jerusalem was built by the Hyksos was not necessarily hostile to Judaism. Erich Gruen has even argued that it was invented by Jews.[40] Much more ominous is Manetho's story

---

[36] Stern, Greek and Latin Authors, 1.78–83.
[37] Hecataeus in Diodorus Siculus, *Bib Hist* 40.3; Stern, *Greek and Latin Authors*, 1.26–29.
[38] Katell Berthelot, *Philanthrôpia judaica: Le débat autour de la 'misanthropie' des lois juives dans l'Antiquité* (Leiden: Brill, 2003) 80–94.
[39] See Berthelot, Ibid., 96–7, who is sympathetic to that view.
[40] Gruen, *Heritage and Hellenism*, 63–64; Berthelot, Philanthrôpia judaica, 97, finds the argument convincing.

about the lepers, which attributes to Moses hostility to Egyptian religion. Here again, the story was not originally concerned with the Jews,[41] and many scholars have questioned whether the references to Jerusalem and Moses were inserted by Manetho or by a later author.[42] The identification of Moses with Osarseph at the end of the second account is especially suspicious, since Osarseph is mentioned earlier in the passage without the identification.[43]

Like Gruen, I think it unlikely that either Manetho or Hecataeus knew the story of the Exodus in its biblical form, or indeed that either had more than an incidental interest in the Jews. Manetho drew on traditional Egyptian polemic against invaders from Asia, which had its roots in the experience of the Hyksos but which was revived in more recent times by the invasions of the Persian kings, Cambyses and Artaxerxes III. But the association of the Jews with this tradition, however incidental, would have highly negative associations for the Jews. They could henceforth be identified with the followers of Seth-Typhon, archetypical enemies of Egypt.[44] The Jews were neither the only nor the primary people who were so identified in the Hellenistic period.[45] They did not pose a threat to Egypt in the way that the Seleucid kings, for example, did. But nonetheless, association with the Hyksos and with Seth-Typhon had negative implications that could be exploited by polemicists.

When we survey the dossier of anti-Jewish polemic presented by Josephus, however, what is striking is how little evidence he presents for such polemic in Egypt or Alexandria. The only Alexandrian author cited who can plausibly be dated between Manetho and Apion

---

[41] For echoes of the Amarna age in this story see Jan Assmann, *Moses the Egyptian. The Memory of Egypt in Western Monotheism* (Cambridge, MA: Harvard, 1997) 23–44.

[42] Berthelot, *Philanthrôpia judaica*, 97–99. Again, she favors the view that the association with the ancestors of the Jews is secondary.

[43] Gruen, *Heritage and Hellenism*, 64, also thinks that the identification of Osarseph with Moses was the work of a Jewish redactor. I find this unlikely. See my comments in "Reinventing Exodus: Exegesis and Legend in Hellenistic Egypt," in Randal Argall, Beverly Bow and Rodney Werline, eds., *For a Later Generation: The Transformation of Tradition in Israel, Early Judaism and Early Christianity* (Harrisburg, PA: Trinity Press International, 2000) 52–62, especially p. 61.

[44] Jan-Willem van Henten and Ra'anan Abusch, "The Jews as Typhonians and Josephus' Strategy of Refutation in *Contra Apionem*," in Feldman and Levison, eds., *Josephus' Contra Apionem*, 271–309.

[45] See especially Ludwig Koenen, "Die Adapatation ägyptischer Königsideologie am Ptolemäerhof," in W. Peremans, ed., *Egypt and the Hellenistic World* (Studia Hellenistica 27; Leuven: Leuven University Press, 1983) 174–90.

is Lysimachus, if indeed he is to be identified with the Alexandrian mythographer and historian who lived around 100 B.C.E.[46] Lysimachus repeats the story of the lepers but adds that Moses instructed them "to show goodwill to no man, to offer not the best but the worst advice, and to overthrow any temples and altars of the gods which they found," (*C. Ap.* 1.309).[47] Moreover, Jerusalem was originally called Hierosyla because of the sacrilegious propensities of the inhabitants. The overthrow of temples was a standard part of the traditional Egyptian account, but the determination to show goodwill to no one was a new development. The implication is that the Jews rejected the laws of Buzyges, and so could be genuinely accused of hatred of humankind.[48] Lysimachus evidently had some animus against Jews, but even here we do not know whether his account was anything more than a passing gibe against a foreign people, or whether his animus against Jews was any greater than his contempt for Asiatics in general. Apion's fellow-emissary, Chaeremon, appears to have embellished the story of the lepers with some motifs from the myth of Osiris, casting the lepers in the role of Seth. But the fragment cited by Josephus has little by way of anti-Jewish polemic, except that the leaders of the lepers were Moses and Joseph (*C. Ap.* 1.288–92).[49] Even in the case of Apion, Josephus cites only a brief version of the account of Jewish origins (*C. Ap.* 2.8–27).[50] Moses was a native of Heliopolis, who erected prayer houses open to the air, all facing eastwards. This account may be confused, but it is not especially hostile. Apion does add a malicious story that relates the origin of the sabbath to a disease of the groin, allegedly called *sabbatosis/sabbo* in Egyptian.

According to Josephus, Apion drew much of his material from Greek authors who were not Alexandrians, such as Mnaseas, Posidonius and Appollonius Molon (*C. Ap.* 2.79, 112). Mnaseas, from Lycia in Asia Minor, lived in the early second century B.C.E.[51] He is the earliest source cited for the legend that Jews worshipped an ass's head in the Jerusalem temple, and he mentions this in connection with a

---

[46] Berthelot, *Philanthrôpia judaica*, 106–7. The main fragment is found in C. Ap. 1.304–311; Stern, *Greek and Latin Authors*, 1.382–86. Stern lists him as "date unknown."

[47] Stern, *Greek and Latin Authors*, 1.384.

[48] Berthelot, *Philanthrôpia judaica*, 107–9.

[49] Stern, *Greek and Latin Authors*, 1.419–21. Schäfer, *Judeophobia*, 30, comments on "the almost complete absence of any open hostility to the Jews."

[50] Stern, *Greek and Latin Authors*, 1.389–97.

[51] Ibid., 1.97–98.

conflict between Jews and Idumeans (*C. Ap.* 2.112–14).[52] A related, though less offensive, story appears in Diodorus, in a passage that is sometimes thought to derive from Posidonius.[53] Allegedly, Antiochus Epiphanes entered the innermost sanctuary of the temple, and found there a statue of Moses as a bearded man seated on an ass, with a book in his hands. This passage also reports the advice given to Antiochus VII Sidetes by his advisers when he was besieging Jerusalem. They rehearse the story of the expulsion of the lepers from Egypt, and urge the king to wipe out the race of the Jews, "since they alone of all nations avoided dealings with any other people and looked upon all men as their enemies." But the king, we are told, being a magnanimous and mild-mannered person, dismissed these charges. It would seem from this story that some quite vitriolic anti-Jewish propaganda circulated in the Seleucid realm, some of it designed to justify the actions of Antiochus Epiphanes in persecuting the Jews. The allegation that Jews annually practiced the ritual murder of a Greek is also told in connection with Antiochus's desecration of the temple.[54] The story of ass-worship is often thought to have originated in Egypt, because the ass was associated with Seth-Typhon.[55] Such colorful slanders may have circulated widely. Their currency is better attested in other parts of the Hellenistic world than in Egypt.

Most of the people cited by Josephus were Hellenistic intellectuals of some prominence. Apollonius Molon was a famous orator who lived on Rhodes and counted Cicero and Caesar among his pupils. The most distinguished of the lot was Posidonius, the Stoic philosopher, who wrote a history of the period 145–85 B.C.E., approximately, continuing that of Polybius. This history has not survived, but it is often thought to have been the source for two passages concerning the Jews: the passage from Diodorus cited above and a passage found in Strabo of Amaseia.[56] The account of Jewish origins in

---

[52] Ibid., 1.99–101. On the story see Bezalel Bar-Kochva, "An Ass in the Jerusalem Temple—The Origins and Development of the Slander," in Feldman and Levison, eds., *Josephus' Contra Apionem*, 320–26.

[53] Diodorus, *Bib. Hist.* 34–35.1.1–5; Stern, *Greek and Latin Authors*, 1.181–85. On the derivation from Posidonius see Berthelot, *Philanthrôpia judaica*, 127–28, and her article "Poseidonios d'Apamée et les Juifs," *JSJ* 34 (2003) 160–98, especially 177–87.

[54] *C. Ap.* 2.89–96.

[55] Bar-Kochva, "An Ass in the Jerusalem Temple," 318–25; van Henten and Abusch, "The Jews as Typhonians," 287–8.

[56] Strabo, *Geog.* 16.2.34–36; Strabo, *Greek and Latin Authors*, 1.294–311. Berthelot, *Philanthrôpia judaica*, 113–23.

Strabo is very different from the usual story of the expulsion of lepers. Moses and his followers left Egypt because they objected to the
Egyptian animal cults, and they also rejected Greek anthropomor-
phism. They held that people should worship God without an image,
and live self-restrained and righteous lives. This has been described
as "a remarkable piece of idealizing ethnography."[57] Strabo goes on
to say that later "superstitious men were appointed to the priesthood, and then tyrannical people," who harrassed both their country and their neighbors. This latter allusion has sometimes been
explained as a reaction to the expansionistic policies of the Hasmoneans,
with whom Posidonius was contemporary.[58] The passage from Diodorus
contains much more hostile sentiments towards the Jews, but they
are attributed to the advisers of Antiochus Sidetes. Diodorus, and
presumably Posidonius, if he is indeed the source, rather approved
of the magnanimity of the king in disregarding the charges.

The implication of Posidonius in anti-Jewish propaganda is of some
importance for the question of anti-semitism in the ancient world,
since it is sometimes argued that Stoic universalism was a factor in
the perception that Jews were misanthropic.[59] (Chaeremon was also
a Stoic philosopher, and Seneca referred to the Jews as "an accursed
race").[60] Jewish particularism was practically the antithesis of the
Stoic ideal of cosmopolitanism. Even the benign account preserved
in Strabo disapproves of the superstition and aggressiveness of contemporary Jewish leaders. Nonetheless, it is unlikely that Stoic philosophy animated the mob in Alexandria. Whatever Posidonius may
have thought about the characterization of Judaism by the advisers
of Antiochus, he surely did not approve of their proposal to extir-
pate the Jews.[61] As we have seen, Chaeremon is not especially polemical. While Seneca regarded the Jews as superstitious, he did not
accuse them of misanthropy. Judaism did not conform to the Stoic
ideal, but the evidence for Stoic involvement in anti-Jewish polemic
is very slight.

While the evidence is limited, it seems that the charge of misanthropy was known in both the Seleucid and the Ptolemaic realms

---

[57] John G. Gager, *The Origins of Anti-Semitism* (New York: Oxford, 1983) 73.
[58] Berthelot, *Philanthrôpia judaica*, 122; "Poseidonios," 175–77.
[59] Berthelot, *Philanthrôpia judaica*, 174–79.
[60] Seneca, *De Superstitione*, in Augustine, *De Civitate Dei* 6.11. Stern, *Greek and Latin
Authors*, 1.431.
[61] This is recognized by Berthelot, "Poseidonios," 198.

by the late second or early first century B.C.E., if not earlier, and derogatory stories about ass-worship and the like circulated widely. Nonetheless, there is little or no evidence of violence against Jewish Diaspora communities in this period.[62] There were occasional disputes over Jewish rights, such as the right to send money to Jerusalem, but no major conflict is reported in the Diaspora, apart from Alexandria, until the time of the Jewish revolt against Rome. At that time violence against Jews became widespread in the Hellenistic cities of Palestine and in Syria. According to Josephus Antioch, Apamea and Sidon were the only Syrian cities that refrained from killing or imprisoning Jews (*Ant.* 2.479).[63] In Antioch, violence subsequently broke out at the instigation of a Jewish renegade. Conflict in Alexandria was also renewed at this time. The revolt against Rome created a new situation, and provided new reasons or pretexts for antagonism towards the Jews. How far the feelings of hatred or fear (*J.W.* 2.478) to which the Gentiles gave vent on this occasion had been building up, and how far they were triggered by the war, is difficult to say. We hear of no similar conflicts in Asia Minor.

IV. *Anti-semitism in antiquity?*

It has become customary to refer to this tradition of anti-Jewish polemic as evidence for "anti-semitism" in antiquity.[64] The term "anti-semitism" was coined in the 19th century, in the context of a growing interest in the characteristics of different races.[65] Strictly speaking, anti-semitism is directed against all semitic peoples, not just the Jews, but it has come to mean an irrational hatred of Judaism, which found its ultimate expression in the Nazi campaign of extermination. To describe ancient attitudes towards the Jews as anti-semitic is to imply that they attest to the same phenomenon as modern anti-semitism, or in the words of Tcherikover, that "the

---

[62] See the survey by S. Applebaum, "The Jewish Diaspora," in S. Safrai and M. Stern, eds., *The Jewish People in the First Century* (CRINT 1.1; Assen: van Gorcum, 1974) 117–83.

[63] Applebaum, "The Jewish Diaspora," 140.

[64] E.g. Gager, *The Origins of Anti-Semitism*; J. N. Sevenster, *The Roots of Pagan Anti-Semitism in the Ancient World* (Leiden: Brill, 1975).

[65] The term was apparently coined by Wilhelm Marr in 1879. See Zvi Yavetz, "Judeophobia in Classical Antiquity: A Different Approach," *JJS* 44 (1993) 1–22; Shulamit Volkov, *Jüdisches Leben und Antisemitismus im 19 und 20 Jahrhundert* (München: Beck, 1990) 27.

inner quality of anti-Semitism is always and everywhere the same."[66]
It also implies that hostility to the Jews in the ancient world was
qualitatively different from prejudice against other peoples.

There are obvious problems with this use of the term "anti-
Semitism."[67] The racial theory of modern anti-semitism has no basis
in the ancient world. Moreover, much of the prejudice against Jews
in western history was grounded in, or legitimated by, Christian
supersessionism, which obviously was not a factor in the attitudes of
the Greeks and Romans.[68] Scholars persist in using the term, for
various reasons. In some cases there is an apologetic overtone, insofar as the original sin is shifted away from Christianity or modern
Europe to ancient paganism. In many cases the usage arises from a
Judeo-centric view of antiquity, to which Christians as well as Jews
are prone. Most scholars who work on ancient Judaism have little
interest in other peoples in antiquity and are eager to believe that
the Jewish experience was unique. Moreover, the primary evidence,
such as the *Against Apion* of Josephus, was compiled by Jews and
transmitted by Christians for apologetic purposes.[69]

In my opinion, this usage is unfortunate and unhelpful, and only
impedes the understanding of Gentile attitudes to Judaism in the
ancient world. One of its by-products is endless quibbling as to what
actually constitutes anti-semitism, or when "mere" anti-Judaism
becomes anti-Semitism.[70] Almost invariably, the answer is a matter
of degree. A certain amount of ethnic animosity is normal, but in
the case of anti-Semitism it is carried to excess. Peter Schäfer has
rightly objected to this kind of casuistry, but he still speaks of the
charge of misanthropy as crossing the line from the "justifiable" to
the "unjustifiable," from "anti-Judaism" to "anti-Semitism."[71] In fact,
if the racial factor in anti-Semitism is left out of account, the only

---

[66] Tcherikover, *Hellenistic Civilization*, 358.
[67] See, for example, Shaye Cohen, "Anti-Semitism in Antiquity: The Problem of
Definition," in David Berger, ed., *History and Hate: The Dimensions of Anti-Semitism*
(Philadelphia: The Jewish Publication Society, 1986) 43–47.
[68] See e.g. Rosemary Ruether, *Faith and Fratricide: The Theological Roots of Anti-
Semitism* (New York: Seabury, 1974).
[69] Gideon Bohak, "The Ibis and the Jewish Question: Ethnic Bias in the Greco-
Roman World," in M. Mor, A. Oppenheimer, J. Pastor and D. R. Schwartz, eds.,
*Jews and Gentiles in the Holy Land in the Days of the Second Temple, the Mishnah and the
Talmud* (Jerusalem: Ben Zvi, 2003) 27–43.
[70] See Schäfer, *Judeophobia*, 197–206, with reference to Gavin Langmuir, *Toward
a Definition of Anti-Semitism* (Berkeley: University of California, 1990).
[71] Schäfer, *Judeophobia*, 206.

basis for a distinction is the scale and severity of the prejudice. Rather than quibble over the point at which to draw the line, it would be better to leave the word "anti-semitism" for its proper, racial, usage, and try to understand ancient conflicts in their own cultural context.

For Schäfer, "the crucial historical questions are (a) whether there was always the same kind of hostility against and hatred of the Jews throughout history, and (b) whether there is something unique about this hostility directed at the Jews which distinguishes the Jews from other ethnic groups."[72] To my mind, the answer to the first question is clearly no. The riots in Alexandria cannot be compared to Hitler's Final Solution. The enormity of the German project cannot be diluted by claiming that it was only an instance of a perennial phenomenon. Hitler's Endlösung was indeed a unique kind of hostility in the experience of the western world, at least. But was the hostility towards the Jews in the ancient world unique in its own context?[73]

To answer that question properly we should have to do a thorough comparative study of ethnic prejudice in the ancient world. To my knowledge, such a study has never been attempted on an adequate scale.[74] The Jews were certainly not the only people in the ancient world who had defamatory stories told about them. Think for example of the cursing of Canaan for looking on his father's nakedness in Gen 9:20–27, or the incestuous begetting of Moab and Ammon by Lot's daughters in Gen 19:30–38. No people endured more ridicule in the Hellenistic world than the Egyptians.[75] The ways of the Egyptians, like those of the Jews, were different from those of the Greeks and Romans.[76] Some of the gibes against them were

---

[72] Ibid., 197.

[73] Van der Horst, *Philo's Flaccus*, 25, recognizes tha "anti-semitism" is anachronistic, and opts for "Jew—hatred." He does not discuss whether this "Jew-hatred" is qualitatively different from other ethnic prejudice.

[74] See Bohak, "The Ibis and the Jewish Question." See also his "Ethnic Stereotypes in the Greco-Roman World: Egyptians, Phoenicians, and Jews," *Proceedings of the Twelfth World Congress of Jewish Studies* (Division B; Jerusalem: World Union of Jewish Studies, 2000) 7–15. Some useful material can be found in A. N. Sherwin-White, *Racial Prejudice in Imperial Rome* (Cambridge: Cambridge University Press, 1967); J. P. V. D. Balsdon, *Romans and Aliens* (London: Duckworth, 1979). S. Davis, *Race-Relations in Ancient Egypt* (New York: Philosophical Library, 1952) relies heavily on the Jewish evidence. I am told that a study of ethnic prejudice in the ancient world by B. Isaac is forthcoming from Princeton University Press.

[75] See, for example, Maren Niehoff, *Philo on Jewish Identity and Culture* (Tübingen: Mohr/Siebeck, 2001) 45–74 ("The Egyptians as Ultimate Other").

[76] For references, see Bohak, "The Ibis and the Jewish Question."

topoi that could be applied to all barbarians. Others were more specific. The charges against them included xenophobia[77] and apanthropia.[78] They were the most superstitious of all people.[79] The animal cults provided endless cause for derision. Moreover, according to Philo, Egyptians were "a seedbed of evil in whose souls both the venom and the temper of the native crocodiles and asps were reproduced" (*Leg.* 166).

Prejudice against Jews was not more widespread than prejudice against Egyptians in the ancient world. Was it different in kind? The most distinctive charge against the Jews, that of misanthropy, of actively hating the human race, is exceptional. It is documented from the late second century B.C.E. in the words of the advisers of Antiochus Sidetes and in Lysimachus. Apion echoes their charges.[80] After the Jewish war, this charge gained credence in Rome.[81] Even this, however, can be viewed as an intensification of the ethnic antagonism that pervades this literature. Such charges were in circulation for centuries, but they did not lead to pogroms in the Seleucid or Ptolemaic kingdoms. As we noted at the beginning, the actions against the Jews in Alexandria lacked precedent. Stereotypes, even misanthropic ones, did not of themselves lead to violent action.

In the corpus of anti-Jewish literature, one passage stands out as reminiscent of Hitler's Final Solution: the advisers of Antiochus Sidetes urge the king "to make an end of the race (*genos*) completely, or failing that, to abolish their laws and force them to change their ways.[82] The king did not act on the advice, and neither did any other ancient ruler. Antiochus Epiphanes tried to change Jewish customs, but he certainly did not contemplate genocide. No such proposal is recorded in the conflict in Alexandria. We do, however, find genocide contemplated in a Jewish text. In the Hebrew text of Esther, Haman says to the king: "There is a certain people scattered and separated among the peoples in all the provinces of your kingdom; their laws are different from those of every other people, and they

---

[77] W. Helck, "Die Ägypter und die Fremden," *Saeculum* 15(1964) 103–116; Bohak, "The Ibis and the Jewish Question."

[78] Philo, *Spec. Leg.* 2.146.

[79] Lucian, *Pro. Imag.* 26; Tacitus, *Hist.* 4.81.1.

[80] *C. Ap.* 2.121: Jews allegedly swore an oath to show goodwill to no alien.

[81] Berthelot, *Philanthrôpia judaica*, 156–71. See especially Tacitus, *Hist.* 5.5.1–2, Stern, *Greek and Latin Authors*, 2.26.

[82] Bib. Hist. 34–35.1.5. Stern, *Greek and Latin Authors*, 1.183.

do not keep the king's laws, so that it is not appropriate for the king to tolerate them. If it pleases the king, let a decree be issued for their destruction" (Esth 3:8–9). Haman does not say that they hate humankind, nor does he mention their refusal to worship the gods of the Persians. (The charge of misanthropy is introduced in the Greek translation, 3:13 d–e). As far as we know, this story is fantasy, not history, but it points to the most basic, persistent feature in the conflicts involving Jews in antiquity, and probably in all ethnic conflicts: their laws and their ways were different.[83] The most basic reason why the Jewish people has been repeatedly involved in conflict over the centuries is that more than any other people it has maintained a distinctive identity and resisted assimilation. To say this is neither to praise nor to blame, but to observe that difference is an essential ingredient in ethnic conflict.

But difference does not always breed conflict. The Jews in Alexandria were no more different from their neighbors than the Jews of Asia Minor, and no more different from the Alexandrians of the Roman era than from their Ptolemaic forebears. Ultimately, the causes of conflict must be sought in specific social and historical circumstances, as we have seen in the case of Alexandria under Roman rule. To speak of anti-semitism as if it were some kind of ahistorical virus is only the obverse of the genuinely anti-semitic tendency to find the cause of conflict in the Jewish, or semitic, character.[84] It is also to fail to appreciate the contingent character of history.

---

[83] Compare the remark of Salo Baron, that the root of the negative attitude towards the Jewish people over the centuries was "dislike of the unlike" (Feldman, *Jew and Gentile*, 124). Tcherikover, *Hellenistic Civilization*, 358, says that the alien character of the Jews is the central cause of the origin of anti-semitism.

[84] For examples, see Feldman, *Jew and Gentile*, 124. The important study of B. Isaac, *The Invention of Racism in Classical Antiquity* (Princeton: Princeton University Press, 2004) appeared after this article had gone to press.

GREEKS AND JEWS: MUTUAL MISPERCEPTIONS IN JOSEPHUS' *CONTRA APIONEM*

ERICH S. GRUEN*

The confrontation of Athens and Jerusalem remains a powerful symbol. The two iconic emblems of Hellenic culture and Jewish tradition have long seemed to define the study of Jewish experience in the world of classical antiquity. A cultural clash between Greek and Jew continues to be the prevailing image.

The *Contra Apionem* of Josephus may not be his best known or his most widely read work. But the text contains considerable material that has helped to shape the view of a collision between the cultures. It was Josephus' last *opus*, composed probably in the late 90s C.E., evidently a reflection upon the place of Judaism in the intellectual and social context of Greco-Roman antiquity—and particularly its place vis-à-vis the Greeks.[1] It merits close scrutiny.

The title, *Contra Apionem* (Against Apion), was probably not the one applied by Josephus himself. Apion plays considerably less than a predominant role in the treatise. One ancient author, the Neo-Platonic philosopher Porphyry, referred to the tract as "Against the Greeks."[2] That may or may not have been Josephus' own title, but it is a perfectly reasonable description. The bulk of the work consists of Josephus' rejoinders to a host of criticisms, calumnies, and slanders by Greek intellectuals or those writing in Greek against Jews and Jewish practices. Hence, this text *prima facie* constitutes a vital repository of information on the attitudes of articulate Hellenes toward the Jews. It also represents a most valuable example of the rhetorical devices employed (with mixed success) by an articulate Jew but drawn from the classical armory in order to respond to and to refute the accusations leveled.[3]

---

* University of California, Berkeley.

[1] On the date, see Gerber (1997), 65–66; Goodman (1999), 50. It certainly came after publication of the *Antiquities* in 93/4; Jos. *CAp.* 1.1, 1.54, 1.127, 2.136, 2.287.

[2] Porphyry, *De Abstinent.* 4.11.

[3] On the rhetoric of the *Contra Apionem*, see Balch (1982), 102–122; Kasher (1996), 143–186; Hall (1996), 231–249; van Henten and Abusch (1996), 296–308; Barclay (1998), 194–221.

What accusations did Greeks bring against the Jews? First and foremost, according to Josephus, they insist that Jews are a relatively new phenomenon in the Mediterranean world. Jews do not go back to distant antiquity, so they need not be taken seriously. After all, Greek historians—the only ones who count—almost never mention the Jews. That is proof positive that Jews merit no attention. Josephus addresses this charge vigorously right at the outset of his treatise (1.1–5).[4] And he proceeds to devote a substantial portion of Book One to that subject, the first half of the treatise. No wonder that some later writers gave the title of the work as "On the Antiquity of the Jews."[5]

In fact, however, Josephus jousts against a plethora of criticisms. The opening round merely sets the stage for repeated bouts against Hellenic censures. As a choice example, Josephus cites Agatharchides, a second century B.C.E. historian and geographer from Cnidus,[6] who mocked the Jewish practice of observing the Sabbath. For Agatharchides, this constituted colossal folly. Jews refuse to take up arms on the Sabbath, and, as a consequence, they were routed by the armies of Ptolemy I and fell helplessly under harsh Egyptian rule (1.205–212).

More significantly, and perhaps more far-reaching, an entire body of literature existed in Greek, stemming from Egypt, primarily from Alexandria, that offered versions of the ancient Hebrews' experiences in Egypt very different from what one would find in the Book of Exodus. Josephus takes them on as a major challenge. The bewildering variety of tales stems ultimately from Manetho, no Greek but an Egyptian writing in Greek in the early third century B.C.E.[7] Manetho himself may not have been referring to the Hebrews at all but to Hyksos, the hostile invaders of Egypt who were eventually expelled by indigenous Egyptians. Later variations, however, amalgamated Hyksos with Hebrews and turned the expulsion into something that

---

[4] Barclay's forthcoming commentary on the *Contra Apionem* leaves open the possibility that Josephus refers to Romans who give credence to Greek historians. But the allusions in 1.6 and, especially, 1.15, make it clear that Greeks are his targets.

[5] Origen, *Contra Celsum*, 1.16, 4.11; Euseb. *HE*, 3.9.4.

[6] On Agatharchides and his geographical work, see Fraser (1972), 516–517, 539–553; Burstein (1989).

[7] On Manetho, see the review of scholarship in Pucci ben Zeev (1993), 224–234, and now Barclay (forthcoming). Josephus introduces this segment by stressing that Egyptians inaugurated the calumnies against Jews (1.223). But this does not dilute the impression that criticism by contemporary Greeks fueled Josephus' response.

looks like an upside-down and fiercely negative version of the Exodus.

That angle of the tale appeared in a work that Josephus tackles directly. Its author was Chaeremon, cited by Josephus as having written a history of Egypt, a man probably identical with the Chaeremon who was both a Stoic philosopher and an Egyptian priest, active in the mid 1st century c.e. (1.288–293).[8] Chaeremon retailed a story that has the goddess Isis appear in a dream to the Egyptian Pharaoh and tell him to expel from the land the polluted peoples who are contaminating the country with their afflictions. The identity of those polluted peoples is no mystery, for Chaeremon names their leaders: Joseph and Moses (1.290).

A more virulent version surfaces in the work of another Greco-Egyptian writer, the mysterious Lysimachus. His date and identity remain uncertain.[9] But it may be not far from that of Chaeremon. Lysimachus has the Jews as afflicted with leprosy, scurvy, and a variety of disgusting diseases, some of them driven out of Egypt into the wilderness and others packed into sheets of lead and drowned in the sea. Those who did leave the country made sure to burn, loot, and ravage on their way out, until they reached Judaea and built Jerusalem (1.304–311). Not a pretty picture of the Jews in Lysimachus' conception.

Then there was Apion.[10] Josephus faced a range of inventive, creative, and diabolical anecdotes or narratives transmitted by the Alexandrian grammarian, historian, and Homeric scholar from whom the *Contra Apionem* derives its name. Apion too retailed a pseudo-Exodus story in his history of Egypt. He makes Moses an Egyptian from Heliopolis (2.8–9). And he has Moses lead the lepers, the blind, and the lame—evidently as undesirable polluters (2.15). As if that were not bad enough, Apion's narrative claims that the Hebrews contracted tumors in their groins, causing them to rest on the seventh day, and

---

[8] For Chaeremon, one should consult the full scale study, including commentary on the fragments, by van der Horst (1984).

[9] See the thorough treatment of Lysimachus by Bar-Kochva (1999–2000b), 471–506 (Hebrew)—although his conjecture on the date (late 2nd century b.c.e.) is speculative.

[10] On Apion, the old study of Sperling (1886) remains useful. See also Gutschmid (1893), 356–371; Schürer (1986), 604–607; van der Horst (2002), 207–221. The forthcoming essay of Jones offers a thorough reassessment of Apion as presented in the *Contra Apionem*. For Josephus, Apion was born an Egyptian, only subsequently obtaining Alexandrian citizenship; 2.28–29, 2.41, 2.65–67, 2.81, 2.85, 2.137–138. Whatever the truth of that, it is clear that Apion wrote from a decidedly Hellenic vantage-point; cf. 2.30–32, 2.73–74, 2.79, 2.89–102, 2.121, 2.135.

thus giving it the name Sabbath because of the Egyptian word *sabbo* which means disease of the groin (2.20–21). That sounds rather nasty.

Apion had other mud to sling as well. He had it in for the Jews of Alexandria in particular. He disputed their claims to Alexandrian citizenship and denied that they had a right to call themselves Alexandrians (2.32, 2.38). He posed the pointed question that if Jews are citizens of Alexandria, why do they not worship the same gods as the Alexandrians (2.65)? And there is more. Apion branded the Jews as sowers of sedition (2.68). He ridiculed the practice of circumcision (2.137). He censured them for slaughtering animals as sacrificial offerings and then rebuked them for not eating pork (2.137). And, having named a number of Greek thinkers with awesome intellectual attainments, Apion maintained that he could not think of any distinguished Jews in the arts, the sciences, or the life of the mind generally (2.135). On that score he echoed the view of Apollonius Molon of Rhodes, the famous rhetorician and man of letters in the 1st century B.C.E. Apollonius called the Jews the dullest of barbarians and the only ones who had contributed no discovery to benefit our lives (2.148).[11] Apollonius and Lysimachus both got a dig in at Moses, characterizing him as a sorcerer and deceiver, and branded Mosaic law as instruction not in virtue but in vice (2.145).

The insults could get worse. A certain Mnaseas, possibly identical with Mnaseas of Patera, a pupil of the great scholar Eratosthenes in the late third century B.C.E., retails a strange story to illustrate the credulity of the Jews (2.112–114).[12] According to Mnaseas, they were taken in by a ruse concocted by an Idumaean in the course of a war between Jews and Idumaeans. This clever fellow promised the Jews that if they ceased to attack his city, he would deliver to them the god Apollo himself, the city's protector. The Jews readily agreed, and the Idumaean proceeded to dress himself in a bizarre attire that, to the untrained eye, would resemble Apollo. The dumfounded and gullible Jews meekly withdrew and kept their distance from this apparition. As a result, the cool Idumaean took the occasion to slip into the Jewish Temple and steal off with a precious object, nothing less than the golden head of an ass (2.112–114). Clearly the Jews do not emerge with much credit in this eccentric tale.

---

[11] On Apollonius and the Jews, see now Bar-Kochva (1999/2000a), 5–58 (Hebrew).
[12] For Mnaseas, see Stern (1974), I, 97–101.

The idea of an ass's image in the Temple in Jerusalem received an embellished version from the indefatigable Apion. He added that Jews not only kept a golden ass's head which turned up when Antiochus Epiphanes plundered the Temple, but that they actually worshipped the animal (2.80). And the story of what Antiochus found in the Temple when he entered it reached its wildest and most malicious form in another tale spun by unknown authors and repeated by Apion. That is the notorious blood-libel fiction. In this fable, Antiochus entered the Temple and there encountered a Greek captive who recounted his tale of woe. Jews had kidnapped him, so the Greek alleged, locked him in isolation in the Temple, fattened him up with lavish feasts, and prepared him for a sacrificial ritual. Indeed, he had learned that Jews did this annually. They would kidnap some innocent and unsuspecting Greek, balloon him into obesity for a whole year, and then feast on his flesh while they swore a mighty oath to maintain hostility against Greeks. This particular Greek, however, managed to escape his fate when Antiochus arrived in the nick of time, just a few days before the prospective victim's time was up (2.89–96).

As a body, this constitutes quite a chilling array of defamatory yarns. The defamations range from censure of Sabbath worship to the slander of ritual murder. Josephus apparently had his work cut out for him in trying to meet the challenge of this smorgasbord of smears. Greek and Greek speaking intellectuals, it seems, had marshaled an arsenal of verbal assaults against the nation of the Jews.

Josephus, as he presents himself, took up the cudgels as standard-bearer for Judaism. The *Contra Apionem* contains an assemblage of counter-attacks. The historian hones his rhetorical stratagems and his polemical weapons, and sallies out to battle.

Josephus fixes his eye on the initial target: the Greek denial that Jews go back to remote antiquity. He dwells on the matter at considerable length. Greeks claimed as proof that their own historians make almost no mention of Jews in their treatment of the distant past. Josephus turns the charge on its head. What do the Greeks know about antiquity? They are mere Johnnys-come-lately. They have not been on the planet long enough to make any such claims. When they write history, it is just modern history, hardly better than journalism; they do not go back much further than yesterday or the day before (1.6–7). Indeed, they did not learn the alphabet until it was taught to them by the Phoenicians (1.10). Homer is their earliest authority—and he could not even write (1.13). Why should anyone

pay attention to Greek historians? They cannot agree among themselves. They constantly snipe at one another. They accuse their rivals
of inaccuracy, sloppiness, and mendacity. Even Thucydides faced the
charge of falsification. And nobody believes Herodotus (1.15–18).
How could anyone trust them? The Greeks do not keep records, so
their historians have to make things up. Even the Athenians, renowned
for their supposed learning, retain no archives to speak of. The earliest laws they can cite only go back to Draco, in the late 7th century. The Arcadians, allegedly the most ancient of Greek folk, did
not even become literate until late in Greek history (1.19–22). In all
these matters, the Hellenes lagged well behind the Egyptians, Babylonians, and Phoenicians—not to mention the Hebrews (1.28–36).

As for the claim that Greek writers never mention the Jews, Josephus
has a barrage of answers. First of all, they only write about people
whom they happened to have encountered on the Mediterranean
coasts. They know nothing about nations that dwell inland. They never
even heard of the Romans until late in their own history (1.60–68).
Secondly, some Greek historians, like Hieronymus of Cardia, who
composed the most influential history of the Successors of Alexander
in the third century B.C.E., though he lived very close to the Jews,
wrote nothing about them out of sheer malice (1.213–214).[13] So the
absence of Jews from the books of Greek historians stems either from
ignorance or from malevolence. But who needs them? The antiquity
of the Jews, as Josephus recounts at excessive length, has authenti-
cation by much earlier and far more trustworthy sources: Egyptians,
Phoenicians, and Babylonians (1.70–160). Josephus revels in his refutations of Greeks ignorant of the great antiquity of the Jews.

The historian then turns to the calumnies and slanders by hostile
intellectuals. Chaeremon's tale of the expulsion of Jews from Egypt
is, according to Josephus, riddled with errors, inconsistencies, and
sheer fabrications. Chaeremon even made Joseph and Moses contemporaries! He did not know enough to be aware that there were
four generations between them (1.293–303). Next on the agenda was
Lysimachus' version that has victims of leprosy and scurvy driven
into the desert or drowned in sheets of lead. Josephus subjects this
narrative to withering scorn. Were Jews the only people who con-

---

[13] On Hieronymus, see the valuable study of Jane Hornblower (1981).

tracted such diseases, all others escaping the epidemic? And, if they were either drowned or tossed helplessly into the wilderness, how did so many of them not only survive but cross the desert, subdue the promised land, found the city of Jerusalem, and build a celebrated temple (1.312–319)?

Josephus hits his stride in taking on Mnaseas' outlandish tale. The notion of an Idumaean who dressed up like some comic Apollo to deceive the credulous Jews is too ridiculous, in Josephus' eyes, to merit much refutation. Did Jews really take this imposter walking about in a costume ringed with an array of lamps on his body to be the god Apollo? Did they leave the gates of the Temple's inner sanctuary unlocked and wide open, so that he could just walk in and make off with the head of an ass? And did he later bring it back so that it would be in the Temple again for Antiochus Epiphanes to find (2.113–120)? Josephus leaves the story in a shambles.

There remained the unspeakable Apion. No need to dwell at any length on Josephus' numerous rebuttals. Apion's chronology for the Exodus was off by several hundred years (2.15–19). Apion had claimed that Jewish wanderers in the wilderness were afflicted by disease of the groin. What, all one hundred and ten thousand of them? And yet they marched through the desert to Judaea in just six days without a problem? Where did the ailments go (2.20–27)? And what about Apion's challenge to Jewish claims on Alexandrian citizenship? Josephus tosses the charge right back at him. Apion himself was born in rural Egypt and only later became a naturalized Alexandrian (2.29–32, 2.40–41). And he is too dumb to know that Jews are not only Alexandrians in Alexandria but Antiochenes in Antioch, Ephesians in Ephesus, and so on (2.38–39). In fact, Jews enjoy civic privileges in Alexandria, so Josephus insists, that were guaranteed to them from the time of Alexander the Great and Ptolemy I (2.42–47, 2.72). He also hurls the charge of sedition back at Apion. Are not the Egyptians, especially those dwelling in Alexandria, the most unruly and violent people in the world (2.68–70)?

Apion even had the gall to blame Jews for not erecting images of the Roman emperor. Does he not know that the Romans themselves exempted Jews from this practice and respected their ancestral prohibition of images? The historian then adds a little twist of the knife. Of course, Greeks do not mind setting up statues to the emperor. They make statues for everyone in sight: parents, wives, children, even their favorite slaves (2.73–78).

Apion knows nothing of Jewish aniconism anyway. Did he not spread the stupid story that Jews house an ass's head made of gold in their temple? Josephus has a field day with that one. He notes a whole series of foreign conquerors, including Roman generals, who entered the Jerusalem Temple—and found nothing therein. But Apion is ignorant of all that, says Josephus. Unsurprisingly so. After all, he has the brains of an ass, as well as the impudence of a dog—an animal which his countrymen, the Egyptians, worship as divine, along with crocodiles, asps, and vipers (2.79–88).

Josephus delivers scathing criticism of the allegation that a captured Greek was fattened up for a year and then chopped up to be eaten. No one with even a minimal knowledge of the rigid restrictions surrounding the practices of the Temple could entertain such an idea for an instant. For Josephus, this is a gratuitous lie perpetrating a gross impiety that could only be conveyed by someone who does not have the smallest regard for the truth (2.97–111).

And that was not all. Apion had the impudence to claim that Jews had produced no men preeminent in wisdom or science, naming among Greeks who earned that distinction Socrates, Zeno, Cleanthes— and Apion himself. Josephus has only to cite his own *Jewish Antiquities* for a gallery of Jewish geniuses. Apion's inclusion of himself among Hellenic sages decisively discredits the idea (2.135–136). Further, his criticism of Jews for sacrificing domestic animals, refraining from pork, and practicing circumcision results in even greater absurdity. Is Apion not aware that all people, including Greeks and Macedonians, slaughter animals for sacrifice? Or that his own Egyptians abstain from pork and carry out circumcision (2.137–142)? The man's ignorance, if we believe Josephus, is simply astounding.

Josephus does not spend much time refuting other Greek indictments. It sufficed, for example, to dismiss Apollonius Molon by pointing out that in different parts of his work he accused the Jews both of cowardice and of temerity. The two traits hardly go together— so much the worse for Apollonius (2.148).

Josephus' more serious and sustained rejoinder to Greek detractors took the form of a lengthy encomium to Jewish laws, customs, and beliefs.[14] In the course of it, he hails Moses as decidedly superior to

---

[14] On this aspect of the work, see Amir (1985–8), 89–105; Rajak (2001), 195–217, and the full scale treatment by Gerber (1997), *passim*; esp. 133–208.

the much praised but undeserving Greek lawgivers like Solon, Lycurgus, and Zaleucus (2.154, 2.161). Spartans and Athenians fall short. The laws of the former are too pragmatic, those of the latter too abstract. Only Moses struck the proper balance (2.172–173). And only Jews really adhere to their laws (2.176–178, 2.182–183, 2.232–235, 2.272). The measures conceived by Plato are reckoned by his fellow Greeks as too utopian to expect compliance. Yet, for Josephus, they are much easier to comply with than the rigorous Jewish code—with which Jews do in fact comply (2.223–224). Greek tradition holds up the Spartans as the most faithful observers of law. But, so Josephus notes, they do so only when fortune smiles upon them. When things go bad, they swiftly forget almost all their conventions (2.225–231).

A common Greek complaint, voiced, among others, by Apollonius Molon, held that Jews were exclusionists. They scorned foreigners, and they were dismissive of all those who did not share their customs. To this Josephus had a sharp rebuttal. He pointed out that Greeks are by no means immune from this attitude. Spartans, in particular, expel aliens from their midst and try to prevent their own citizens from going abroad lest they become corrupted by others' practices. And even the supposedly liberal Athenians executed Socrates and persecuted other philosophers when they propounded ideas that did not cohere with traditional Athenian beliefs (2.258–268). Finally, Josephus, in condemning Greek infringements of their own laws, cites sodomy, incest, and indulgence in every imaginable unnatural and disgusting pleasure (2.275). That is the flourish he employs to conclude his denunciation of the Hellenes.

The message of the treatise seems to ring out loud and clear. A fierce antagonism held between the cultures, at least at the level of savage verbal exchange. As is plain, the *Contra Apionem* ranks as a prime document for that antagonism. Josephus composed a vigorous apologia for Jews under attack.[15] And it contains a substantial proportion of the evidence for a split between Athens and Jerusalem.

Yet the matter is not so simple. A closer examination of the text suggests more ambiguity and complexity than meets the eye. And a

---

[15] This is the standard interpretation. See, e.g., Reinach (1930), xv–xx; Balch (1982), 114–122; Schäublin (1982), 316–340; Bilde (1988), 118–120; *idem* (1996), 94–111; Kasher (1996), 150–157; Barclay (1996), 362–363; Gerber (1997), 78–88; Rajak (2001), 197; Barclay (2004), 109–111. Goodman (1999), 45–58, doubts that there was a tradition of Jewish apologetic, but acknowledges such an objective in this work.

number of the accusations leveled at Jews by Greeks seem on inspection surprisingly peculiar and paradoxical.

Consider the opening charge to which Josephus devotes a substantial amount of text: i.e. the Greek denial that Jews date back to early antiquity. Josephus takes great pains to refute that allegation. A noteworthy fact, however, needs to be stressed here. Josephus does not attach the accusation to any particular author or authors. This contrasts with most of the rest of the text where he regularly cites and addresses specific writers. The view that Jews are recent arrivals in the Mediterranean has only vague and unidentified perpetrators. That causes some misgivings right away.

Further, there is something particularly odd about this alleged Greek complaint. Greeks did not normally find it necessary to debunk other nations or other ethnic groups for their relative youth in the history of the world. Quite the contrary. Hellenes readily acknowledged, in admiring fashion, the great antiquity of Egypt. Herodotus had no difficulty in recording a range of Greek borrowings from Egyptian culture, including the worship of Dionysus, the belief in transmigration of souls, and various philosophical and religious precepts.[16] Aristotle conceded that Egypt is the oldest of nations, the first to create political institutions, and the first to discover the mathematical arts.[17] Isocrates noted that the Spartans adopted their social and political system in imitation of Egypt.[18] Nor did Greek writers like Herodotus hesitate to recognize that Greeks owed their very literacy to the teachings of the Phoenicians.[19] Numerous other instances of these acknowledged borrowings can readily be cited. The famous anecdote of the Egyptian priest who told Solon that, by comparison with Egypt, all Greeks are children, comes to us from a Greek, Plato, with no hint of embarrassment.[20]

The fact needs stress. It seems quite unlikely that Greek writers would see the lack of a long chronological pedigree as a reason for reproach. And it is even less likely that they would fasten this label upon the Jews for whom it was manifestly specious. No wonder that Josephus failed to provide a single name for any Greek author who

---

[16] Herodotus, 2.49, 2.123.
[17] Aristotle, *Pol.* 7.1329b.20–34; *Met.* 1.1.981b.
[18] Isocrates, *Busiris*, 17–18.
[19] Herodotus, 5.57–59.
[20] Plato, *Tim.* 22b.

held such a view. One cannot avoid the strong suspicion that he has concocted a confrontation on this issue. It certainly allowed Josephus to discredit the idea quite easily and unequivocally. A neat set-up.[21]

One can say much the same about Josephus' sniping at Greek historians as untrustworthy on the grounds that they disagreed with one another (1.15–18). That is a cheap shot.[22] Of course, historians quarrel with one another—to this very day. That does not itself diminish their credibility. Josephus was hardly immune. He came under heavy criticisms from other historians as well (1.2, 1.46–47, 1.53, 1.56). This begins to look more and more like an artificial construct.

In fact, Josephus, in his more sober moments, draws heavily on Greek historians himself—even when he does not cite them. He gives as reason for the antiquity and accuracy of Jewish records the fact that their archives record an unbroken succession of High Priests who go back for two thousand years (1.36). That is a variant on the closely comparable tale told by Herodotus who has the Egyptians tell the naive Greek historian Hecataeus of Miletus that they can trace an unbroken succession of high priests and kings who go back for three hundred and forty one generations, or about 11,340 years.[23] And when Josephus responds to the critics of his own historical writing—again without naming any names—he pilfers the thought and language directly from Thucydides and Polybius. He stresses his own commitment to personal, eyewitness testimony, and rejects those who treat his work like a schoolboy's submission for a prize essay (1.53–56). That comes straight out of Thucydides and Polybius.[24]

More significantly, Josephus is not averse to citing Greek authors, whether apparently discredited historians or other writers, so long as they advance his own agenda—even if he has to press their statements into service. When useful for his purpose, they suddenly become credible and reliable. He even quotes Herodotus as speaking of the Syrians in Palestine who practice circumcision and concludes that he must be referring to Jews (1.168–171). In all likelihood Herodotus,

---

[21] Goodman (1999), 52–53, rightly raises the suspicion that some of the arguments against which Josephus tilts were artificial creations. That possibility is noted also by Droge (1996), 117–118. Neither pursues the matter.

[22] Cohen (1988), 3–9, recognizes the weakness, even absurdity, of Josephus' position here, but nevertheless takes this as an authentic historiographical debate and polemic. See also Schäublin (1982), 320–321; Bilde (1996), 98–101; Barclay (forthcoming).

[23] Herodotus, 2.142–143.

[24] Thucydides, 1.22.4; Polybius, 3.31.12–13.

who never mentions Jews, alluded to the Philistines.[25] Josephus would
not inquire further. He sought out Greek sources who acknowledged
(even indirectly) the existence of the Jews. He cites a certain Choerilus
who recorded a people from the Solyman hills among the troops
accompanying Xerxes on the Persian expedition to Greece. Josephus
takes this to be an allusion to Hierosolyma and thus a reference to
Jews from Jerusalem (1.172–175).[26] A bit of a stretch. He has still
better material from Clearchus, a pupil of Aristotle. Josephus found
a useful anecdote in Clearchus who reports that his teacher encountered a learned Jew in Asia Minor and was much impressed by his
erudition. Clearchus added the tidbit that this (unnamed) Jew was
not only Hellenic in language but in his very soul (1.176–182).[27]

Most suitable for Josephus' ends was the early 3rd century historian Hecataeus of Abdera. He quotes or paraphrases at great length
from excerpts attributed to Hecataeus—or, at least to someone whom
he took to be or presented as the Greek historian Hecataeus. The
extended snippets disclose Hecataeus' great admiration for Jewish
adherence to their laws, the splendor of their temple, their military
skills, and the high esteem in which they were held by Hellenistic
kings (1.183–204). Josephus further cites a number of Greek authors
who attest to the antiquity of the Jews, even if they do not have all
the facts straight (1.216–217). And he notes three in particular who
are demonstrably accurate and trustworthy: Demetrius of Phalerum,
Philo the Elder, and Eupolemus (1.218). Here, misconception or
deceit cannot be gainsaid. We may be confident that each of these
writers was, in fact, a Jew, writing under a Greek pseudonym. That
is surely true of Hecataeus and almost as surely of Philo, Demetrius,
and Eupolemus. Josephus ought to have known this—and probably
did.[28] But whether he deliberately passed them off as Greeks or was

---

[25] Gutschmid (1893), 565–567; Reinach (1930), 33; Stern (1974), 2–4; Barclay
(forthcoming).
[26] See the discussions of Gutschmid (1893), 567–578; Reinach (1930), 35; Barclay
(forthcoming).
[27] On the passage from Clearchus, see now Bar-Kochva (1997/8), 435–481
(Hebrew); Barclay (forthcoming).
[28] That "Hecataeus" was a Jewish author has been firmly established by Bar-
Kochva (1996a), 54–121, 143–181. An extensive commentary on these fragments
will appear in Barclay (forthcoming). For the fragments of Philo, Demetrius, and
Eupolemus, Jewish writers whom Josephus misidentified, see Holladay (1983), 51–156;
(1989), 205–299. For Wacholder (1974), 2–3, Josephus knew the truth but was deliberately ambiguous.

himself deceived matters little for our purposes. More to the point, he was perfectly happy, even proud, to parade Greek authors, or what he took to be Greek authors, as confirming the favorable impressions and the prestige that Jews enjoyed among the intelligentsia of the Mediterranean world.

So, what happened to the chasm between Jew and Greek? Where did the animosity disappear to? Josephus in fact lets slip a telling phrase: he says that Jews are more distant from Greeks in geography than in their way of life (2.123). Indeed he goes further still. He singles out certain Greek intellectuals for high praise, notably Plato. Josephus particularly likes Plato's criticism of Hellenic myths and his rebuke of those naive persons who believe in them, for they represent gods as men and women with all the faults and vices that attach to mortals—only more so (2.239–256). In Josephus' conception, Plato is here more akin to Moses, indeed follows Moses on this and other matters (2.257). The idea that the Greek intelligentsia got much of its best ideas from Jewish thinkers and the books of Moses had already been voiced by other Jewish writers. Josephus readily picks up the theme. He proclaims that Hellenic philosophers, whether they knew it or not, were really following the precepts of Moses (2.281). And he is able to cite the Greek biographer Hermippus of Smyrna who wrote a life of Pythagoras in the 3rd century B.C.E. to show that some Greeks bought this idea as well. Hermippus affirmed that the great Pythagoras adopted many aspects of Jewish law into his own teaching (1.162–165). Whatever the truth of these claims— and there is good reason to be skeptical—what matters is that Josephus retailed them and presented them as authentic.[29] The same man who composed the *Contra Apionem* to underscore the divide between Jews and their detractors also finds the Greeks as intellectual heirs to the Jews and as reproducers of Jewish doctrines.[30]

What is going on here? The more one reads, the more one wonders how real is this confrontation'. How should we interpret the verbal assaults by Greek writers and the rhetorical rejoinders by Josephus? It is hard to escape an increasing sense of mendacity and manipulation. An important point requires notice—one that is obvious enough

---

[29] Hermippus' own comments may have been mocking ones. But Josephus' selective excerpt evidently omitted that feature. So, rightly, Barclay (forthcoming).

[30] Some of the internal tensions in Josephus' treatment are noted by Barclay (1996), 364–366.

but all too easily forgotten. What we possess of these ostensibly hostile writers are simply excerpts—excerpts carefully chosen for us by Josephus. It would be foolish indeed to infer that what survives through that medium is representative or characteristic of the authors and works as a whole. Very far from it.

One example can serve as pointed illustration. Agatharchides, as noted earlier, criticized Jews who observed the Sabbath, declined to take up arms, and thus got smashed by Ptolemy I. This passage, however, did not derive from an anti-semitic work. Nor is there reason to believe that Agatharchides even censured the observance of the Sabbath. He simply offered instances of human folly driven by superstition. The prime exhibit indeed involved a Hellenistic princess who perished because she delayed escape when stopped by a dream. The Jewish failure served him only as a parallel (1.205–212).[31] That is not the impression one would get, however, from Josephus' presentation of the excerpt. He represents it tendentiously as anti-Jewish.

Another instance delivers a similar lesson: Mnaseas' narrative of the Idumaean who put on a fancy get-up, posing as Apollo, and completely hoodwinking the Jews (2.111–114). The story makes no sense as it stands, and we have no idea of the context. The brief selection that Josephus provides seems deliberately designed to make it preposterous and thus to allow him to shoot it down with ease.

The pseudo-Exodus stories packaged under the names of Chaeremon and Lysimachus neatly serve as set-ups for demolition by Josephus (1.288–293, 1.304–311). It warrants mention that the quoted or paraphrased excerpts are a good deal shorter than Josephus' refutation of them. Once again, they seem chosen, indeed manipulated, to highlight their inconsistencies, chronological blunders, exaggerated numbers, ignorance of Jewish tradition, and inexplicable omissions. Another point needs stress. Neither of these authors wrote about the Jews *per se*. They composed histories of Egypt in which the Jews just briefly came into play—and probably in passing. Even the excerpts do not make much of the Jews themselves. They focus on the Pharaoh's efforts to rid the land of pollution. Lysimachus indeed seems to admire Moses for rallying his people in the wilderness (1.309). And both authors, in pointing to successful Jewish assaults on Egypt, may actually be drawing on Jewish sources for whom this was a point of

---

[31] Cf. the remarks of Barclay (forthcoming), who sees a sharper critique of the Jews here.

pride.[32] Josephus' packaging bears the principal responsibility for saddling these authors with anti-Jewish motivation, thereby to make them easier for the historian to knock over.

Even the arch-villain Apion may not be quite so evil as he seems.[33] He too almost certainly did not write a history of the Jews. He did produce a work on Egypt in which the Jews naturally cropped up (2.10).[34] It is entirely possible that almost everything Apion had to say about Jews appears in the selections supplied by Josephus—unless, of course, he had anything favorable to say. What Apion reports about Moses is at least not obviously hostile. He observes that Moses set up open-air prayer houses in each district of his home town Heliopolis, that he erected pillars instead of obelisks, created the relief of a boat and perhaps a statue that cast a shadow paralleling the course of the sun (2.10–11). Josephus makes mincemeat of this, interpreting it as a graven image which Moses would never have dreamed of (2.12–14). What Apion actually had in mind seems impossible to fathom. But he would surely not have pilloried Moses for erecting graven images. This small selection contains nothing of an anti-Jewish character.

Apion merits a closer look. The majority of blasts leveled at him by Josephus in the treatise direct themselves against errors, ignorance, and stupidity rather than prejudice. This holds, for example, in Josephus' mockery of Apion for listing the most eminent Greek sages and including himself among them (2.135–136). Josephus skewers him for that boast. Apion doubtless included no Jews in that select company of wise men. But he may very well have excluded all others besides Greeks as well. It is Josephus who puts the spotlight on the Jews. He also lambasts Apion for his version of the Exodus story, making hash of his etymological connection between Sabbath and the Egyptian *sabbo* that signified disease of the groin (2.20–27).[35] The connection may indeed be specious, and the joke

---

[32] See the arguments of Gruen (1998), 55–70. Cf. the treatment of Droge (1996), 134–141.

[33] For a comparable approach, see Jones (forthcoming).

[34] See Gellius, 5.14.4, 6.8.4, 10.10.2; Tatian, *Orat. Ad Graec.* 38; Euseb. *PE*, 10.11.13. Reference to a work on the Jews appears in Julius Africanus, *apud* Euseb. *PE*, 10.10.16, and Clement, *Strom.* 1.21.101.3. But these probably depend on inference from Josephus. See the convincing arguments of Jones (forthcoming). Cf. also Schürer (1986), 606–607; *contra*: Motzo (1912–13), 459–464.

[35] Cf. Scheller (1955), 298–300. See now Dillery (2003), 387–389, who sees Josephus' assault as, in part, an attack on Apion's repute as a *grammatikos*.

sardonic, but the purpose need not have been malicious—except in Josephus' formulation.

Much the same can be said about Apion's questioning of Jewish rights to civic privileges in Alexandria (2.33–42). One might consider the possibility that Apion, who acquired Alexandrian citizenship rather than possessing it by birth, could have reason to question that privilege for a whole range of immigrants—not just Jews as Jews (2.32). It was Josephus who converted this position into a glorious opportunity to wax eloquent about the generous privileges bestowed upon Jews from the time of Alexander the Great through the Ptolemies and to the Romans (2.42–50, 2.61–64, 2.71–72). Insofar as Apion did have occasion to assail the Jews in particular we know the context: he served as spokesman for the Alexandrians in 40 C.E. at a hearing before the emperor Caligula, where he sought to blame the Jews for the recent upheaval in that city.[36] There he confronted a rival Jewish delegation, and the rhetorical exchange must have been a heated one. It is in that setting that Apion most probably delivered accusations of sedition and failure to set up statues of the emperor (2.68, 2.73).[37] But a notable fact needs to be registered. Although Josephus reports Apion's role as Alexandrian envoy to Rome in his *Jewish Antiquities*, he makes no mention of it in the *Contra Apionem*. Why? An answer can be surmised. It would spoil his picture. In the latter treatise the historian seeks to suppress specific circumstances and postulate a wider Hellenic hostility to Judaism. The broader scene furthers his design of presenting himself as champion of Jewish principles and traditions.

The misrepresentations multiply. Apion's story of the golden ass's head in the Temple, whatever its origin, would not, from a pagan point of view, constitute an attack on erecting graven images (2.80–88).[38]

---

[36] Jos. *Ant.* 18.257–259.

[37] It does not follow that all or most of Apion's remarks on the Jews in his written work stemmed from that political hearing, as is claimed by Motzo (1912–13), 461–463.

[38] The belief or purported belief that Jews paid homage to an ass in the Temple circulated in different versions, whether as ass's head, statue of an ass, or Moses seated on an ass; Diod. 34/35.1.3; Tac. *Hist.* 5.4.2; Plut. *Quaest. Conviv.* 4.5.2; Jos. *CAp.* 112–114. For efforts to sort out the entangled tales, see, esp., Bickermann (1980), 245–255; Bar-Kochva (1996b), 310–326. The stories may have originated in Egypt, later incorporated into the narrative of Antiochus IV's assault on Jerusalem. That the Jewish nation is here being assimilated in hostile fashion to Seth-Typhon, the enemy of Osiris in Egyptian tradition and the god whose sacred animal was an ass, is now a scholarly consensus; e.g. van Henten and Abusch (1996), 284–289;

But it served Josephus' purpose to make his point about the purity of Jewish piety. As for the blood-libel tale, the annual ritual murder of a Greek, Josephus evidently plucked out that slander precisely because it was preposterous (2.89–96). Few Greeks could have believed it. The libel appears almost nowhere else in all the Greco-Roman literature of antiquity. And, of course, we do not know in what context Apion made reference to it.[39] For Josephus who dug it out, however, it provided the useful occasion for a tirade against Apion's stupidity and an encomium of the Temple and its rituals (2.97–111).

The calculated selectivity of snippets and the deliberate repression of context mark the *Contra Apionem* throughout. The labors of modern scholars who assembled the fragments of Greek writers from this treatise and constructed an epidemic of anti-Judaism that had to be resisted and refuted show just how effectively Josephus has shepherded his readership. The *Contra Apionem* is not a genuine antidote to a wave of Hellenic hostility toward Judaism. Josephus ransacked his texts to find the most outrageous claims that he could most readily rebut with zest and panache, a collection of straw men to be knocked over. And he massaged his material to simulate a confrontation in which he could take up the banner for his countrymen. This was not an authentic crusade but a rhetorical showpiece.

Why do it? Some have suggested that it supplied a means to encourage Jewish proselytism.[40] If so, then Josephus has been exceedingly

---

Schäfer (1997), 55–62; Bar-Kochva (1996b), 318–325. If so, however, it is remarkable that that connection is nowhere explicitly made. The nearest to it is Plutarch, *De Iside et Osiride*, 31, who, in fact, questions it. Cf. Bickermann (1980), 246. Whatever its origins, the claim that Jews revered an ass hardly represents a major pagan critique of Judaism that Josephus felt obliged to refute. Schäfer (1997), 60–61, regards it as an invention of Apion. Feldman (1988), 212–215; (1996), 257–258, even considers association with the ass as having positive features.

[39] It appears elsewhere only in the Suda, ascribed to a certain Damocritus; see Stern (1974), 530–531. And this may well derive from Apion's own report. The tale had more than one formulation, pieced together in the source employed by Apion; Bickermann (1980), 225–245; Bar-Kochva (1995/6), 347–374 (Hebrew). Like the ass stories, it too may have originated in Egypt and was subsequently blended into the narrative on Antiochus IV. But Josephus' claim (2.90–91), that Antiochus' propagandists fashioned it to justify his assault upon the Jews, widely accepted by moderns, has little to recommend it. Cf. Schäfer (1997), 65. Why should the partisans of Antiochus worry about producing an apologia to defend his actions against Jews? And to what audiences? Insofar as any retrospective explanations were needed for Antiochus' attack, they cited Jewish misanthropy and practices contrary to custom, not ritual murder; see Diod. 34/5.1.3–4. In any event, there is no indication that this "blood-libel" had much circulation and demanded a response from Josephus.

[40] Bilde (1988), 120–121; Mason (1996), 208–224.

subtle and the message is muted. To be sure, the work contains references to an openness to converts, a welcome to those who wish to share Jewish principles and practices, indeed a pride in the fact that many have already chosen to do so (2.123, 2.209–210, 2.261, 2.282–286). But it is hard to conceive of anyone rushing to conversion as a consequence of reading this tract. Another suggestion proposes that Josephus responded to anti-Jewish propaganda circulating in Flavian Rome where he was writing, in the wake of the Jewish rebellion.[41] If that be the case, however, it is most peculiar that the criticisms that appear most commonly in Roman writers, namely those regarding observance of the Sabbath, dietary laws, and circumcision, barely play any role at all in the *Contra Apionem*. Even in the circles in which Josephus might have moved in Rome, he would hardly have picked up conversations about Agatharchides, Chaeremon, or Apion![42]

A more personal motive may play a role. Josephus himself had come under censure for his previously published works. The issue surfaces right at the beginning of the *Contra Apionem*, precisely with regard to the antiquity of the Jews (1.2–3). As we have seen, this could hardly have been a matter of widespread concern to Greeks. But it evidently did stimulate some critics who charged Josephus with exaggeration on that score. Others, according to Josephus, had written rival histories of the Jewish war, challenging his version (1.46–47). And, as has already been noted, some described his work as a schoolboy's exercise, questioning its reliability and its veracity (1.53, 1.56; cf. 1.127, 2.136, 2.287). Josephus elected not to respond to his critics with a personal apologia or polemic. Rather, he chose a different and more elevated cause. In essence, Josephus wrapped himself in the mantle of Judaism as a whole. The reply to his critics transmogrified into a retort to attacks on Jewish values and Jewish character generally.

The attacks themselves, to be sure, did not all stem from Josephus' fertile imagination. Jewish traditions and practices had often been a subject of amusement or derision. But the historian, in numerous

---

[41] Goodman (1999), 55–57.

[42] A recent study by Barclay (2004), 111–121, suggests that Josephus sought to undermine the widespread belief, in Rome and elsewhere, that associated Jews with Egyptians. But there is no evidence that the Romans held this putative association (insofar as they took it seriously) against the Jews. It is difficult to believe that Josephus felt impelled to slander Egyptians in order to reassure Romans that Jews were quite distinct from them.

instances, applied exaggeration, embellishment, and contrivance. He selected, condensed, trimmed, and paraphrased in order to make the judgments easier targets for his own rejoinders. Josephus, in brief, presents himself not as acting from personal pique but as defending the integrity of his own people everywhere.

The audience for such a treatise remains a matter of conjecture. None can proclaim a definitive answer (though some have approached such a proclamation). A growing number of scholars now concur that Josephus had Gentiles as his target readership, whether Romans among whom he dwelled when composing his work or wider circles in the Greco-Roman world who might have been sympathetic to Jews. For those who conjecture a missionary purpose, such a readership needs to be postulated.[43] But that purpose is itself questionable.[44] Others imagine an array of readers across the spectrum, ranging from hostile libelers of Jews who were being answered, those influenced by the slanders who needed to be convinced, those either ignorant of Jews or interested in Judaism, those close to the administration in Rome or governing circles in the Roman empire, and educated Jews who needed an arsenal to use against their opponents.[45] If this is what Josephus had in mind, he would have required the mechanisms and marketing of a modern publishing house. One might observe that some of the description of Jewish practices and customs would seem too basic for a Jewish audience, thus suggesting Gentile targets (2.180–219).[46] But this means no more than that non-Jews may have been a purported audience for the purpose of the rhetoric, not that they were an intended one. Certainly one can rule out the idea that Josephus expected Greeks to welcome this tract. They could only have read it with fury, disdain, or incredulity. And how many Romans would take an interest in Josephus' sniping at obscure Greek and Egyptian writers, quarreling about Jewish antiquity, and claiming the superiority of Judaism over Hellenic institutions? Josephus needed to make a case to his fellow-Jews.[47]

---

[43] See Bilde (1988), 120; Mason (1996), 223; cf. Feldman (1988), 230–243; but see Gerber (1997), 374–379.

[44] See above.

[45] Kasher (1996), 150–157 proposes this motley assemblage. Barclay (2004), 111, 121–126, puts principal stress on a putative Roman or "Romanized" readership.

[46] So Goodman (1999), 50–51.

[47] Rajak (2001), 197, recognizes Jews as the audience, but sees the purpose as supplying them with an armory for their defense.

The *Contra Apionem* is a shrewd and effective treatise. But it should not be taken as a genuine deposit of Hellenic thrusts against the Jews nor as a selfless championship of Judaism against its enemies. Josephus' own agenda prevails. The *Contra Apionem* may, in some ways be his cleverest work. But it is not authentic reflection of a war between Athens and Jerusalem.

Contra Apionem Bibliography

Amir, Y. "Θεοκρατία as a Concept of Political Philosophy: Josephus' Presentation of Moses' *Politeia*," *SCI* 8–9 (1985–8) 83–105.

Balch, D. "Two Apologetic Encomia: Dionysius on Rome and Josephus on the Jews," *JSJ* 13 (1982) 102–122.

Barclay, J. M. G. *Jews in the Mediterranean Diaspora* (Edinburgh, 1996).

—— "Josephus v. Apion," in S. Mason, *Understanding Josephus: Seven Perspectives* (Sheffield, 1998) 194–221.

—— "The Politics of Contempt: Judaeans and Egyptians in Josephus's *Against Apion*," in J. M. G. Barclay, *Negotiating Diaspora: Jewish Strategies in the Roman Empire* (London, 2004) 109–127.

—— *Contra Apionem: Translation and Commentary* (forthcoming).

Bar-Kochva, B. "The Hellenistic Blood-Libel—Content, Origins, and Transformations," *Tarbiz* 65 (1995/6) 347–374 (Hebrew).

—— *Pseudo-Hecataeus on the Jews: Legitimizing the Jewish Diaspora* (Berkeley, 1996a).

—— "An Ass in the Jerusalem Temple—The Origins and Development of the Slander," in Feldman and Levison (1996b) 310–326.

—— "Aristotle, the Learned Jew, and the Indian Kalanoi," *Tarbiz* 67 (1997/8) 435–481 (Hebrew).

—— "The Anti-Jewish Treatise of Apollonius Molon," *Tarbiz* 69 (1999–2000a) 5–58 (Hebrew).

—— "Lysimachus of Alexandria and the Hostile Traditions Concerning the Exodus," *Tarbiz* 69 (1999–2000b) 471–506 (Hebrew).

Bickermann, E. "Ritualmord und Eselkult: Ein Beitrag zur Geschichte antiker Publizistik," in E. Bickermann, *Studies in Jewish and Christian History*, vol. 2 (Leiden, 1980).

Bilde, P. *Flavius Josephus between Jerusalem and Rome* (Sheffield, 1988).

—— "*Contra Apionem* 1.28–56: Josephus' View of his own Work in the Context of the Jewish Canon," in Feldman and Levison (1996) 94–114.

Burstein, S. M. *Agatharchides of Cnidus: On the Erythraean Sea* (London, 1989).

Cohen, S. J. D. "History and Historiography in the *Against Apion* of Josephus," in A. Rapoport-Albert, *Essays in Jewish Historiography* (*History and Theory*, Beiheft 27, 1988) 1–11.

Dillery, J. "Putting him Back Together Again: Apion Historian, Apion *Grammatikos*," *CP* 98 (2003) 383–390.

Droge, A. J. "Josephus between Greeks and Barbarians," in Feldman and Levison (1996) 115–142.

Feldman, L. H. "Pro-Jewish Intimations in Anti-Jewish Remarks Cited in Josephus' *Against Apion*," *JQR* 78 (1988) 187–251.

—— "Reading Between the Lines: Appreciation of Judaism in Anti-Jewish Writers Cited in *Contra Apionem*," in Feldman and Levison (1996) 250–270.

Feldman, L. H. and J. R. Levison, *Josephus' Contra Apionem: Studies in its Character and Context* (Leiden, 1996).

Fraser, P. M. *Ptolemaic Alexandria* (Oxford, 1972).

Gerber, C. *Ein Bild des Judentums für Nichtjuden von Flavius Josephus: Untersuchungen zu seiner Schrift Contra Apionem* (Leiden, 1997).

Goodman, M. "Josephus' Treatise *Against Apion*," in M. Edwards, M. Goodman, and S. Price, *Apologetics in the Roman Empire* (Oxford, 1999) 45–58.

Gruen, E. S. *Heritage and Hellenism: The Reinvention of Jewish Tradition* (Berkeley, 1998).

Gutschmid , A. von, *Kleine Schriften*, vol. 4 (Leipzig, 1893).

Hall, R. G. "Josephus' *Contra Apionem* and Historical Inquiry in the Roman Rhetorical Schools," in Feldman and Levison (1996) 229–249.

Holladay, C. R. *Fragments from Hellenistic Jewish Authors, Vol. I: Historians* (Chico, 1983).

—— *Fragments from Hellenistic Jewish Authors, Vol. II: Poets* (Atlanta, 1989).

Hornblower, J. *Hieronymus of Cardia* (Oxford, 1981).

Jones, K. R. "Apion the Grammarian in Josephus' *Contra Apionem*" (forthcoming).

Mason, S. "The *Contra Apionem* in Social and Literary Context: An Invitation to Judean Philosophy," in Feldman and Levison (1996) 187–228.

Motzo, B. "Il κατὰ Ἰουδαίων di Apione," *Atti della R. Accademia delle scienze di Torino* 48 (1912–13) 459–468.

Pucci ben Zeev, M. "The Reliability of Josephus Flavius: The Case of Hecataeus' and Manetho's Accounts of Jews and Judaism," *JSJ* 24 (1993) 215–234.

Kasher, A. "Polemic and Apologetic Methods of Writing in *Contra Apionem*," in Feldman and Levison (1996) 143–186.

Rajak, T. "The *Against Apion* and the Continuities in Josephus' Political Thought," in T. Rajak, *The Jewish Dialogue with Greece and Rome: Studies in Social and Cultural Interaction* (Leiden, 2001).

Reinach, T. *Flavius Josèphe, Contre Apion* (Paris, 1930).

Schäfer, P. *Judeophobia* (Cambridge, Mass., 1997).

Schäublin, C. "Josephus und die Griechen," *Hermes* 110 (1982) 316–341.

Scheller, M. "σάββω und σαββάτωσις," *Glotta* 34 (1955) 298–300.

Schürer, E. *The History of the Jewish People in the Age of Jesus Christ*, vol. III.1, rev. and ed. by G. Vermes, F. Millar, and M. Goodman (Edinburgh, 1986).

Sperling, A. G. *Apion der Grammatiker und sein Verhältnis zum Judentum* (Dresden, 1886).

Stern, M. *Greek and Latin Authors on Jews and Judaism*, vol. I (Jerusalem, 1974).

Van der Horst, P. W. *Chaeremon: Egyptian Priest and Stoic Philosopher* (Leiden, 1984).

—— "Who was Apion?" in P. W. van der Horst, *Japheth in the Tents of Shem* (Leuven, 2002).

Van Henten, J.-W. and R. Abusch, "The Jews as Typhonians and Josephus' Strategy of Refutation in *Contra Apionem*," in Feldman and Levison (1996) 271–309.

Wacholder, B. Z. *Eupolemus: A Study of Judeo-Greek Literature* (Cincinnati, 1974).

HEBREW AND IMPERIALISM IN JEWISH PALESTINE[1]

Seth Schwartz*

For Keith Hopkins, *bona anima*

A study of the social history of the Hebrew language in antiquity has several lessons to teach. It first of all demonstrates the complex, sometimes paradoxical, interdependence, of social and political history: sociolinguistics, like all other inquiries into systems of group behavior, can never really be undertaken without also considering questions of power. This is not to say that purely cultural factors are insignificant, only that they cannot be extricated from the political: children, to be sure, grow up speaking in an ostensibly wholly natural way the language of their environment, but that environment is shaped by decisions made by their parents and others. To take a particularly clear example: the descendants of immigrants "normally" (that is, in countries which tend to integrate their immigrants—which itself depends on the state's political and cultural disposition) lose their ancestral languages in three generations. But immigrant groups which are especially self-enclosed, either because, like most Amish or Hasidim, they have a rigorously separatist religious ideology, or, like some European immigrant groups in the American upper Midwest before the middle of the twentieth century, they live in geographical isolation (because of the government's provision of incentives to immigrants to develop remote farmland), or, like some Hispano-Caribbeans in the United States, they live in relative economic isolation, may retain ancestral languages far longer. So, language use is always among other things an aspect of a larger

---

* Jewish Theological Seminary.
[1] An earlier version of this paper appeared as "Language, Power and Identity in Ancient Palestine," in *Past and Present* 148 (1995) 3–47. I have not changed my basic approach in the new version, but have changed many details, and have introduced a quadripartite schema to replace the old tripartite one. I have also eliminated the section on the Diaspora, and abbreviated that on the post-Destruction period, which I now think require far more detailed treatments than I provided then, and than there is space for here.

complex of social, political and cultural, including religious, choices.
Not infrequently, as in the case of ancient Hebrew, it has a certain
ideological freight, not discernible in politically blind ethnographic
description. The social history of Hebrew in antiquity also shows
that the widespread assumption that shared language is a necessary
component of group identity is so simplistic as to be nearly useless
as a working hypothesis: the Jews have not been united by shared
Hebrew speech since the Iron Age, and then in practice they shared
their Canaanite language with such neighbors as Ammonites, Moabites
and even Phoenicians; but it is undeniable that Hebrew has often
played a role in the group integration of the Jews. I argue that this
role was far more complex than assumptions about language characteristic of romantic nationalism would lead us to expect.[2] Finally
a study of the social history of Hebrew constitutes a warning against
any broad and inadequately theorized notion that "hellenization" is
a sufficiently precise tool in the analysis of changes in Jewish, or in
general eastern Mediterranean and Near Eastern, culture in the millennium which began with Alexander the Great's defeat of Darius
III, king of Persia, in 332 B.C.E. It would, for example, be simply
false to say that the rise of Greek in the Hellenistic period generated a decline in Hebrew, or that the revival of Hebrew for some
purposes in late antiquity implied a decline in Greek. Hebrew usage
was only obliquely related to vicissitudes in the usage of Greek, if it
was related to them at all. It was, however, intimately related to the
policies and preferences of the Macedonian and Roman imperial
rulers of Palestine.

In this paper I argue that there were four stages in the social history of Hebrew. In the first, which lasted until c. 300 B.C.E., Hebrew
was commonly spoken by Israelites/Jews in Palestine, but this fact
played only a small role in their construction of their group identity. In this respect they were probably typical of the small nations
living around the eastern Mediterranean, and unlike the Greeks, who
began to consider shared language an essential element in their corporate identity no later (and possibly much earlier) than the fifth
century B.C.E.

---

[2] For the conceptual background of the above, see K. Woolard and B. Schieffelin,
"Language Ideology," *Annual Review of Anthropology* 23 (1994) 55–82.

In the second stage, from 300 B.C.E. to 70 C.E., Hebrew was no longer commonly spoken, having been replaced by Aramaic. Hebrew, however, remained important because it was still the language of the Jerusalem temple and of the Pentateuch. In part because of consistent imperial patronage, these institutions gradually became the central symbols of Jewish corporate identity in the three or four centuries after their respective foundation (c. 500 B.C.E.) and compilation (c. 400 B.C.E.). By the third century B.C.E., Hebrew began to be used on coins and the like in a way, which may have been intended to evoke these symbols, and thus Jewish identity. But the temple and the Torah also became real repositories of power, so that there developed around both of them closely related classes of intermediaries. These men used Hebrew to distinguish themselves from the rest of the population, and since intermediation of the Torah was in theory open to all males, mastery of Hebrew could also be a path to prestige, and study of it may have been widespread in certain circles. In this second stage, then, Hebrew, no longer commonly spoken, became a *commodity*, consciously manipulated by the leaders of the Jews to evoke the Jews' distinctness from their neighbors, and the leaders' own distinctness from their social inferiors.

The third stage began with the destruction of the temple in 70 C.E. and came to a gradual end with the Christianization of the Roman Empire in the course of the fourth century. In this period, the temple and the Torah lost their political power, and retained only an attenuated symbolic importance, and that probably only for a minority of Jews. In the absence of a significant class of intermediaries, Hebrew lost its practical importance, but retained in some circles an evocative or symbolic power.

In the fourth stage (c. 350–c. 600 C.E.), the Jews regained limited religious autonomy, and so the Torah, but no longer the temple, and its intermediaries, reemerged as symbolically and in a small way even politically important—but they were now geographically decentralized. Hebrew therefore experienced a revival, but had lost its old connection with the temple staff; instead, it was now used to mark the sanctity, and the Jewishness, of synagogues, and the social distinctiveness primarily of rabbis and similar religious experts.

In this paper, I will concentrate on the first two periods.

PALESTINE BEFORE ALEXANDER

The observation that different nations speak different languages, attested in a few scattered near eastern texts of the Bronze Age, becomes commonplace in texts of the Iron Age. A familiar example is the catalogue of Trojan allies in the Iliad (in which, however, only one group, the Carians, is distinguished by language, as *barbarophonos*);[3] collections have been made of comparable Egyptian and Akkadian texts,[4] in which language, side by side with physical appearance and behavior, appears as a feature of national differentiation much more prominently than in Homer.

In Mesopotamian and Egyptian texts (and iconography), these "ethnographic" catalogues tend to serve an imperialist function—emphasizing the diversity, strangeness and ferocity of enemies overcome and reduced to tribute (in Akkadian the same word, *nakru*, means both enemy and foreigner).[5] But the tribute-bearing nations, too, among them the Israelites, had observed that language could be a feature of national difference: this is at most implicit in the story of the Tower of Babel in Genesis 11. This story is not, of course, an empire-glorifying list of subject nations but, at least in its original form, a myth about how the creator god imposed linguistic diversity on humanity. No similar myths are preserved from elsewhere in the Near East, but they may be assumed to have existed in Egypt, where Iron Age and later liturgical texts commonly praise various creator gods for diversifying human speech.

But recognition of linguistic diversity and the occasional mocking of foreign, especially Egyptian, speech[6] do not imply any particular self-consciousness about a national language. Indeed, the Pentateuch (in its present form c. 400 B.C.E.), which is concerned to promote the separateness of the Israelites/Jews, has apart from the Babel story little to say about language at all. Certainly it does not, as some

---

[3] Homer, Iliad 2.816–77, at 867.

[4] To which I am indebted for some of the observations that follow: see S. Sauneron, "La differentiation des langages d'après la tradition égyptienne," *Bulletin de l'Institut Français d'Archéologie Orientale* 60 (1960) 31–41. C. Zaccagnini, "The Enemy in the Neo-Assyrian Royal Inscriptions: The 'Ethnographic' Description," in H. Nissen and J. Renger, eds., *Mesopotamien und seine Nachbarn: 25e rencontre assyriologique internationale*, 2 volumes (Berlin: D. Reimer, 1982) ii, 409–24.

[5] Zaccagnini, "Enemy in Neo-Assyrian Royal Inscriptions," 410–11.

[6] Cf. Ps 119.1; Ezek 3.5–6; Ps 81.6.

later texts do, praise Hebrew as God's language, or prescribe its use in public cult or private prayer: Hebrew is never even mentioned. There is in the entire Hebrew Bible a single passage in which Hebrew—now for the first time identified as a language separate from its neighbors ("Judahite")—is definitely associated with Israelite identity (Neh 13.22–30):[7]

> In those days too I [Nehemiah] saw that the Judahites had taken Ashdodite, Ammonite and Moabite wives. And their sons spoke half Ashdodite [or, "their sons, half spoke Ashdodite"] . . . and could not speak Judahite. And I fought with them and cursed them and beat some of them and pulled out their hair, and I made them swear by God: "You shall not give your daughters to their sons nor marry your sons or yourselves to their daughters. Did not Solomon king of Israel sin on account of such (women)? And among the many nations there was no king like him, and he was beloved of his God, and God made him king of all Israel, yet even him did foreign wives cause to sin. Shall we then listen to you and do all this great evil, to commit a trespass against our God by marrying foreign wives?" And one of the sons of Yoyada' son of Eliashib the high priest was son-in-law of Sanballat the Horonite, and I put him to flight. Remember them, O God, for having defiled the priesthood and the covenant of the priests and Levites. For I purified them [the priesthood] of every foreign thing.

Even here, the function of the statement that the children of mixed marriages could not speak Judahite is not clear; it does not figure in Nehemiah's actual argument with the perpetrators, where he denounces mixed marriage as a violation of the Law, a trespass against God, a source of impurity and sin, but not as a linguistic crime.[8]

Why was Hebrew apparently not central to the self-understanding of the Israelites? I would suggest, in brief and as a partial explanation only, that the extreme political fragmentation of the eastern Mediterranean basin—a consequence of topography and of the political

---

[7] For translations of and commentaries on this difficult passage, see H. G. M. Williamson, *Ezra, Nehemiah* (Word Biblical Commentary 16, Waco: Word Books, 1985) 391–402; Joseph Blenkinsopp, *Ezra-Nehemiah* (London: SCM Press, 1988) 361–6. More problematic is Isa 19.18: "On that day there will be five towns in the land of Egypt speaking the language of Canaan and swearing by Yahweh-of-Hosts". For background, see the discussion of Christine Hayes, *Gentile Impurities and Jewish Identities: Intermarriage and Conversion from the Bible to the Talmud* (Oxford; New York: Oxford University Press, 2002) 27–8, 45–73.

[8] Blenkinsopp's and Williamson's failure to notice the isolation and uniqueness of the verse is typical; Hayes, *Gentile Impurity*, 30, acutely notes that only priestly intermarriage is described in terms of impurity.

practice of most of the imperial powers who ruled the area—was not accompanied by a corresponding linguistic diversity.[9] We should imagine the entire region from the Amanus to Pelusium and from the desert to the sea as a linguistic continuum in which each group could understand its neighbors' languages—languages which were hardly more diverse than the dialects of Greek. In the book of Ruth, for example, it is assumed that Judahites and Moabites spoke mutually comprehensible languages.[10] Yet, notwithstanding the occasional inter-ethnic friendships between kings or aristocratic families, there was a powerful tendency towards particularism confirmed and exploited by the policies of Assyrians, Chaldaeans and Achaemenids, who ruled the area from the ninth to the fourth centuries. So, you loathed your neighbors—but spoke their language (and sometimes married their daughters).

The case of the Israelites and their neighbors may then serve as a warning against the common assumption, usually tacit and unthe-orized, derived from modern nationalist ideology and confirmed for classicists and ancient historians by the example of the Greeks (mean-ing especially the classical Athenians), that shared language is nec-essarily a significant component of national identity—from the actors' perspective. The Israelites of the Iron Age shared a language but apparently attached little importance to this fact, for they shared it also with their neighbors; later, the Jews did not share a language but still often thought of themselves as a nation.

There are two substantial surviving corpora of writing from the Mediterranean world of the Iron Age (say 700 to 300 b.c.e.) which we would recognize as literary, the Greek and the Israelite. Comparison of these corpora is a good way of determining what is peculiar about Israelite writing; without attempting to present a rigorous argument, I would like to suggest that some of these peculiarities have *some* relation to the non-coincidence among the Israelites of language and national self-definition. I give two examples.

---

[9] On the fragmentation of the Mediterranean basin see in general Nicholas Purcell and Peregrine Horden, *The Corrupting Sea: A Study of Mediterranean History* (Oxford: Blackwell Publishers, 2000).

[10] See E. Ullendorf, "The Knowledge of Languages in the Old Testament," *BJRL* 44 (1961–2) 462–3. For an account of the relationship between Hebrew and its "Canaanite" neighbors, Phoenician, Ammonite, Moabite and Edomite, see Angel Saenz-Badillos, *A History of the Hebrew Language* (Cambridge: Cambridge University Press, 1993) 38–44; for northwest Semitic (which consists of the Canaanite and Aramaic families) as a continuum, see ibid., 36.

First, the absence of an elaborate metalanguage to describe different types of written (and spoken?) discourse. There are words for different genres, "psalm," "song," "dirge" and "prophetic speech," but no words for the stylistic components of these genres (as in the Greek iambs, dactyls, cola and so on) nor, for that matter, for "poetry" and "prose," though we would say that the genres mentioned are generally speaking written in poetry. Even within genres, there is remarkable stylistic lability: poetry gives way to prose and prose is studded with poetry—often not marked but simply slipped into. The absence of terminology, and the lability, imply (but only imply) an absence of linguistic self-consciousness which in turn has important social-historical implications: literate (and articulate) Iron Age Israelites did not think about language in the same way as Greeks of the same period did; to the extent that Israelites were conscious of "style," it was not for them disembedded from its social function. Hence there was no use for a word for "poetry," which describes so many different types of expression as to be socially meaningless. Nor was there any use for words describing units smaller than the generic: a prophet apparently learned how to speak "prophecy," and a psalmist to sing "psalms."[11]

Greek, especially but not only Athenian, practice was utterly different. Use of an elaborate prosodic terminology was accompanied by the sense that certain forms were appropriate for certain occasions, but also, at least by the end of the Archaic period (c. 500 B.C.E.), that the conventions were only that: they could be stretched, manipulated, selectively violated.[12] Hence, to take just one example, Greeks, starting with Aristophanes's *Acharnians* at the latest, wrote parody, the most self-conscious of literary styles, while scholars have notoriously striven in vain to detect convincing examples of parody (as opposed to satire) in Israelite literature.[13] I would suggest that

---

[11] My discussion here is indebted to James Kugel, *The Idea of Biblical Poetry* (New Haven: Yale University Press, 1981) especially 59–95.

[12] For a complex and nuanced account of the gradual emergence of language as an important criterion of identity among the Greeks (or at least some of them), see J. M. Hall, "The Role of Language in Greek Ethnicities," *Proceedings of the Cambridge Philological Society* 41 (1995) 83–100; cf. Edith Hall, *Inventing the Barbarian* (Oxford; New York: Oxford University Press, 1989) 6–13; Gregory Nagy, "On the Death of Sarpedon," in Carl Rubino and Cynthia Shelmerdine, eds., *Approaches to Homer* (Austin: University of Texas Press, 1983) 189–91; G. Nagy, *The Best of the Achaeans* (Baltimore: Johns Hopkins Press, 1979) 115–7.

[13] The evidence for parody in the Bible is limited and sketchy: see discussion in David Stern, "The Alphabet of Ben Sira and the Early History of Parody in Jewish

these opposite characteristics of Iron Age Hebrew and Greek writing reflect utterly different attitudes to the desirability of sophistication and elaborateness in the manipulation of language. This is not to say that there was no Israelite eloquence or "high style," only that genres remained embedded in the social contexts, which generated them.[14]

Secondly, the Israelites' attitude toward their language may also help explain the tendency of some Israelite/Jewish texts of the latter part of this period to slip back and forth not only between styles, but also between languages. Ezra-Nehemiah (c. 350 B.C.E.) and Daniel (compiled c. 165 B.C.E. but containing, especially in the first half of the book, material perhaps a hundred and fifty years older) notoriously begin in Hebrew, shift into Aramaic (in one case to quote an alleged Achaemenid document, in the other to quote a speech), and then "get stuck" in Aramaic, continuing the narrative in that language. Only later do they return to Hebrew.[15] Such a phenomenon, whatever other explanations there might be for it, is possible only in a context, presumably primarily scribal (a class evidently non-existent or of little importance in most Greek cities not ruled by Persia), which is not only thoroughly bilingual, but also unselfconscious about what language it happens to be using.[16]

Literature," in Hindy Najman and Judith Newman, eds., *The Idea of Biblical Interpretation: Essays in Honor of James Kugel* (Leiden: Brill, 2004) 423–48, especially 425. The book of Jonah has been thought a satire of Israelite prophecy (Morton Smith, *Palestinian Parties and Politics that Shaped the Old Testament*, 2nd ed., [London: SCM Press, 1987] 123; cf. Harold Bloom, *Ruin the Sacred Truths* [Cambridge, MA: Harvard University Press, 1989] 22–4).

[14] Thomas Cole, *The Origins of Rhetoric in Ancient Greece* (Baltimore: Johns Hopkins Press, 1991), distinguishes eloquence from rhetoric (in a Greek context) in part on the basis of the latter's self-consciousness; but his restriction of this characteristic to post-Platonic writing has been widely criticized: see reviews by R. Martin, *Classical Philology* 88 (1993) 77–84; D. A. Russell, *Journal of Hellenic Studies* 112 (1992) 185–6.

[15] There are brief surveys of the language problem in John J. Collins, *Daniel: A Commentary on the Book of Daniel* (Hermeneia: Minneapolis: Fortress Press, 1993) 24; Philip R. Davies, *Daniel* (Sheffield: JSOT, 1985) 35–9.

[16] Achaemenid scribes, even modest ones, needed a high level of bilingualism, since from the time of Darius I all public documents were customarily written in Aramaic; the scribe was expected to be able to compose an Aramaic text from dictation in a different language and conversely to read out such a text in the language of his audience. Significantly, the book of Nehemiah itself reports this practice: Ezra, a scribe by profession, had his associates read out the "Law of Moses" *meforash*, a word normally understood as a calque of the Old Persian *huzvarishn*—the term applied to the practice just described; in other words, the Hebrew text of the *torat Moshe* was read in Aramaic, or vice versa (Neh 8.1–8). Like Ezra himself, many Jewish writers (and readers?) of the fifth-fourth centuries B.C.E. must have come from scribal circles. See Muhammad A. Dandamaev and Vladimir G. Lukonin, *The*

In sum, the Israelites shared a language but tended not to consider it an essential component of their corporate identity. In this respect it was the Israelites, not the Greeks, who approximated to the norm in the eastern Mediterranean basin of the Iron Age. This view of language lies at the root of some of those characteristics of Israelite writing which are most striking for the western reader: the apparent absence of literary self-consciousness, the poverty of Hebrew literary and prosodic terminology, the incomplete differentiation of poetry and prose, and the unproblematized bilingualism of some of the works.

The Languages of Palestine, 300 b.c.e.–70 c.e.

The bilingualism of such texts as Ezra-Nehemiah and Daniel hints at one of the most significant, though relatively little examined, cultural developments in the history of the ancient Near East: the changing use of Aramaic. Before c. 800 b.c.e., Aramaic was the language of several ethnic groups and small kingdoms situated at the edge of the Syrian desert; subsequently, until 332 b.c.e., it was used as an administrative language in the Assyrian and Achaemenid Empires, and in this latter period it gradually replaced, almost completely, a large number of spoken languages in the eastern Mediterranean basin. Apparently no one compelled people to stop speaking their native languages; nor are there likely to have been Aramaic schools in every village comparable to the Qur'anic schools which slightly over a millennium later helped bring about the replacement of Aramaic, Coptic and Greek by Arabic. Yet by 300 b.c.e. or slightly later, a whole host of local languages, Hebrew, Ammonite, Moabite, Edomite, the unknown languages of the Lebanese, Syrian and south-eastern Turkish hinterland (some of which may in fact have been dialects of Aramaic, while others may not have been Semitic at all), and in many places possibly Phoenician[17]—not to mention the various dialects of Akkadian,

---

Culture and Social Institutions of Iran (Cambridge; New York: Cambridge University Press, 1989) 113–16; J. Naveh and J. C. Greenfield, "Hebrew and Aramic in the Persian Period," in William D. Davies and Louis Finkelstein, eds., *The Cambridge History of Judaism*, vol. 1 (Cambridge; New York: Cambridge University Press, 1984) 115–16.

[17] The Aramaization of Phoenicia may have been slower and less thorough than that of Palestine, Syria and Mesopotamia: see E. Lipínski, "Géographie linguistique de la Transeuphratène à l'époque Achémenide," *Transeuphratene* 3 (1990) 105–6.

too—had lost currency and were spoken, if at all, only by a small number of people.[18] It is true that Aramaic is fairly closely related to the Canaanite (but not Akkadian) languages, including Hebrew, which it replaced, and conversely it seems never to have been much more than an administrative and immigrants' language in Achaemenid Egypt;[19] but a comparable situation would be to imagine the Italians simply giving up their own language and switching to French—easier, presumably, than switching to Russian or Japanese, but still a remarkable change (and one unlikely to happen, it may be added, without intense political pressure, as, for example, on Corsica).

The mechanics of the Aramaization of the eastern Mediterranean basin have never been adequately explained, though the Assyrian and Neo-Babylonian practice of large-scale transfer of populations surely played a role in the Aramaization of Mesopotamia, and it would be reasonable to suppose it to have been a factor in Syria-Palestine, too.[20] However it happened, I would suggest that it tends to confirm one of the conclusions of the previous section, namely that national and tribal groups in the Near East generally did not consider language an essential component of their group identity.

But how thorough was the Aramaization of Palestine? The language of common speech is of course unrecoverable, and evidence for written language is poor; moreover, the written material is obviously difficult to use as evidence for spoken language since in some cases writing may reflect no more than scribal practice. And in all cases writing is necessarily related to speech in highly complex and sometimes highly attenuated ways. Besides, literacy was presumably limited along social lines, and ancient Palestinian society was rigidly stratified according to status and probably class, so that we can scarcely do more than guess at the language(s) used by the lower levels of society.

---

[18] For a good survey, see J. C. Greenfield, "Aramaic in the Achaemenian Empire," in Ilya Gershevitch, ed., *The Cambridge History of Iran*, 7 volumes, (Cambridge: Cambridge University Press, 1968–91) 2.698–713.

[19] See D. B. Redford, "Egyptian," in John Kaltner and Steve McKenzie, eds., *Beyond Babel: A Handbook for Hebrew and Related Languages* (Leiden: Brill, 2002) 109–37.

[20] See H. Tadmor, "The Aramaization of Assyria: Aspects of Western Impact," in Nissen and Renger, eds., *Mesopotamien und seine Nachbarn*, volume 2, 449–70. In Mesopotamia, though, the Assyrian and Babylonian kings had settled vast numbers of "Aramaeans" and other western Semites, whereas many settlers in Syria-Palestine must have been of east Semitic and Iranian-speaking background: see Bustenay Oded, *Deportations and Deportees in the Neo-Assyrian Empire* (Wiesbaden: Reichert, 1979) 26–32.

There have in fact been several different such guesses. Until the middle of the twentieth century, the common view about the relative importance of Hebrew and Aramaic was roughly as follows: by the third century B.C.E., Hebrew had given way to Aramaic, certainly for common speech, and probably for most other purposes, too. The language of later Hebrew literature is artificial—the result of efforts by native speakers of Aramaic and/or Greek to write in a dead classical language. This consensus was challenged early in the century by the semiticist M. H. Segal, who argued that the language of the Mishnah (c. 200 C.E.), was written not, as had previously been thought, in an Aramaic-calque language (that is, in a version of Hebrew whose peculiarities stemmed from mechanical translation from Aramaic), but in a formalized version of the Hebrew vernacular commonly spoken in Judaea until the Bar Kokhba Revolt (132–5 C.E.), and still used by the children of Judaean emigrants to Aramaic-speaking Galilee, among them the rabbis, in the late second century.[21]

Initially, Segal's argument convinced few outside a circle of Zionistically inclined Hebraists, and it soon required modification when it became clear from fragments of early manuscripts of the Mishnah found in the Cairo Genizah that its language was far more heavily Aramaized than Segal, who worked from late manuscripts and printed texts, had supposed. Nevertheless, the discovery of the Dead Sea Scrolls at Qumran in 1947, which included many texts written in the third-first centuries B.C.E. in a Hebrew sharing features with the language of both the Pentateuch and the Mishnah, and the slightly later discovery of the early second century "Bar Kokhba letters," some of which were written in colloquial-sounding Hebrew, convinced many that Segal had basically been right: it was now possible to trace a more or less steady evolution in written Hebrew,

---

[21] For surveys of the question, see Nahum Waldman, *The Recent Study of Hebrew* (Cincinnati: Hebrew Union College Press, 1989) 91–8; James Barr, "Hebrew, Aramaic and Greek in the Hellenistic Age," in William D. Davies, ed., *The Cambridge History of Judaism*, vol. 2, 79–114; *New Documents Illustrating Early Christianity*, ed., G. H. R. Horsley, 5 vols. (North Ryde: Ancient History Documentary Research Centre, Macquarie University, 1981–9) vol. 5, 19–26; Emil Schürer, *The History of the Jewish People in the Age of Jesus Christ*, rev. and ed. G. Vermes et al., 3 vols. (Edinburgh: T&T Clark, 1973–87) vol. 2, 20–8. M. H. Segal's most accessible statement of his position is to be found in his *A Grammar of Mishnaic Hebrew* (Oxford: Clarendon Press, 1927) 1–20. Most recently Segal's views have been taken up and refined by M. Bar Asher, e.g. in "Mishnaic Hebrew: An Introductory Survey," *Hebrew Studies* 40 (1999) 115–51.

from early biblical to late biblical (e.g., Chronicles, Ezra-Nehemiah, Ecclesiastes) to Qumranic and finally rabbinic.[22] This evolution could not be explained solely as a consequence of the progressive influence of spoken Aramaic and Greek on a classical literary language. It seemed more reasonable to suppose that the language of these texts reflected and was influenced by a still vigorous Hebrew vernacular. Most have agreed with Segal that this vernacular disappeared a few generations after the Bar Kokhba Revolt, which put an end to large scale Jewish settlement in Judaea, though it has more recently been argued, not very convincingly, that Jews in northern Palestine spoke Hebrew into the Middle Ages.[23]

As a historian, I may challenge this consensus of semiticists and sociolinguists only with diffidence; and it must be admitted that the arguments from Hebrew literary writing seem compelling, at least to the non-professional. Yet the consensual view seems to me to require revision, if not complete reversal, for the following reasons.

First, the consensus breaks down when it comes to determining who exactly the speakers of colloquial Hebrew could have been. The evidence for Hebrew in non-literary—epigraphical and documentary—writing is slender, though not entirely non-existent. In the great corpora of non-literary writing from pre-70 C.E. Judaea—the hundreds of inscribed ossuaries from first century Jerusalem and the vast collection of ostraca used at the southern Judaean fortress of Masada in 66–74 C.E.—Aramaic and Greek are used almost to the exclusion of Hebrew.[24] The greatest authority on the languages of Palestine,

---

[22] William Schniedewind, "Qumran Hebrew as Antilanguage," *JBL* 118 (1999) 235–52, has argued, however, that Qumran Hebrew does not comfortably fit on the spectrum which begins with biblical and ends with rabbinic Hebrew.

[23] See Steven Fraade, "Rabbinic Views on the Practice of Targum, and Multilingualism in the Jewish Galilee of the Third-Sixth Centuries," in Lee Levine, ed., *The Galilee in Late Antiquity* (Cambridge, MA: Harvard Univeristy Press, 1992) 253–84; Fraade bases his argument on late antique epigraphy, the *piyyut*, and on a document from the Cairo Genizah which can be interpreted (probably incorrectly—Haggai Ben-Shammai, personal communication) to refer to the persistence of colloquial Hebrew in Tiberias as late as the ninth century. Cf. A. Tal, "Is There a Raison d'etre for an Aramaic Targum in a Hebrew-Speaking Society," *REJ* 160 (2001) 357–78; Tal's failure to cite Fraade is baffling, not to say shocking. For a balanced account of the emergence of the post-Dead Sea scroll consensus, see James Barr, "Which Language Did Jesus Speak?," *BJRL* 50 (1970–1) 9–29.

[24] Of the hundreds of ostraca from Masada, the Hebrew prepositive article appears six times in epithets and nicknames, and Hebrew forms appear eleven times in indications of filiation: see J. Naveh, *Masada, I: The Aramaic and Hebrew Ostraca and Jar Inscriptions* (Jerusalem, 1989) 8–9. I discuss the Hebrew jar inscriptions below. Of

and the most moderate and nuanced of the Hebrew "survivalists," E. Y. Kutscher, concluded from the ossuary inscriptions that Aramaic—originally a language of administration and trade—was predominant in Jerusalem, the multi-ethnic administrative, commercial and religious capital of Judaea, while Hebrew predominated in the countryside (though Kutscher admitted that some Hebrew was spoken in Jerusalem and some Aramaic in the countryside).[25] But this view cannot be maintained—and not only because it is so transparently motivated by a romantic desire to attribute Hebrew speech to the Judaean "folk". In a suggestive observation, Kutscher himself had noted the use of Aramaic in place-names in the Judaean countryside, presumably dating from the post-exilic period (i.e., after 500 B.C.E.); and the ostraca from Masada, published long after his death, seem to demonstrate the primary use of Aramaic by the Judaean rebels who occupied the site. There is no compelling reason to think that they were all, or even mostly, of Jerusalemite origin. Furthermore, the best evidence for the survival of Hebrew comes from literature, presumably mostly a metropolitan and elite rather than a rustic product.

Secondly, the sociological models presupposed by scholars of socio-linguistic inclination in trying to smooth out the complexities and contradictions of the fragmentary evidence have generally been overly

---

the 177 Jerusalem ossuary inscriptions found in J.-B. Frey, *Corpus Inscriptionum Iudaicarum*, vol. 2 (Rome, 1952) #1210–1387, 24 use Hebrew forms (The updated collection of L. Y. Rahmani, *A Catalogue of Jewish Ossuaries in the Collection of the State of Israel* [Jerusalem: IAA, 1994], does not change the picture; it may or may not be meaningful that Hebrew is more abundant in the Jerusalem than in the Masada texts); in these cases, this is, as in the Masada texts, a matter of prepositive articles in epithets, and use of the Hebrew forms *ben* (son of), *bat* (daughter of) and *eshet* (wife of) instead of the Aramaic *bar*, *berat* and *atat*. Longer texts are in Aramaic or Greek, with the exception of a handful of Jerusalemite inscriptions of manifestly priestly provenance (*CIJ* 1388, 1394), the funerary graffiti of the priestly *benei* Hezir; an apparent street sign in or near the temple precinct: B. Mazar, "A Hebrew Inscription from the Temple Area in Jerusalem," *Qadmoniot* 3 (1970) 142–44; and note also the interestingly enigmatic epitaph of a priest written in Aramaic but in Paleo-Hebrew script, found just north of Jerusalem: Joseph Naveh, "An Aramaic Tomb Inscription Written in Paleo-Hebrew script," *IEJ* 23 (1973) 82–91), and the Masada jar inscriptions, which concern the priestly gifts. There may be some justice to Naveh's argument that precisely such small matters as onomastic habits reflect spoken language more accurately than do longer texts, but even if this were so, which is not self-evident, the texts would say little about the extent of the diffusion of spoken Hebrew, especially, perhaps, outside priestly circles.

[25] Edward Y. Kutscher, *The Language and Linguistic Background of the Isaiah Scroll* (1 Q Isaᵃ, Studies on the Texts of the Desert of Judah 6; Leiden: Brill, 1974) 8–15, 89–95.

simple. The influential characterization of Jewish Palestine as "diglossic," i.e., using two languages, one for formal and the other for informal communication (the "high" and "low" or "home" language,
respectively) as applied to any premodern, more or less rigidly stratified
society, would necessarily imply a social distinction: the elites mostly
use the high language, perhaps even in informal circumstances (with
appropriate distinctions in register), and peasants, artisans, and so
on, know and use only the low language.[26] But which language was
which in Jewish Palestine? Kutscher had after all recognized the frequency of Aramaic and Greek—the former, at least, a low language
in most schemes—in the funerary inscriptions of well-to-do Jerusalemites
(not to mention Judaean literary writing); but Hebrew, in various
registers, both "classical" and "vernacular," was a significant vehicle
of literary expression—also an elite activity; and the "vernacular"
register of Hebrew was allegedly the language of the Judaean peas-
antry. The "diglossia" model thus fails to explain the ancient Palestinian
evidence, because it was developed to describe the linguistic situation in certain more or less industrialized developing nation-states
(whether it was up even to this task is a different question). Such
entities are generally characterized by relatively permeable social
boundaries, wide dissemination of education, prominence of the
media, and so on, so that many individuals are proficient in both a
common language, learned and spoken at home, and a high language, which is learned in school and used for some purposes by
the media.[27] Jewish Palestine, by contrast, had a mixed elite of tem-

---

[26] That is, the situation is unlikely to have been diglossic in the strict sense, for
diglossia involves the use in certain public situations of a language which is not
actually spoken as a "home" language by anyone, though the two languages are
closely related and the high language may be widely understood: see C. A. Ferguson,
"Diglossia," *Word* 15 (1959) 336–37. It was, however, certainly diglossic in the looser
sense in post-Ferguson discussion, in that it was characterized by the use of two or
more languages—or dialects, or registers of one language—in various contexts. For
discussion, see A. Hudson, "Diglossia: A Bibliographic Review," *Language in Society*
21 (1992) 617–8. The utility of so broad a conception of the phenomenon as a
principle of social classification is not obvious, for diglossia in this sense is a feature of all but the simplest societies.

[27] My characterization of the emerging nation-state is indebted to Ernest Gellner,
Nations and Nationalism (Oxford: Blackwell, 1983) 19–38. See Ferguson, "Diglossia,"
331, on the importance of schools in spreading the high language. Ferguson's own
description of the conditions in which diglossia occurs (p. 338) is quite mistaken;
more satisfactory is J. Fishman, "Bilingualism With and Without Diglossia; Diglossia
With and Without Bilingualism," *Journal of Social Issues* 23 (1967) 29–38. For general criticism of diglossia, and dismissal of its applicability to ancient conditions, see

ple staff and landowners—who interacted with each other, with the country's foreign rulers, and with the general populace in various and complex ways—a patchwork of competing ethnic and religious groups, and a profound yet often bridged division between city and country. Normal as this may have been for the ancient Mediterranean world, it was quite different from the societies from which sociolinguists generate their models; in Jewish Palestine, the preconditions for diglossia in the strict sense did not exist.[28]

A third failure of the consensual view is its obliviousness to ideological factors in the use of languages. There are no doubt many reasons for this blindness: the tendency among some linguists (as also among many social scientists and historians) to privilege observation over explanation; the tendency of positivist historians to treat writing as unmediated "evidence" and so pay little attention to content, context, social function and other inconveniences; a related scholasticism, which causes confusion between the beliefs expressed in a classical literary corpus and those actually held in a society; and the ideological position of some Zionist scholars, whose zeal to establish Hebrew as the Jewish national language ironically prevented them from acknowledging the ideological uses to which the same language may have been put in the past.[29]

K. Versteegh, "Dead or Alive? The Status of the Standard Language," in J. N. Adams, Mark Janse and Simon Swain, eds., *Bilingualism in Ancient Society: Language Contact and the Written Word* (Oxford; New York: Oxford University Press, 2002) 52–7.

[28] The multilingual model, which often complements the diglossic model, supposes that many or most Judaeans could get by in two or even three spoken languages; see, e.g., B. Spolsky, "Jewish Multilingualism in the First Century," in Joshua Fishman, ed., *Readings in the Sociology of Languages* (Leiden: Brill, 1985) 35–50. No doubt among some male members of the upper classes—Josephus may provide an example—trilingualism of a limited sort (in Greek, Aramaic and Hebrew) was not uncommon, and certainly there are no grounds for excluding the possibility of widespread multilingualism a priori. It is a well-attested phenomenon in other societies; note, for example, the case of the Indians of the Vaupés, in Colombia, who are reported all to speak at least three languages fluently: J. Jackson, "Language Identity of the Vaupés Indians," in Richard Bauman and Joel Sherzer, eds., *Explorations in the Ethnography of Speaking*, 2nd ed. (Cambridge; New York: Cambridge University Press, 1989) 55–6. But there is no evidence, and no good reason to believe in its absence, that most Jews in ancient Palestine were multilingual. This is obviously a different question from that of the multilingualism of Palestinian Jewish society as a whole (see D. G. K. Taylor, "Bilingualism and Diglossia in Syria and Mesopotamia," in Adams, et al., *Bilingualism in Ancient Society*, 298–300).

[29] For a general survey of these issues, see Woolard and Schieffelin, "Language Ideology". Of course, there have always been scholars sensitive to the ideological component of Hebrew usage, and their ranks seem to be growing, notwithstanding

However generated, this blindness to ideology seems to me critical, for it is precisely from the third century B.C.E. onwards that the Hebrew language began to be ideologized, so that its use was no longer a matter of indifference, but came to acquire symbolic weight and social importance. The literary works, coins, documents and so forth in which Hebrew is used are most convincingly considered *not* simply as "evidence" of a linguistic situation: what they are in fact evidence of is the ideological function of the Hebrew language in ancient Jewish society, and it is as such that I will consider them in what follows. There I will assume that although Hebrew may have been a spoken language in some circles of Palestinian Jewish society in the third century B.C.E. and following, there is no reason to think that these circles included large numbers of the Judaean "folk". In fact, they are more likely to have consisted of priests and experts in the Torah: Hebrew was thus, apart from its symbolic functions, a sociolect, whose use marked membership in an elite or sub-elite class. All of the suppositions underlying the belief that Judaean villagers preserved the Hebrew language for centuries after the fall of the kingdom of Judah in 586 B.C.E.—their isolation, their cultivation of "purity," and their ferocious resistance to foreign influence, even apart from conventional assumptions about the importance of language for national identity—are questionable. Indeed, the real story of rural Judaea is more likely one of flux and stasis, contact and withdrawal, accommodation and resistance, and obviously has far more complex linguistic implications.

---

the persistence of distinguished holdouts like M. Bar Asher. For example, Rabin, Rosén and Yadin, to mention only the most important among scholars of an earlier generation, at least acknowledged the role of Hebrew in the ideology of the various Judaean revolts: C. Rabin, "Hebrew and Aramaic in the First Century," in S. Safrai and M. Stern, eds., *The Jewish People in the First Century*, 2 vols. (Compendia Rerum Iudaicarum ad Novum Testamentum, vol. 2: Philadelphia: Fortress Press, 1976) 1007–39; H. Rosén, "Die Sprachsituation im römischen Palästina," *Die Sprachen im römischen Reich der Kaiserzeit* (Beihefte der Bonner Jahrbücher 40; Cologne, Rheinland-Verlag, 1980) 215–39; Y. Yadin, *Bar Kokhba* (London: Weidenfeld and Nicolson, 1971) 124; and see below. None of these scholars, however, ever attempted to work out the less obvious implications of Hebrew's significance in revolutionary propaganda. Some important steps in this direction have now been taken by S. Weitzman, "Why Did the Qumran Community Write in Hebrew?," *JAOS* 119 (1999) 35–45, W. Schniedewind, "Qumran Hebrew as an Antilanguage," and at least in a limited way Hannah Cotton, "The Languages of the Legal and Administrative documents from the Judaean Desert," *Zeitschrift für Papyrologie und Epigraphik* 125 (1999) 219–31.

In sum, the evidence from Palestine in the sixth to the third centuries B.C.E. is consistent with the view that the Jews, like almost all other national and tribal groups in the Levant and Mesopotamia, generally came to adopt Aramaic as their normal means of communication. The contrary view is based on a simplistic reading of the evidence, characterized by insensitivity to its content and context, and correspondingly to the social and political functions of languages in premodern societies. In what follows, I will provide a different account of the uses of Hebrew in Hellenistic and Roman Palestine.

Despite the ascendancy of Aramaic and, later, of Greek throughout the Near East, the survival of Hebrew after 300 B.C.E. was not a unique phenomenon. New texts continued to be composed in Akkadian, Old Egyptian and Phoenician down to the end of the Hellenistic period (31 B.C.E.), and in the case of Egyptian well beyond this date (the latest hieroglyphic inscription whose date is known was made in 394 C.E.—it fell victim not to Hellenization or Romanization but to Christianization).[30] If we can trust a hostile testimony quoted in a papyrus of the third century C.E., Idumaeans in Egypt continued to use their ancestral language in their temples almost four centuries after their homeland had been conquered by the Judaeans.[31] Akkadian, hieroglyphic and Phoenician writing, too, are found especially, though not exclusively, in temples. It seems likely that the liturgy of the Jerusalem temple was performed in Hebrew, despite the fact that (like the other languages just mentioned) it was no longer commonly spoken. Some psalms included in the canonical Psalter, which was probably used in the temple liturgy, were composed in third century B.C.E. or even later, and sectarian groups continued to compose Hebrew psalms for their own use—which may have reflected that

---

[30] For Akkadian, see the discussion in Susan Sherwin-White and Amélie Kuhrt, *From Samarkhand to Sardis*: A New Approach to the Seleucid Empire (London: Duckworth, 1993) 149–61; for Egyptian, see the texts collected in Miriam Lichtheim, *Ancient Egyptian Literature*, vol. 3 (Berkeley: California University Press, 1980); David Frankfurter, *Religion in Roman Egypt: Assimilation and Resistance* (Princeton: Princeton University Press, 1998) 248–56; Redford, "Egyptian," 110; for Phoenician, Fergus Millar, "The Phoenician Cities: A Case Study in Hellenisation," *Proceeding of the Cambridge Philological Society* 29 (1983) 55–71, especially 60–3 (isolated Phoenician words and letters on coins to the end of the second century C.E.).

[31] See *Griechische Papyri im Museum des Oberhessischen Geschichtsvereins zu Giessen*, vol. 1, ed. E. Kornemann and P. Meyer (Leipzig and Berlin: B. G. Teubner, 1910–12) #99; F. Zucker, *Doppelinschrift spätptolemaischer Zeit aus der Garnison von Hermopolis Magna* (Berlin, 1938) 13.

of the Jerusalem temple—into the first century c.e.[32] But while little is known about the non-liturgical use of the pre-Aramaic languages of the Near East (except Egyptian), perhaps because of the fragmentary character of the evidence,[33] we do possess, as indicated above, a significant and wide-ranging body of Hebrew (in addition to Aramaic and Greek) writing produced in Hellenistic and Roman Palestine. It would be a mistake to think of Hebrew in this period as a purely liturgical language, like the archaic Latin of the revived Arval Brethren in early Imperial Rome, or Old Slavonic and Syriac in modern eastern churches. How then can we account for the language's position?

A brief discussion of the policies of the Achaemenid emperors is a good starting point. The Achaemenids, as suggested earlier, promoted Aramaic; whether this promotion consisted of its explicit establishment by Darius I as the official language of administration, or the mere encouragement of a language which was already in widespread scribal use, will scarcely have affected the cultural consequences of the promotion, which were considerable and may in general be compared to those of the *non-exclusive* use of Greek for administrative purposes in Hellenistic and Roman Egypt.[34] Among the specific consequences of Aramaization was the rise of an international elite or sub-elite literary culture in Mesopotamia, Syria, Asia Minor and, to a lesser extent, Egypt. This culture was distinct from its cuneiform predecessor in that scribes copied Aramaic literary texts on papyrus and leather, not on clay and wax tablets, and did so not purely for their own training, but apparently (also?) to satisfy

---

[32] For a survey, see Schürer, *History of the Jewish People*, 3.1, 187–96; 452–5.

[33] The Hellenistic Akkadian administrative documents, discussed by Sherwin-White and Kuhrt, *From Samarkhand to Sardis*, 149–61, which demonstrate that in the Seleucid Empire it took at least a century for Greek to be established as the exclusive language of administration, may at least hint at what is missing. For the situation in Egypt in a slightly later period (notwithstanding the marginal survival of all forms of Egyptian writing well into late antiquity, the position even of Demotic, though it continued to be strong throughout the Hellenistic period, very quickly eroded under Roman rule, for all practical purposes ceasing to exist as a functional writing system by the first century c.e.) see Roger Bagnall, *Egypt in Late Antiquity* (Princeton: Princeton University Press, 1993) 230–60.

[34] See Dandamaev and Lukonin, *Culture and Social Institutions of Iran*, 112–13; Greenfield, "Aramaic in the Achaemenian Empire," 698; Keith Hopkins, "Conquest by Book," in *Literacy in the Roman World*, Journal of Roman Archaeology Supplement, volume 3 (Ann Arbor, MI: Dept. of Classical Studies, University of Michigan, 1991) 133–58.

the needs of a market of readers.[35] Aramaic thus came to compete with earlier languages on all levels: it became the language not merely of government business and public life, but also of common speech and upper class literary expression; and the end of Achaemenid rule, and so of government patronage of Aramaic, did not lead to any discernible resurgence of the pre-Aramaic languages, for Aramaic was already established as a language of speech and high culture, and was in any case partly replaced by a new international language, Greek.

But other Achaemenid policies functioned to preserve the pre-Aramaic languages. The emperors liked to be thought patrons of native temples where, as suggested above, the old languages were often still used. For example, Cyrus had come to Babylon in 539 B.C.E. as restorer of the temple of Marduk following the alleged depredations of Nabonidus,[36] and the Achaemenids are also known to have autho-rized the collection and promulgation of the laws of the subject nations; the Demotic Chronicle provides a report of the codification of Egyptian law at the initiative of Darius I.[37] In Judah, too, the cen-tral temple in Jerusalem—in which the Hebrew language was used—was rebuilt with government support, which it received to the exclusion of other traditional holy places; and the so-called Law of Moses—whatever precisely its relationship to our Pentateuch may have been, and whatever the age of its sources—now compiled in the Hebrew language (and also in an Aramaic recension, like the Egyptian code?), and imposed on the Judahites, probably including those living out-side their native country, with some Achaemenid support.[38]

---

[35] See A. Leo Oppenheim, *Letters from Mesopotamia* (Chicago: University of Chicago Press, 1967) 42–53; Elias J. Bickerman, *The Jews in the Greek Age* (Cambridge, MA: Harvard University Press, 1988) 51–65; Sebastian Brock, "Three Thousand Years of Aramaic Literature," *Aram*_1 (1989) 17–8. On the association of Aramaic with leather and papyrus, see Greenfield, "Aramaic in the Achaemenian Empire," 698.

[36] For discussion and literature, see P. Briant, "The Seleucid Kingdom and the Achaemenid Empire," in Per Bilde et al., eds., *Religion and Religious Practice in the Seleucid Kingdom* (Studies in Hellenistic Civilization 1; Aarhus: Aarhus University Press, 1990) 53–4, 58–60.

[37] For the text and translation of this account, see *Die sogenannte demotische Chronik des Pap. 215 der Bibliothèque Nationale zu Paris*, ed. W. Spiegelberg (Leipzig: J. C. Hinrichs, 1915) 30–2; Dandamaev and Lukonin, *Cultures and Social Institutions of Iran*, 125. The laws were officially published in Demotic, for the use of native judges, and in Aramaic ("the writing of Ashur"), for Persian officials.

[38] That construction of the temple and imposition of the Law were not uncon-tested is demonstrated by the partisan accounts in the books of Ezra and Nehemiah. On the connection between the Demotic law and the Law of Moses, see E. J.

These developments had complex and ramified effects on language, some of which I will now try to untangle. The temple, and especially the Law, came to be the central symbols of Jewish nationhood—so potent that, if we can believe Josephus, at the time of the Jewish revolt against Rome in 67 C.E. the mere public display of a scroll of the Law was enough to make men take up arms.[39] These two symbols were closely associated, too, for the Law itself expected the priests of the temple to be among its authoritative interpreters and the executors of its imposition on the people of Judaea;[40] as far as we can determine, the priests did play an especially important role, at least before the destruction of the temple in 70 C.E., and the high priest was recognized as the final legal authority.[41] The transformation of the temple and the Law of Moses from institutions of real but limited importance into the central items in the symbolic language of ancient Judaism must not be thought self-explanatory—after all, the Egyptian law, also codified at imperial initiative and invested with imperial support, seems never to have played as important a role as that of the Torah in Judaea.[42] Yet we know too little about the history of Palestine from 400 to 200 B.C.E.—a period evidently crucial to the emergence of the temple and the Torah as ideologically central—to be able to suggest a complete explanation. I will indicate only a few factors which I consider to have been important for

---

Bickerman, *The Jews in the Greek Age*, 29–32; for a discussion of the Achaemenid context of the Pentateuch, see J. Blenkinsopp, *The Pentateuch* (London: SCM Pres, 1992) 239–42; in all likelihood this imperial support was sporadic, weaker and vaguer than the tendentious biblical accounts indicate: see the papers collected in James W. Watts, ed., *Persia and Torah: The Theory of Imperial Authorization of the Pentateuch*, SBL Symposium Series 17 (Atlanta: Scholars Press, 2001).

[39] Josephus, *Autobiography*, 134–5.

[40] See, for example, Deut 17.8–13.

[41] See Seth Schwartz, *Josephus and Judaean Politics* (Leiden: Brill, 1990) 69–70; E. J. Bickerman, *Studies in Jewish and Christian History*, 3 volumes (Leiden: Brill, 1976–86) 2.69–74; Bickerman, *Jews in the Greek Age*, 140–7.

[42] Though various versions of Darius's law-code may, if it is somehow related to a Demotic law-code of the third century B.C.E. found in Hermopolis, have survived into the high Roman Empire, and may have functioned in some circles as a kind of national symbol. On the "Hermopolis code," see Girgis Mattha, *The Demotic Legal Code of Hermopolis West* (Cairo: Institut français d'archéologie orientale du Caire, 1975); a fragment of a Greek translation of this code, probably made in third century B.C.E. but copied in the late second century CE, is published in *The Oxyrhynchus Papyri* 46, ed. J. R. Rea (London: Egypt Exploration Fund, 1978) #3285; the suggestion about the ideological function of the text in the Roman period is made by Joseph Mélèze-Modrzejewski, *Les Juifs d'Egypte* (Paris, 1991) 89–91.

this development, and will refer the reader to a more detailed treatment elsewhere.[43]

First, from the Achaemenids to Nero, almost every imperial and native ruler of Palestine supported the temple and the Torah.[44] This consistent support (probably absent in Egypt)[45] for these centralizing institutions allowed their staff to impose their values and practices on the Judaeans without serious competition from radical dissenters, who either left the country, withdrew to the desert, or behaved very discreetly. It so functioned by empowering the central authorities to establish administrative, judicial and other networks throughout the country, embodying views and practices that, however roughly, approximated to their own, in part because small-town strong men, who necessarily wielded power on the local level, were ideologically speaking forced to meet the authorities halfway.[46]

The uniqueness of the temple and the Torah gave them a peculiar force as centralizers of ideology—even though it was a uniqueness more theoretical than real. Several shrines outside Jerusalem dedicated to the worship of Yahweh maintained a shadowy existence for centuries after the construction of the Jerusalem temple in the late sixth century B.C.E.,[47] and the Law as actually practiced in the Judaean countryside, and probably even in Jerusalem, was varied and often strikingly different from that laid down in the Pentateuch.[48]

---

[43] See S. Schwartz, *Imperialism and Jewish Society, 200 B.C.E. to 640 C.E.*, (Princeton: Princeton University Press, 2001) 49–99.

[44] The only certain exception is Antiochus IV, who suspended the Torah between 167 and 164 B.C.E.

[45] On the Ptolemies and Egyptian law, see H. J. Wolff, "Law in Ptolemaic Egypt," in A. E. Samuel, ed., *Essays in Honor of C. B. Welles* (New Haven: Yale University Press, 1966) 67–77. In the third century B.C.E., the Ptolemies empowered Egyptian priests to judge according to Egyptian laws, but gave neither the priests nor the laws exclusive jurisdiction over any inhabitant of Egypt; the Egyptian law was voluntary an imperial concession intended to spare the feelings of native subjects. In the second century B.C.E. the system collapsed.

[46] For an account of this process, see Smith, *Palestinian Parties and Politics*, 121–4.

[47] For a brief survey, see ibid., 68–70.

[48] For a possible case, though from the post-Destruction period, see Tal Ilan, "Notes and Observations on a Newly Published Divorce Bill from the Judaean Desert," *HTR* 89 (1996) 195–202 (a possible case of initiation of divorce by a woman—an ostensible violation, or at least radical reinterpretation, of the biblical rule on the subject; note, however, the criticisms of Adiel Schremer, "Divorce in Papyrus Se'elim Once Again: A Reply to Tal Ilan" (and Ilan's response), *HTR* 91 (1998) 193–204. More to the point may be P. Benoit, J. T. Milik and R. de Vaux, *Les grottes de Murabba'at*, Discoveries in the Judaean Desert 2 (Oxford, 1961 [= P. Murab.]) #18, a loan contract from Judaea, 55/6 C.E., which seems to evade, though not

Yet the most prominent non-Jerusalemite shrines were located out-side Judaea—that is, outside the jurisdiction of the high priest. And in the official ideology, local, non-Pentateuchal varieties of the Law were nevertheless part of a larger conception of the Law provided that their practice could somehow be reconciled with Pentateuchal prescriptions: the ideological uniqueness of the Torah was thus pre-served by co-optation.[49]

The emergence of the temple and Torah as the central symbols of Judaism cannot be adequately explained, or even traced. That said, it seems likely that the "Antiochan persecution" and the sub-sequent, and ultimately successful, Judaean revolt (167–152 B.C.E.) did much to simplify and consolidate the symbolic system of the Jews.[50] It may be significant that the earliest story to presuppose that the Torah scroll itself possesses symbolic importance is in the account of the persecution in 1 Maccabees 1.56–7, composed a generation or two after the events it describes: in the course of the persecution, Torah scrolls were not confiscated and discarded, but ripped to shreds and burnt—something not easily done to parchment. The absence of this information in the parallel account in 2 Maccabees casts doubt on the episode's historicity, but not on the significance of the claim as an indicator of the ideological position of its post-revolt, pro-Maccabean author.

The emergence of the temple as ideologically central is somewhat easier to trace, since admiration for it and its staff is the theme of a long series of ancient Jewish literary works, from Chronicles (c. 350

---

ignore, the pentateuchal prohibition of interest and cancellation of debts during the sabbatical year. Notwithstanding the scholarly tradition on this text, it has no con-nection with the rabbinic *prozbol*. See Schwartz, *Imperialism and Jewish Society*, 68–9.

[49] Alternatively, one may adopt the admirably complex formulation of J. Blenkinsopp, according to which the Torah may be thought of as a large and unsystematic body of practice, customary and prescribed, including both the Pentateuch and other nor-mative material—a body in which at some point, perhaps not much earlier than 250 or 200 B.C.E. (and even then not necessarily for all Jews), the Pentateuch came to dominate: see *Wisdom and Law in the Old Testament* (Oxford; New York: Oxford Univeristy Press, 1983) 74–5. But this formulation may slightly overestimate the actual (as opposed to the ideological) role of the Pentateuch after 200 B.C.E.

[50] See 1 Maccabees 1.41–64; 2 Maccabees 6. The most important single work on the background of the persecution and revolt remains E. J. Bickermann, *Der Gott der Makkabäer* (Berlin: Schocken Verlag, 1937); more recent literature is clearly and briefly discussed in Daniel J. Harrington, *The Maccabean Revolt: Anatomy of a Biblical Revolution* (Wilmington: M. Glazier, 1988). For the effect of the persecution and revolt on Judaism, see Shaye Cohen, *The Beginnings of Jewishness: Boundaries, Varieties, Uncertainties* (Berkeley: California University Press, 1999) 109–39.

B.C.E.) to 2 Maccabees (c. 100 B.C.E.) to Josephus's *Jewish War* (c. 80
C.E.), and is reflected also in works of pagan writers, from Hecataeus
of Abdera (fl. 300 B.C.E.) onwards.[51] Admittedly, this admiration sometimes has an anxious edge to it and there certainly were at various
periods small groups of Jews who rejected the temple's sanctity and/or
the fitness of its staff. Even the book of Ezra reflects a certain dis-
appointment at the meanness of the temple completed by Zerubbabel
in 515 B.C.E. Nevertheless, that the centrality of the temple was not
simply the fantasy of a small group of authors themselves of priestly
background is demonstrated by a series of events from the feuds of
the late sixth and fifth centuries B.C.E. (both among the Judaeans
themselves and between them and their neighbors) over access to
and control of the temple, to the apparently widespread enthusiasm
generated by the emperor Julian's plan, in 361 or 362 C.E., to rebuild
it. And once Zerubbabel's small shrine was replaced by Herod's vast
complex (20 B.C.E.), which for the first time made possible pilgrim-
age on a large scale, the temple became a massive economic "black
hole," sucking in and consigning to oblivion (often in fact to the
strong-boxes of rapacious Roman generals) vast quantities of surplus
Jewish silver—not all of it, we must suppose, given under duress.[52]

For my purposes, these developments are important because the
Hebrew language was closely associated with these two central symbols, Torah and temple, and so came itself to have a certain symbolic force: it became, not the national language of the Jews, but
the language whose representation symbolized Jewish nationhood.
The earliest indication of this development may date back to the
middle or later fourth century B.C.E. Most documentary writing from
Achaemenid Judaea—inscriptions on coins, seals, bullae and so on—
is Aramaic, though some probably quite early bullae, made at a time
when Hebrew was still commonly spoken, bear Hebrew inscriptions
in Aramaic script. All Achaemenid Judaean coins give the name of
the province in its Aramaic form (Yehud) and in Aramaic script,
but the latest type of Achaemenid coin features two examples bearing

---

[51] See M. Stern, *Greek and Latin Authors on Jews and Judaism*, 3 volumes, (Jerusalem,
1974–84) vol. 1, passim.
[52] There is no good single treatment of the history of the temple; for a general
survey, see Schürer, *History of the Jewish People*, rev. and ed. Vermes et al., 2.227–313.
The temple as economic "black hole" is well discussed by Martin Goodman, *The
Ruling Class of Judaea* (Cambridge; New York: Cambridge University Press, 1987)
51–75; cf. Schwartz, *Imperialism and Jewish Society*, 87–99.

inscriptions in Hebrew and in Paleo-Hebrew script, one of which, interestingly, gives the name of the high priest, and the other that of a governor who may also have been high priest.[53] By the early third century B.C.E., though, Hebrew alone is used in inscriptions on the coins, written in Paleo-Hebrew script; and the name of the province now has its old Hebrew form, Yehudah. Official stamps of Hellenistic Judaea, of either the early third or early second centuries B.C.E., likewise use the old Hebrew script. However, it is difficult to know how these inscriptions functioned; it may be worth pointing out that the iconography of the coins is not terribly distinctive— under the Achaemenids it consisted of a repertoire of motifs borrowed in part from Athenian coinage and then, under Ptolemy I, imitations of Alexandrian issues. Both sets of coins feature a large number of anomalous types which are difficult to interpret but not distinctively "Judaean," at least not in any obvious way.

The interpretation of the coinage of the Hasmoneans (ruled from 152 to 37 B.C.E.; minted coins starting c. 120) is characterized by a different set of complexities. As I suggested above, the revolt which was the dynasty's *raison d'etre* had tended to magnify the symbolic centrality of the Torah and the temple; this was perhaps accompanied by the first explicit and unambiguous uses of Hebrew as a national symbol—at least, such a use of the language was retrospectively attributed to the rebels. The quasi-official chronicle of the revolt and the rise of the Hasmonean family, 1 Maccabees, was composed in archaizing Hebrew;[54] the author of 2 Maccabees (an account of the revolt composed in Greek and unconnected with 1 Maccabees) emphasized, with an uncertain degree of accuracy, that rebels and martyrs of the persecution used Hebrew in some circumstances (2 Macc 7; 12.37). The attribution of symbolic importance to Hebrew— whether by the rebels themselves or by their successors—may help explain why the earliest Hasmonean coins, minted under John

---

[53] On the coins, see Y. Meshorer, *Ancient Jewish Coinage*, 2 volumes (New York: Amphora Books, 1982) 1.14–17; L. Mildenberg, "Yehud-Münzen," in H. Weippert, *Palästina in vorhellenistischer Zeit* (Munich: C. H. Beck, 1988) 721–8; D. Barag, "A Silver Coin of Yohanan the High Priest and the Coinage of Judaea in the Fourth Century B.C.E.," *Israel Numismatic Journal* 9 (1986–7) 4–21. On seals, bullae, etc., see the survey in Ephraim Stern, *Material Culture in the Land of the Bible in the Persian Period* (Warminster: Aris and Phillips, 1982) 202–13. On Paleo-Hebrew script, see J. Naveh, *On Sherd and Papyrus: Aramaic and Hebrew Inscriptions from the Second Temple, Mishnaic and Talmudic Periods* (Jerusalem: Magnes Press, 1992) 11–36 (in Hebrew).

[54] See Jonathan Goldstein, *I Maccabees* (Garden City: Doubleday, 1976) 14.

Hyrcanus I (reigned 134–104 B.C.E.), bore legends exclusively in the Hebrew language and in the presumably increasingly incomprehensible Paleo-Hebrew script, accompanied by a distinctive iconography no longer simply imitated from Hellenistic royal issues and Greek city coins.[55] Yet John's son Alexander (reigned 103–76 B.C.E.) minted coins with inscriptions in three languages: Hebrew (in Paleo-Hebrew script), Aramaic and Greek, with no concomitant variation in iconography. What might this mean?[56]

The role of Hebrew in the two Judaean revolts against Rome is less ambiguous. The silver coins of both the Great Revolt (66–74 C.E.) and the Bar Kokhba Revolt (132–135 C.E.) bear inscriptions exclusively in Hebrew and in Paleo-Hebrew script, at a time when ability to read this script must have been very rare indeed, even among those literate in Hebrew;[57] the inscriptions are accompanied by appropriate images, usually connected to the temple cult. There seems little doubt that the language functions on these coins practically as a talisman—an important element in the iconography of these powerful and ubiquitous expressions of Judaean national defiance.[58]

---

[55] The fullest collection is to be found in Meshorer, *Ancient Jewish Coinage*, volume 1; *contra* Meshorer, the first coins were issued not by Alexander Jannaeus but by John Hyrcanus I: see D. Barag, "Jewish Coins in Hellenistic and Roman Time," in Tony Hackens et al., eds., *A Survey of Numismatic Research, 1985–1990*, 2 volumes (International Society of Professional Numismatists, special publications, 12; Brussels: International Numismatic Commission, 1992) 1.106. Hasmonean coins were all small denomination bronze, intended only for local use. Seleucid royal and municipal silver coins continued to circulate extensively in Hasmonean Palestine.

[56] I will refrain from speculation here, and simply point out that the coins of the Hasmoneans' successor, Herod, were inscribed exclusively in Greek, with a gradual return, more pronounced under Herod's heirs, to "normal" (i.e., Greek style) iconography, including portraits of monarchs.

[57] The survival of one or two texts of the first century C.E. in the old script, and the use of a few Paleo-Hebrew letters as stone-cutters' marks and on food-rationing tags from Masada no more demonstrates general literacy in Paleo-Hebrew than the use of Greek letters by mathematicians demonstrates general literacy in Greek nowadays: see Naveh, *On Sherd and Papyrus*, 11–23. On the difficulties the engravers of the coins of both revolts had with the Paleo-Hebrew legends, see Leo Mildenberg, *The Coinage of the Bar Kokhba War* (Aarau: Sauerländer, 1984) 22.
    The standard collection of the coins of the first revolt is the outdated but not yet replaced work by Leo Kadman, *The Coins of the Jewish War of 66–73 C.E.* (Tel Aviv: Schocken, 1960), see especially his comments on the iconography of the coins, 83–95.

[58] There is some evidence that Bar Kokhba insisted on the use of Hebrew in his revolutionary administration: see Cotton, "The Languages of the Documents from the Judaean Desert". In contrast, the documents produced by the rebels of the Great Revolt encamped at Masada are overwhelmingly Aramaic: see n. 24 above. On the language of the Bar Kokhba coins, see Mildenberg, *Coinage of the Bar Kokhba War*, 69–72.

I suppose, then, that for most of the Jews of Palestine, Hebrew was important mainly as an item in a complex of symbols—a fact to which Judaean revolutionaries gave a fairly unambiguous material expression but which was, if less conspicuous, no less true in more peaceful times. These symbols no doubt shaped the Jews' consciousness in various unknowable ways and created among them the feeling that Hebrew was somehow "their" language, but in practice Hebrew impinged on their lives rather little. This is because those contexts in which Hebrew was used were remote from most people's regular experience: a passage in Josephus' *Jewish War* creates the impression that copies of the Pentateuch could not normally be found in Judaean villages[59]—not surprisingly, given the undoubted expense of parchment scrolls.[60] This implies that there was in most villages no time or place for reading the Torah—at least until several centuries later, when synagogues—where a portion of the Torah was probably read weekly—became more common in rural Palestine.[61] It is also unlikely that, at least before 70 C.E., elementary education in the Torah (and so in the Hebrew language) was provided for most boys, though it was certainly common in some circles; the late rabbinic tales about the establishment of a "state" school system in the first century or even earlier are probably idealizations.[62] Whatever the typical Judaean peasant knew of the contents of the Pentateuch, he knew from oral report, presumably in Aramaic.

---

[59] Josephus, *Jewish War* 2.228–31.

[60] This is not the only possible interpretation of the passage, and it may be worth remembering that substantial collections of books could be found in some Egyptian villages; however, Greek books in Egypt were written on (relatively inexpensive) papyrus while, if we may extrapolate from the Dead Sea scrolls, Jewish holy books, as early as the second and first centuries B.C.E., were written on parchment: on Egypt, see Rafaella Cribiore, *Gymnastics of the Mind: Greek Education in Hellenistic and Roman Egypt* (Princeton: Princeton Unviersity Press, 2001) 132–47; on use of parchment for Jewish holy books, see M. Goodman, "Sacred Scripture and 'Defiling the Hands'," *JThS* 41 (1990) 105; M. Haran, "Book-Scrolls at the Beginning of the Second Temple Period: The Transition from Papyrus to Skins," *HUCA* 44 (1983) 111–33. The implication of *Against Apion* 2.175, that Torah scrolls could be found in every Jewish settlement is an idealization and reflects, if anything, conditions in the diaspora.

[61] For discussion see Schwartz, *Imperialism and Jewish Society*, 215–39; Lee Levine, *The Ancient Synagogue: The First Thousand Years* (New Haven: Yale University Press, 2000) 42–73, concludes from the same evidence that the synagogue was a "dominant institution" in Jewish Palestine already in the first century. But the archaeology clearly indicates that it became ubiquitous in the countryside only in the fifth century or later.

[62] For detailed, and highly skeptical, discussion, see Catherine Hezser, *Jewish Literacy in Roman Palestine* (Tübingen: Mohr Siebeck, 2001) 39–68.

The transformation of the Torah and the temple into important symbols may be supposed to have enhanced their practical significance as, respectively, the civic and religious constitution of the Jews and the place where (among other things) it was authoritatively inter- preted. The Pentateuch was unique among ancient law-codes, national epics and the like in that it required general acquaintance with itself (a fact whose significance was much exaggerated by ancient Jewish apologists) and was in theory, unlike the temple, not the exclusive province of a class restricted by birth.[63] In practice, this meant that most Jews knew something of the Torah as applied in daily life. But despite the exoteric character of the Torah, its practical importance, its complexity, and the technical impossibility of widespread mastery of it in the conditions of a pre-modern agrarian economy, combined to generate a powerful, though by the first century loosely organized and to some extent fragmented class of intermediaries, responsible for preserving and interpreting it. The priests were, as suggested above, given by the Torah itself a special role in its own interpre- tation and execution. But the public character of the Jewish Law— as opposed to Egyptian or Babylonian—meant that access to intermediation of it was not restricted to priests, but was open to all—all, that is, with enough wealth to finance study. Village scribes, local arbitrators, and so on—probably for most Jews the most con- spicuous representatives of the class—were not necessarily priests. Thus, knowledge of the Torah, even when not accompanied by priestly birth and political connections, was a path to prestige. Even in the absence of evidence we would have to suppose that among some Judaeans knowledge of the Torah was zealously cultivated. Hebrew, as the language of the priestly curators of the temple, and of the mixed (priestly and lay) intermediaries of the Torah, became, in short, a language whose use (and this vagueness is intentional: it seems possible, but is uncertain, that members of this class actually spoke Hebrew among themselves) both distinguished a class and helped determine admission to it—a class whose legitimacy was in turn presumably confirmed by the language's symbolic power.

The function of Hebrew in the ideology of the intermediary/priestly class is well illustrated by a passage from the *Book of Jubilees*, an imi- tation and expansion of the book of Genesis, allegedly narrated by an

---

[63] See Albert Baumgarten, "The Torah as a Public Document in Judaism," *Studies in Religion* 15 (1985) 17–24.

"angel of the (divine) Presence," composed in Hebrew in the second century B.C.E. (it survives now in full only in translation into Ge'ez):

> And the Lord God said to me [the angel], "Open [Abraham's] mouth and his ears so that he might hear and speak with his mouth in the language which is revealed because it ceased from the mouth of all the sons of men from the day of the fall [of Babel?]." And I opened his mouth and his ears and his lips and I began to speak to him in Hebrew, in the tongue of creation. And he took his father's books— and they were written in Hebrew—and he copied them. And he began studying them thereafter. And I caused him to know everything that he was unable to understand. And he studied them in the six months of rain.

It is impossible here to trace the effects of this development in the masses of literature produced by this class from the third century B.C.E. to the third century C.E. But some observations may be made. Almost all surviving Palestinian literary writing from this period (whether or not it was composed in Hebrew) is informed by familiarity with the Pentateuch, and much of it actually imitates the Pentateuch and the other biblical books: Jubilees imitates Genesis, Ben Sira Proverbs, the Temple Scroll Deuteronomy, 1 Maccabees the Deuteronomic histories, and so on. That is to say, one of the consequences of the centrality of the Pentateuch and the concomitant rise of a class of intermediaries—for which the literature just mentioned is important evidence—is the pervasiveness of literary classicism, that is, the tendency to emulate a more or less discrete body of writing which has come to be thought uniquely valuable and significant.[64] The self-consciousness which classicism implies was not in fact completely non-existent before the third century B.C.E., but only from then onwards was it a defining characteristic of Judaean literature; it also conforms with the growing importance of Hebrew in the same period as a symbolic commodity and is, like it, an aspect of the ideologization of the language which I have previously discussed.

Imitation is only one possible response to the development of a classical literature; in the Jewish case, as in the Greek, it was accompanied or followed by the rise of detailed study, explication and commentary—in short, scholasticism. Jubilees, for example, contains

---

[64] For an illuminating, slightly different, account of this phenomenon, see H. Najman, *Seconding Sinai: The Development of Mosaic Discourse in Second Temple Judaism*, (Leiden: Brill, 2003).

elements of both classicism and scholasticism, since it is simultaneously an imitation and expansion of Genesis, and an attempt to work out the details of biblical chronology and solve other exegetical problems raised by the biblical text. In the first century B.C.E., if not earlier, the sectaries of Qumran produced commentaries on biblical books, a genre later taken up, though in very different forms, by Philo, the rabbis and the Church Fathers.

Hebrew After 70 c.e.

The status of Hebrew after the destruction of Jerusalem in 70 c.e. and the concurrent "normalization" of the constitutional condition of Palestine as a Roman province demands a more detailed discussion than it will receive here. In brief, the failed revolts, of 66–70 and 132–135, drastically reduced the numbers of the priests, scribes and sectaries who had constituted the temple staff and the class of intermediaries of the Torah. So, for example, Josephus claimed that in the early and mid-first century, there had been 20,000 priests, 6,000 Pharisees and 4,000 Essenes (many of the sectaries were probably also priests). The number of priests who survived the destruction is unknown, but the sects seem to have passed out of existence. The rabbis were probably the remnant of these classes of intermediaries, but in the second century there were never more than a few dozen rabbis active at any one time. The replacement of the Torah as the law of the land by Roman provincial law—a corollary of full annexation—necessarily reduced the attractiveness as legal authorities of those intermediaries who had survived. And Roman victory itself rendered adherence to the Torah religiously problematic. Josephus' *Jewish Antiquities* can be read as a plea, to both Jews and Romans, to continue to uphold the validity of the Torah—evidently something which could no longer be taken for granted. His contemporary, the author of *4 Ezra*, consigned the re-establishment of the covenant between God and Israel to an apocalyptic future.[65]

Under these circumstances, it is unsurprising that Hebrew disappears nearly completely from documentary and epigraphical texts definitely dated between 70 and Constantine's conquest of the East

---

[65] The above summarizes Schwartz, *Imperialism and Jewish Society*, 103–61. This final section of the paper abbreviates, revises and updates "Language, Power and Identity," 31–35.

in 324, except for a brief and significant revival at the time of the Bar Kokhba revolt, described above. The only Hebrew text definitely datable to this period is the Mishnah (the Tosefta and tannaitic midrashim may also belong in this period, but there is no consensus on this point). The language of the Mishnah differs considerably from that used in most pre-70 texts, whose language is archaizing or biblicizing. Mishnaic Hebrew is often said to correspond to the colloquial register of the language (how would we know?), but its resemblance to the language of 4 Q MMT—apparently a letter from a Qumran sectary to a member of a different sect or a non-sectarian Jerusalem priest—, of the ostraca from Masada marking priestly gifts, and of the "Bar Kokhba letters" suggests a different characterization.[66] The Hebrew of the Mishnah reflects a pre-70 priestly/scribal Hebrew *koine*, whether spoken or exclusively written.[67] In fact, the rabbis consistently avoided the archaic register of Hebrew in their extant writings, and were strongly conscious of the differences between *leshon hakhamim* ("the languages of the sages") and the biblicizing language of pre-70 Judaean writing. Unlike their predecessors, they rejected classicism, and embraced scholasticism exclusively. Perhaps use of this language was one of several strategies (in addition, for example, to avoidance of writing altogether) the rabbis adopted to perform or enact the distinction between their own lore and the "written Torah". In any case, it seems overwhelmingly likely that the use of Hebrew was for them as much an expression of ideology as for their priestly and sectarian forebears in the Second Temple period. In sum, Hebrew—*leshon hakhamim* or *leshon ha-qodesh* (probably, "temple language")—functioned for the rabbis as a sociolect, a means of marking themselves off from other Jews and emphasizing their partial continuity with the intermediary classes of the Second Temple period.[68]

---

[66] See Naveh, *On Sherd and Papyrus*, 24–5.

[67] For a historical-linguistic characterization of the language of the Mishnah, see M. Bar Asher, "Mishnaic Hebrew: An Introductory Survey".

[68] *Leshon ha-qodesh* is more widely, and earlier, attested as a term for Hebrew in rabbinic sources than "*leshon hakhamim*," and may be used in a fragmentary Qumran text: see E. Eshel and M. Stone, "Leshon Haqodesh in the End of Days in the Light of a Fragment from Qumran," *Tarbiz* 62 (1993) 169–77. On the meaning of the term, formed on the paradigm of such biblical phrases as "*sheqel ha-qodesh*" and "*hin qodesh*" ("*sheqel/hin* according to the temple standard"): see J. Greenfield, "Languages of Palestine, 200 B.C.E.–200 C.E.," in Herbert Paper, ed., *Jewish Languages: Theme and Variations* (Cambridge, MA: Harvard University Press, 1978) 149. Avigdor Shinan's frequently repeated claim that the term means "synagogue language" is

This claim may be confirmed by the epigraphical remains found
in the catacombs of Beth Shearim, probably in use from the third
to the fifth centuries. Most of these texts were written in Greek, but
Palestinian Jewish Aramaic is common, too, and there is a sprin-
kling of texts in other languages, Palmyrene, for example, probably
because some of the people buried in the necropolis came from the
diaspora. Only catacomb 20 contains many texts in a Hebrew very
close to that of the Mishnah, and almost every male commemorated
in these texts has the title "rabbi," and many have names associated with the patriarchal dynasty.[69] These rabbis may not in fact be
"our" rabbis, i.e., the men behind the Mishnah and the Palestinian
Talmud,[70] but the Talmud itself informs us that by the third or
fourth century there were many rabbis in northern Palestine who
were not part of what we regard as the rabbinic movement but were
nevertheless authorized to teach, and to judge in accordance with,
the laws of the Torah (Y. Bikkurim 3.3—"*ilen demitmenin biksaf*").[71]
At Beth Shearim then, Hebrew was still used to distinguish intermediaries of the Torah, whatever their precise identity may have
been, from other Jews.

In late antiquity (350–650), Hebrew once again became not only
a significant medium of Jewish literary expression, but also a common symbolic marker of Jewishness. Though most Jewish inscriptions continued to be written in Greek and Aramaic, Hebrew in this
period returned to occasional epigraphical use, both in epitaphs and
in dedicatory inscriptions in synagogues (there are no Palestinian
Jewish documentary texts from this period). This Hebrew revival,
which has been frequently discussed, seems to me connected to the
fact that only under Christian rule were the Jews once again granted
limited autonomy, not as a nation, as before 70, but as a collection
of discrete local religious communities.[72]

---

unlikely: in no extant source is the synagogue called "*ha-qodesh*" or its occasional
Aramaic equivalent, "*bet qudsha*": A Shinan, "Lishan Bet Qudsha in the Aramaic
Targums to the Torah," *Bet Miqra* 66 (1976) 472–4.

[69] See B. Mazar et al., *Beth Shearim*, 3 volumes (New Brunswick: Rutgers Univeristy
Press, 1971) 3, 52–65; Naveh, *On Sherd and Papyrus*, 25.

[70] See S. Cohen, "Epigraphical Rabbis," *JQR* 72 (1981–2) 1–17.

[71] The classic account is Gedalia Alon, "Those Appointed for Money," *Jews,
Judaism and the Classical World* (Jerusalem: Magnes Press, 1977) 374–435.

[72] For recent discussion, see Nicholas R. M. De Lange, "The Revival of the
Hebrew Language in the Third Century C.E.," *JSQ* 3 (1996) 342–58; S. Schwartz,
"Rabbinization in the Sixth Century," in P. Schäfer, ed., *The Talmud Yerushalmi and
Graeco-Roman Culture* III (Tübingen: Mohr Siebeck, 2002) 55–69.

Conclusion

The vicissitudes of Hebrew use in antiquity demonstrate the inextricable connections of social and cultural with political history, but also the complexity of those connections. Hebrew's emergence under Achaemenid and Macedonian rule as a symbol of Jewish nationhood and as a sociolect, distinguishing priestly and scribal intermediaries of the authority of the temple and the Torah, cannot be understood in abstraction from the practices of their imperial rulers. These governed by regulating local particularisms, and so, they were responsible for the spread of Aramaic and Greek as both administrative and spoken languages. But the Persian and Hellenistic emperors, in regulating local particularisms also supported them, and thereby contributed to the marginal preservation of Hebrew as symbol of Jewish nationhood and of the privileges enjoyed by the staffs of the national institutions. When Palestine was subjected to direct Roman rule, Hebrew was marginalized still further—preserved mainly by the remnants of the intermediary class, implausibly zealous to reestablish their authority over the Jews through their expertise in the surviving Jewish national institution, the Torah. The revival of partial Jewish autonomy under Christian rulers was connected, in its turn, to a revival of Hebrew as a symbol of Jewish particularity—much as altered versions of pre-Roman and pre-Hellenistic languages, like Coptic and Syriac, came in some oblique way to serve the interests of the national churches of the Jews' neighbors in precisely the same period.

THE MOTIVATIONS OF THE MACCABEES AND JUDEAN RHETORIC OF ANCESTRAL TRADITION

Brent Nongbri*

Introduction

The study of the history of the region around Jerusalem in the second century B.C.E. has come of age in recent years.[1] The groundbreaking works of Elias Bickerman,[2] Victor Tcherikover,[3] and Martin Hengel[4] paved the way, showing that a simple model of Jews resisting Greek influence was inadequate as a historical description of Palestine in the middle of the second century. Building on these classic treatments, more recent scholars have refined the methods and conclusions of earlier generations.[5] While some have pointed to the fact that "Judaism" and "Hellenism" need not be mutually exclusive categories, others have questioned the validity of the dichotomy and

* Yale University.

[1] Quotations from the Septuagint are drawn from Rahlfs' 1979 edition. Quotations from Josephus are drawn from the 1955 edition of Niese. Translations are my own unless otherwise noted.

[2] *Der Gott der Makkabäer: Untersuchungen über Sinn und Ursprung der makkabäischen Erhebung* (Berlin: Schocken Verlag/Jüdischer Buchverlag, 1937); English trans. by H.R. Moehring, *The God of the Maccabees: Studies on the Meaning and Origin of the Maccabean Revolt* (Leiden: Brill, 1979).

[3] *Hellenistic Civilization and the Jews* (reprint ed. Peabody, Mass.: Hendrickson Publishers, 1999).

[4] *Judentum und Hellenismus: Studien zu ihrer Begegnung unter besonderer Berücksichtigung Palästinas bis zur Mitte des 2 Jh.s. v.Chr.* (Tübingen: Mohr/Siebeck, 1973); English trans. by J. Bowden, *Judaism and Hellenism: Studies in their Encounter in Palestine during the Early Hellenistic Period* (one vol. ed. Philadelphia: Fortress Press, 1981). One of the most impressive aspects of all these works is the breadth of materials the authors have mastered. The present contribution seeks only to suggest another angle by which we might view just a few of the sources.

[5] These recent works are too numerous to recount here. Of special note are the superb opening chapter ("Hellenism and the Hasmoneans") of Erich Gruen's recent book, *Heritage and Hellenism: The Reinvention of Jewish Tradition* (Berkeley: University of California Press, 1998); John J. Collins, "Cult and Culture: The Limits of Hellenization in Judea" in *Hellenism in the Land of Israel*, eds. J. J. Collins and G. E. Sterling (Notre Dame: University of Notre Dame Press, 2001) 38–61; and Martin Goodman, "Jewish Attitudes to Greek Culture in the Period of the Second Temple" in *Jewish Education and Learning*, eds. G. Abramson and T. Parfitt (Chur: Harpwood Academic Publishers, 1994) 167–74.

even the categories themselves.[6] Wayne A. Meeks' summary of these developments is particularly apt:

> [S]tudies of language usage, trading patterns, political institutions, and other elements began to suggest to more and more scholars that Judea and Galilee were far from being pure Jewish islands in a sea of Hellenism. Even the Maccabee revolt and its aftermath came more and more to look not like the ultimate defense of Judaism from Hellenism, but like a continuing struggle between different ways of adapting to Hellenism . . . Indeed, "Judaism" was in some senses a Hellenistic religion.[7]

Meeks' point that Maccabean identity took shape in, and is a product of, the Hellenistic world should prompt us to ask: Why, when so much work has been done in reading the events in Judea between 200 B.C.E. and 169 B.C.E. in terms of shifting regional political tensions among Ptolemies, Seleucids, and Romans, do we continue to frame questions about the actions of Antiochus IV and the Maccabees from 169 to 163 B.C.E. in terms of a stable, well-defined "Judaism" fighting off Greek influences?[8] 2 Maccabees describes events that way, but some caution is in order.

---

[6] See Gruen, *Heritage and Hellenism*, xiv. For questions about the validity of the dichotomy itself, see Dale B. Martin, "Paul and the Judaism/Hellenism Dichotomy: Toward a Social History of the Question," in *Paul Beyond the Judaism/Hellenism Divide*, ed. T. Engberg-Pedersen (Louisville: Westminster John Knox Press, 2001) 29–61 and in the same volume Philip S. Alexander, "Hellenism and Hellenization as Problematic Historiographical Categories," 63–80. Early reviewers of Hengel expressed doubts along these same lines; in a review of *Judentum und Hellenismus* Arnaldo Momigliano wrote that "His book really deals with the Hellenization of an unknown entity," *Journal of Theological Studies* 21 (1970) 149–53. Much of the current discussion was anticipated early on in a characteristically blunt and provocative essay by Morton Smith, "Terminological Boobytraps and Real Problems in Second-Temple Judaeo-Christian Studies" in *Traditions in Contact and Change: Proceedings of the XIV Congress of the International Association for the History of Religion*, eds. P. Slater and D. Wiebe (Waterloo, Ont.: Wilfred Laurier University Press, 1983) 295–306.

[7] "Judaism, Hellenism, and the Birth of Christianity" in Engberg-Pedersen, *Paul Beyond the Judaism/Hellenism Divide*, 24–5. To be sure, there is nothing like uniform agreement on these points and there are scholars who have taken up reactionary positions attempting to reassert the dichotomy; foremost among this group is Louis Feldman. For a particularly bold example of his take on matters, see his review of Collins and Sterling's *Hellenism in the Land of Israel*, "How Much Hellenism in the Land of Israel?" *Journal for the Study of Judaism in the Persian, Hellenistic and Roman Period* 33 (2002) 290–313.

[8] Take the excellent work of Tessa Rajak as an example. After her most recent extended discussion of the complexities of the terms "Judaism" and "Hellenism," she asserts that there were still "those moments when Jews saw themselves as diametrically opposed to what Greeks stood for, in the broadest sense . . . Not only the

As Bickerman noted long ago, the Maccabean documents "were produced in order to make history, not report it."[9] Since the Hasmonean house eventually usurped the ancestral high priesthood, all our major sources—1 and 2 Macc and Josephus—all (in different ways and for different reasons) needed to legitimate the Maccabees.[10] 1 and 2 Macc explain the rise of the Maccabees in terms of a fight for the "covenant of the fathers" or "Judaism."[11] The authors of these documents sharply differentiate between the Maccabees and those who held power in Jerusalem before them. While 2 Macc 3:1 makes an exception for the virtuous high priest Simon III, the overall impression is that the pious Maccabees in Modein were people of a different sort than the Judeans in Jerusalem.

Josephus and modern scholarship tend to reinforce this impression, but we may legitimately ask if some of the similarities between the Maccabees and their contemporaries and predecessors have been overlooked.[12] To be sure, no Judeans before the Maccabees openly attacked the representatives of the Seleucid king, but as we shall see,

---

most important, but also the most formative of such experiences was the revolt of the Maccabees," *The Jewish Dialogue with Greece and Rome: Studies in Cultural and Social Interaction* (Leiden: Brill, 2002) 7. As I see it, the chief difficulty with this formulation is the phrase "moments when Jews saw themselves." If that read "moments when a relatively small number of literate Jews strategically chose to portray themselves and other Jews," I would entirely agree. The difference is crucial, especially when we want to consider the motivations of the Maccabees. It is important that we be attuned to the rhetoric of the Maccabean literature.

[9] *The God of the Maccabees*, 4.

[10] The legitimate line of priestly succession was already broken when Menelaus bought the priesthood and deposed Jason ca. 172 B.C.E., if 1 and 2 Maccabees are to be believed over against Josephus, who states that Menelaus was of Oniad stock, *Ant.* 12.237–9. For more on this point, see below. For this project, I have left aside the veiled references to the Maccabees in Daniel. For a discussion of these passages, see the relevant sections of John J. Collins' commentary in the Hermeneia series, *Daniel: A Commentary on the Book of Daniel* (Minneapolis: Fortress Press, 1993).

[11] I follow Martin Goodman in taking very seriously the notion that our ancient sources for this period may tell us more about the times in which the sources were composed than about the years following 169 B.C.E. See his "Jewish Attitudes to Greek Culture in the Period of the Second Temple," 171.

[12] An important exception to this statement is a brief but extremely useful article by Seth Schwartz, "A Note on the Social Type and Political Ideology of the Hasmonean Family" *JBL* 112 (1993) 305–9. Schwartz argues that the Maccabees, like the Tobiads, were "village strongmen," ambitious rural up-and-comers who exploited upheaval in Jerusalem for their own ends. It will be clear throughout the present paper that I agree with much of Schwartz's presentation of the Maccabees and Tobiads, though I have reservations about his emphasis on the "rural" concerns of these families.

just what the Maccabees hoped to accomplish with these attacks does
not look all that different from the goals of others who preceded
them in the struggle for prestige in Jerusalem. The primary difference
between the actions attributed to Mattathias and his posterity and
the actions of the political players active in and around Jerusalem
in the years leading up to the revolt is the Maccabean rhetoric of
"ancestral tradition."[13] It will thus be informative to examine how
the Maccabees might be similar to some of the other powerful families in Judea and how the Maccabean rhetoric of "ancestral tradition" functions.

In order to re-contextualize the Maccabees in this way, I shall
provide a quick summary of the period before the Maccabees with
an eye to the fights between families and their alliances with the
regional powers, building on the valuable work of Seth Schwartz.[14]
Then I shall examine the motivations of the Maccabees, first with
a brief analysis of Antiochus IV's edict of 167 B.C.E. followed by a
reevaluation of Mattathias' origins and the nature of Judas' actions
in "the revolt." Finally, I shall point out similarities between the
Maccabees' use of "ancestral traditions" and the use of the notion
of "the ancestral constitution" in Athens. By considering some of the

---

[13] As several colleagues have pointed out to me, the Maccabees appear different
to us at an intuitive level because they stayed in power longer (ergo they had more
popular support) than the previous contenders for power in Jerusalem. This reasoning does not seem entirely sound to me; the staying power of Judas and his successors can be attributed to shrewd political moves, and the main difference from
their predecessors seems to be that they chose their alliances more wisely. See Dov
Gera, *Judea and Mediterranean Politics 219 to 161 B.C.E.* (Leiden: Brill, 1998) 239–54.
It is useful as a starting point to note similarities between the actions of the Maccabees
and those of other groups in similar positions within the Hellenistic world. Thomas
Fischer has noted that the Hasmonean's usurpation of priestly power and stubborn
stance towards the Seleucids fits the regional pattern, since that time period was
one of "continuous uprisings and striving for independence throughout the Seleucid
empire, particularly in the fringe areas." He further observes similarities in "the
manner in which the residents of those areas sought support from the new leading
powers in East and West, the Parthians and the Romans. Classical sources are copi-
ous in this context: the city ruler of Pergamum; the Parthians themselves; the rulers
of Bactria and Media (Diodotus, Molon, Timarchus); the native dynasts in Persis,
in Commagene, in Elam and in Judea. In the course of time all gained freedom
from Seleucid rule, as did the coastal cities of Asia Minor, and later those of Syria
and Phonecia" (13). "Hasmoneans and Seleucids: Aspects of War and Policy in the
Second and First Centuries B.C.E." in *Greece and Rome in Eretz Israel: Collected Essays*,
ed. A. Kasher, et al. (Jerusalem: The Israel Exploration Society, 1990) 3–19.
[14] "A Note on the Social Type and Political Ideology of the Hasmonean Family,"
305–9. See n. 12 above.

similarities between the Maccabees and other Judean families, we shall see the Maccabees' deployment of the idea of "ancestral traditions" is best understood not as conservative response to Greek incursion, but rather as a part of the Maccabees' innovative strategy for taking over Jerusalem and running the temple and cult as they saw fit.

FAMILY FEUDS IN JUDEA, PART 1: THE TOBIADS

To begin with, I want to look at the stories of the Tobiad family in the third and second centuries B.C.E., for which we mainly rely on Josephus. Fortunately, there is a good deal of high quality secondary literature that offers various reconstructions of the history of Judea from the time of Antiochus III's capture of Palestine in 200 B.C.E. to the first Egyptian campaign of Antiochus IV in 169 B.C.E. I shall provide a summary here of these scholars' conclusions about the major political actors in Palestine during that time period.

The main characters in Josephus' description of this time period are the members of two families, the high priestly Oniads and the Tobiads, a Judean family based in the trans-Jordan. Both these families seem to have had a history in the later biblical texts. The Oniads were the high priests dating back to the Persian era,[15] and the Tobiads also seem to have roots reaching back to the time of Nehemiah.[16]

---

[15] On the history of this family, see Frank Moore Cross' most recent reconstruction in *From Epic to Canon: History and Literature in Ancient Israel* (Baltimore: Johns Hopkins University Press, 1998) 151–72 along with the cautionary remarks of Lester L. Grabbe, *Judaism from Cyrus to Hadrian* (Minneapolis: Fortress Press, 1992) 1.112–14. See also Deborah W. Rooke, *Zadok's Heirs: The Role and Development of the High Priesthood in Ancient Israel* (Oxford: Oxford University Press, 2000) 243–75 and now the relevant sections of James C. VanderKam, *From Joshua to Caiaphas: High Priests after the Exile* (Minneapolis: Fortress Press, 2004).

[16] The name "Tobiah" makes multiple appearances in the later biblical literature. In Ezra 2:60, "the sons of Tobiah" are listed among the returnees who "were not able to proclaim the house of their father and their seed, whether it was from Israel . . . and they were excluded from the priesthood as unclean" (so also Nehemiah 7:62). According to Ezra 2:60, they came back in the time of Cyrus (just after 538 B.C.E., but according to 1 Esdras 5:37, they returned in the time of Darius (522–20 B.C.E.). In the MT (but not the LXX) a certain Tobiah is a named figure in Zechariah's crowning of Joshua as high priest (Zech 6:10–14). In Nehemiah, Tobiah ("the Ammonite") actively opposes Nehemiah's building project. He appears to be a powerful man in Jerusalem, since "many in Judah were bound by an oath to him" (Neh 6:18) and he later established some kind of presence in the temple through an alliance with the high priest Eliashib, which outraged Nehemiah (Neh

While the families became related by marriage, they appear to have had distinct political alliances both before and after 200 B.C.E. The first of the Oniads whom Josephus describes in detail is Onias II, who seems to have been high priest in the middle to late part of the third century B.C.E.[17] According to Josephus, Onias II refused to pay taxes to the reigning Ptolemy and thus brought the risk of Ptolemaic action against Jerusalem.[18] Josephus reports that Joseph, the son of Tobias (and thus Onias II's nephew), went to Egypt to appease Ptolemy with gifts and in addition to averting Ptolemaic punishment of Jerusalem, he secured for himself tax-farming rights for all of Coele-Syria (*Ant.* 12.154–79). Beyond granting Joseph the

---

13:4–10). We also know of a "Tobiah, servant of the king" from Lachish Ostracon No. 3 (on which see Klaas A. D. Smelik, *Writings from Ancient Israel: A Handbook of Historical and Religious Documents*, trans. G. I. Davies [Louisville: Westminster/John Knox Press, 1991], 116–31) and a slave-trader in the trans-Jordan called Tobiah from the Zenon Papyri (on which see Tcherikover, *Hellenistic Civilization and the Jews*, 60–72). B. Mazar has argued that all the "Tobiah"s can be arranged into a straight genealogy and further that the family can be traced back through the exile to monarchic times; see his "The Tobiads," *Israel Exploration Journal* 7 (1957) 137–45, 229–38, particularly 235. The argument is unconvincing, but the repeat appearances of powerful men named Tobias in Jerusalem politics with trans-Jordanian associations suggest that some familial connection is probable at least from the time of Tobiah "the Ammonite."

[17] I regard the social structures outlined in these stories as basically historical. Josephus' account of Joseph and Hyrcanus' courting of the king and his entourage with gifts is quite similar to the picture painted of another "Tobias" courting the king earlier in the century preserved in the Zenon Papyri. See *Corpus Papyrorum Judaicarum*, ed. V. Tcherikover (Cambridge: Harvard University Press, 1957–64) nos. 1, 4, and 5. Tcherikover and others before him were clearly correct that Josephus misdates these episodes to the reign of Ptolemy V Epiphanes (ruled 203–181 B.C.E.). They should rather be placed in the reign of Ptolemy III Euergetes (ruled 246–221 B.C.E.). See Tcherikover, *Hellenistic Civilization and the Jews*, 128–30. Dov Gera rejects altogether the historicity of Josephus' account of the Tobiads. See his essay "On the Credibility of the History of the Tobiads (Josephus, *Antiquities* 12, 156–222, 228–236)" in *Greece and Rome in Eretz Israel: Collected Essays*, ed. A. Kasher, et al. (Jerusalem: The Israel Exploration Society, 1990) 21–38 and more recently *Judaea and Mediterranean Politics 219 to 161 B.C.E.* (Leiden: Brill, 1998) 36–58. The biblical parallels he highlights are well worth noticing and they do call into question the details of the stories, but even Gera notes that "the historical setting of the story [of Joseph] is convincing" ("On the Credibility," 31) and that the author of the tale has "intimate knowledge of the period" (*Judaea and Mediterranean Politics*, 56). Excavations have confirmed that Josephus is at least correct in his location of the Tobiad fortress at 'Arāq el Amīr, if not in his dating of it. On the site, see the bibliography and discussion in Grabbe, *Judaism from Cyrus to Hadrian*, 1.188–9.

[18] Josephus attributes this action to Onias' avarice (*Ant.* 12. 157–9) but that Onias would risk having Jerusalem occupied by Egyptian forces for the sake of personal greed is suspicious. If his refusal to pay taxes is believable, it is likely he had political motivations rather than (or in addition to) greed.

tax collecting rights, Ptolemy also gave him a force of 2000 soldiers, which he used to enforce the tax collection in Syrian cities (*Ant.* 12.180–5). He held this prominent position for twenty-two years.

Josephus then focuses on Joseph's son Hyrcanus, who like his father, went to Alexandria and won the favor of the Ptolemy.[19] Upon his return to Judea, his brothers (with Joseph's approval) attacked him, and he retreated to the trans-Jordan where he levied taxes on the inhabitants there (φορολογῶν τοὺς βαρβάρους, *Ant.* 12.222).[20] Presumably, Hyrcanus had secured himself some kind of fighting force to carry out this tax collection. After noting the deaths of Joseph and Onias II and the ascension of Seleucus IV, Josephus describes continued fighting among the Tobiads that left the population "divided into two camps" (διέστη τὸ πλῆθος, *Ant.* 12.228); again the implication is that both Onias and the Tobiad brothers on the one hand and Hyrcanus on the other had fighting forces. After describing Hycanus' fortress in the trans-Jordan, Josephus claims that Hyrcanus, fearing reprisals for his attacks on locals in the trans-Jordan, committed suicide upon the ascension of Antiochus Epiphanes.[21]

---

[19] Josephus places Hyrcanus' actions in Alexandria at the time of the birth of a son to Ptolemy Euergetes; so the time period is around 187 B.C.E. (birth of Ptolemy Philometor) or shortly after 185 B.C.E. (birth of Euergetes' second son, Physcon), *Ant* 12.196. Tcherikover has convincingly shown that given the various contradictions in Josephus' chronology, the most likely date for such a trip would have been between 205 and 200 B.C.E. (*Hellenistic Civilization and the Jews*, 130).

[20] Although Josephus makes no clear indication, Tcherikover makes the plausible case that the family's reason for hostility toward Hyrcanus was his usurpation of the tax farming rights that had formerly belonged to Joseph, *Hellenistic Civilization and the Jews*, 135–6.

[21] Tcherikover has teased out of Josephus' brief account just about all that can be surmised, and on the whole, I agree with his portrayal of an up and coming family advancing its cause on the international scene by making alliances with foreign leaders. For Tcherikover, however, Joseph and Hyrcanus represent the early "Hellenizing" force in Judea, in opposition to the priests (131–42). Hengel concurs, stating that people like the Tobiads faced "representatives of a theocracy faithful to the Law" (*Judaism and Hellenism*, 50). We have an advantage over Tcherikover and Hengel, though, in our access to recent archaeological finds suggesting that the Oniads were just as "Hellenized" as the Tobiads may have been. See, e.g., the coins of Onais I's father, which have cursive Aramaic script with the common Athenian Owl on the reverse and what appears to be the head of Athena on the obverse. See Arnold Spaer, "Jaddua the High Priest," *Israel Numismatic Journal* 9 (1986–7) 1–3 and Plate 2:1–2. This coin is one of several from Judea with paleo-Hebrew or Aramaic script bearing Greek images that predate the arrival of Alexander the Great. See Dan Barag, "A Silver Coin of Yohanan the High Priest and the Coinage of Judea in the Fourth Century" Idem, 4–25.

Before his death, Hyrcanus seems to have established what amounted to a petty kingdom of his own even though he failed to take Jerusalem. If Josephus is to be taken seriously, divisions within the Tobiad family led to serious outbreaks of violence in Jerusalem.[22] Hyrcanus' own relations with Jerusalem, however, may have been better than Josephus lets on, since 2 Macc 3:10–11 states that in the time of Onias III, the temple held the money of "Hyrcanus, son of Tobias, a man of high authority" (σφόδρα ἀνδρὸς ἐν ὑπεροχῇ). In any event, the Tobiads, who had questionable status in the Persian period (see n. 15 above), had become quite powerful, and as we shall see, the Tobiads continued to be a force in the Maccabean wars.[23]

Family Feuds in Judea, Part 2: The Later Oniads

Josephus next relates further intrigues among the Tobiads and the Oniads but shifts the focus to the latter. After the reign of Simon II, the high priesthood fell to Onias III, but according to Josephus, it was then given to his brother. In a rather convoluted summary, Josephus writes:

> At about the same time, upon the death of Onias the high priest, Antiochus gave the high priesthood to his brother Jesus; for the child that Onias left was still an infant . . . But Jesus, (this was the brother of Onias), was denied the high priesthood by the king, who was angry

---

[22] Josephus' brief note at the beginning of the *Jewish War* gives the same impression: "At the time when Antiochus, who was called Epiphanes, had a quarrel with the sixth Ptolemy about his right to all of Syria, sedition fell upon the powerful men among the Judeans (στάσεως τοῖς δυνατοῖς Ἰουδαίων ἐμπεσούσης) and they had an ambitious rivalry over power; as each of those who were of dignity could not stand to be subject to their equals. However, Onias, one of the high priests, prevailed, and threw the sons of Tobias out of the city," 1.31.

[23] Aside from the notice in Josephus discussed below, 1 Macc. 5:13 indicates that Judeans under attack write a letter to Judas noting that "all our brothers who are among the Tobiads (πάντες οἱ ἀδελφοὶ ἡμῶν οἱ ὄντες ἐν τοῖς Τουβίου) have been killed" (see also 2 Macc. 12:17). These are clearly references to the Tobiad forces in the trans-Jordan. See Israel Shatzman, *The Armies of the Hasmoneans and Herod: From Hellenistic to Roman Frameworks* (Tübingen: Mohr/Siebeck, 1991) 20 and the literature cited there. Hengel suggested that after his failure to take Jerusalem, Hyrcanus established his own temple at ʿArāq el-Amīr in competition with the Jerusalem temple (*Judaism and Hellenism*, 273–5). Given the existence of other Judean temples at Elephantine and Leontopolis, we cannot exclude Hengel's suggestion, but the archaeological evidence is questionable, and in light of the lack of literary evidence, I regard Hengel's proposal as just an interesting conjecture.

with him and gave it to his younger brother, Onias; for Simon had these three sons, and to each of them came the high priesthood, as we have made clear. This Jesus changed his name to Jason, and Onias was called Menelaus. When the former high priest, Jesus, rebelled against Menelaus, who was appointed after him, the populace was divided between them. And the offspring of Tobias took the part of Menelaus, but the majority of the people joined with Jason; on account of which Menelaus and the offspring of Tobias were distressed, and retired to Antiochus making clear to him that they, having left behind the laws of their country and the civic life entailed therein (βούλονται τοὺς πατρίους νόμους καταλιπόντες καὶ τὴν κατ᾽ αὐτοὺς πολιτείαν), wanted to follow the king's decrees and to have the Greek civic life; they then asked permission to build a gymnasium in Jerusalem (*Ant.* 12.237–41).

Josephus seems to have telescoped a good deal of material at this point, and it is here that 2 Macc and (to a lesser degree) 1 Macc become more important sources. First, however, we must step back to an earlier point in Josephus' *Antiquities*, which outlines another political move of the Oniads. When Antiochus III's forces were on the verge of defeating the Egyptian army at the turn of the third century, the ruling powers of Judea turned coat and switched their hundred-year old allegiance with the Ptolemies over to the Seleucids.[24] Much has been made of Antiochus' response to the Judeans actions in the supposed decree that Josephus presents. The relevant section is below:

> Let all the members of the nation conduct themselves as citizens in accordance with ancestral laws (πολιτευέσθωσαν δὲ πάντες οἱ ἐκ τοῦ ἔθνους κατὰ τοὺς πατρίους νόμους, *Ant.* 12.142).

For Bickerman, the content of these laws was clear. The decree's " 'laws of the fathers' meant Torah. Only Torah and nothing but Torah."[25] Tcherikover agreed the Law of Moses was meant but noted an important caveat. He pointed out that

> the "theocracy" of Jerusalem, for example, with the authority of the High Priest, and the priestly class grouped about the temple, all rested on the right of the Jews "to live according to their ancestral laws"; the Mosaic law, however, knows nothing of the High Priest as head of the nation, nor of the Temple at Jerusalem.[26]

---

[24] Josephus, *Ant.* 12.133: "the Judeans willingly went over to him and welcomed him to their city."
[25] *The God of the Maccabees*, 34.
[26] *Hellenistic Civilization and the Jews*, 83–4.

Tcherikover's solution to the problem is an appeal to "oral tradition" as a means of accounting for the differences.[27] It seems that a
more prudent solution is simply to note that we do not know the
exact content of these "ancestral laws," just that they seem to have
upheld the status quo of a priestly aristocracy and were not coter-
minous with what came to be regarded as "normative" Mosaic law.

In any event, Antiochus III did uphold that status quo, and Simon
II and Onias III were able to hold on to the high priesthood in
spite of the Tobiad incursions. The serious trouble seems to have
come from within the Oniad family. While Josephus says that Antiochus
gave Jesus/Jason the high priesthood when Onias III died, 2 Macc
relates that while Onias III was alive, Jason bribed the king for the
high priesthood and for the right to build a gymnasium and establish Jerusalem as a *polis* (2 Macc 4:7–9).[28] The remainder of 2 Macc
4 laments Jason's various "Greek" influences on the city.[29] Jason's
time as high priest was limited, though. According to 2 Macc 4:23,
after three years he sent Menelaus[30] to deliver money to the king,
at which point Menelaus "outbid" Jason for the office of high priest.

---

[27] So also Hengel, *Judaism and Hellenism*, 271.

[28] For the argument that 2 Macc 4:9 implies the restructuring of Jerusalem as a
polis, see Tcherikover, *Hellenistic Civilization and the Jews*, 161ff. and 404–9.

[29] This chapter of 2 Macc. is really the only place in the literature describing
these events in which "Greekness" is the major issue. See John J. Collins, *The
Hellenization of Jerusalem in the Pre-Maccabean Era* (Jerusalem: Ingeborg Rennert Center
for Jerusalem Studies, 1999) 1–3. According to 2 Macc, Jason encouraged "Greek
ways," (4:10) "introduced new customs contrary to the law" (4:11), built a gymnasium (4:12), "induced the noblest of the young men to wear the Greek hat" (4:12),
brought about "an extreme of Hellenization" (4:13), encouraged the priests to neglect
their duties and put "the highest value upon Greek forms of prestige" (4:15). As
Seth Schwartz has aptly noted, "1 Macc. is completely unconcerned with distinctions between 'Greek' and 'non-Greek' gentiles." See his "Israel and the Nations
Roundabout: 1 Maccabees and the Hasmonean Expansion" *JJS* 42 (1991) 22–3.

[30] 2 Macc does not mention that Menelaus was a son of Simon II. In 2 Macc.,
Menelaus is instead identified as the brother of another Simon, the προστάτης τοῦ
ἱεροῦ, "overseer of the temple," who is of the tribe of Benjamin (ἐκ τῆς Βενιαμιν
φυλῆς, 3:4; although most scholars prefer to follow a Latin manuscript here that
reads *de tribu Balgea*, "the watch of Balgea," thus maintaining that Menelaus was of
priestly, but not high priestly stock. For a full discussion, see Tcherikover, *Hellenistic
Civilization*, 403–4. We later read of another brother of Menelaus, a certain Lysimachus,
who oversees temple affairs while Menelaus is away with the king (2 Macc 4:29).
Lysimachus gathered a force of three thousand men, attacked a crowd of Judeans
and died (2 Macc 4:39–41). The picture of a new family on the rise fits quite well
with what we saw of the Tobiads, but Josephus' genealogy is not impossible. It is
difficult to see why Josephus would fabricate such a connection. On the other hand,
there is clearly motivation for 1 and 2 Macc either to omit Menelaus altogether or
to obscure his priestly legitimacy.

2 Macc 4:26 reports that when Menelaus ousted Jason as high priest, the latter was "forced as a fugitive into the region of Ammon"[31] and Menelaus began selling various temple paraphernalia, which brought rebuke from the deposed Onias III who had taken refuge at the sanctuary of Daphne near Antioch.[32] Menelaus then had him murdered. At this point, Antiochus IV had made his second invasion against Egypt (5:1), and upon reports of Antiochus' death, Jason, with a thousand troops, took Jerusalem but "he did not take the leadership" (τῆς μὲν ἀρχῆς οὐκ ἐκράτησεν), and he fled back to Ammon after his attack, but was unwelcome there and ended up in Egypt where he eventually died (5:5–8). This depiction is thus not quite Josephus' "civil war," but it does testify to family battles and, if 2 Macc is to be believed, the rise of yet another priestly family (the brothers Simon, Menelaus, and Lysimachus) to power in Jerusalem.

Apparently, Jason's attack was enough to catch the attention of the king: "When word of what had happened fell before the king, he took it to mean Judea was in revolt. So, raging inwardly, he broke camp from Egypt and took the city" (2 Macc 5:11). 2 Macc reports that 80,000 were killed and an equal number put into slavery. Menelaus, however, remained in good standing with the king and more firmly in control with some of Antiochus' forces to help keep the peace.

Finally, before moving on, we should note that after Menelaus died,[33] it seems that a certain Alcimus became high priest. 1 Macc relates that shortly after Demetrius' coup in Antioch (162 B.C.E.), there was an embassy of "all the unlawful and impious men from Israel" (πάντες ἄνδρες ἄνομοι καὶ ἀσεβεῖς ἐξ Ἰσραηλ, 1 Macc 7:5) led by one "impious" Alcimus (Ἄλκιμον τὸν ἀσεβῆ, 1 Macc 7:9), whom Demetrius appointed as high priest and instructed to "take vengeance on the sons of Israel" (1 Macc 7:9).[34] Only later (7:14), do we find

---

[31] Jason's flight to the trans-Jordan seems odd in light of Josephus' statement that the Tobiads took Menelaus' side in the fight against Jason (*Ant.* 12.237–41, quoted above).

[32] Onias' presence there is yet another indication that "Hellenization" was not as large a factor in these disputes as most assume.

[33] 2 Macc 13:4–7 later reports that the king had Menelaus killed, believing he was "the cause of all the trouble" in Judea.

[34] 2 Macc 14:3 is also unclear on Alcimus' origins. He appears there as one who "had formerly been high priest" but who no longer "had safety nor further access to the holy altar" (καθ' ὁντιναοῦν τρόπον οὐκ ἔστιν αὐτῷ σωτηρία οὐδὲ πρὸς τὸ ἅγιον θυσιαστήριον ἔτι πρόσοδος).

out that Alcimus was in fact of good priestly stock ("a priest from the seed of Aaron" ἱερεὺς ἐκ σπέρματος Ααρων, according to the Hasidaioi, who sided with Alcimus and thereafter abandoned Judas' army).[35] Alcimus arrived in Jerusalem with an army under the command of Bacchides and took control. Here again, it seems a member of yet another priestly family active in Jerusalem was able to secure power through a foreign alliance.

The Maccabees, Part 1: Antiochus IV's Decree

In stark contrast to all such political intrigue, the scholarly portrayal of the Maccabees is generally one of pious country priests reacting with holy wrath to what are read as Antiochus IV's religious persecutions of Judaism; it was only the later members of the Hasmonean dynasty that had political, high priestly pretensions in Jerusalem.[36] All of these views need to be nuanced, and to do so, it will be necessary to question some standard interpretations of the decree of Antiochus IV.

The author of 1 Macc presents the king's actions as a series of events with no clear logical ties to one another: Antiochus attacks Egypt (1:16–19), "goes up against Israel" and robs the temple (1:20–28), and two years later sends a tax collector to Jerusalem who plunders the city, tears down its walls, builds new walls and the *akra*, and stations there "sinful" people (ἔθνος ἁμαρτωλόν ἄνδρας παρανόμους, 1:34). Finally, Antiochus himself sends out a decree, which our author describes in the famous passage in 1:41–9:

---

[35] Alcimus' seems to have been in control ca. 162–159 B.C.E. In his history of the high priesthood, Josephus claims that Alcimus was "of the family of Aaron but not of this house" γένους μὲν τοῦ Ἀαρῶνος οὐκ ὄντα δὲ τῆς οἰκίας ταύτης, *Ant.* 20.235. I am uncertain what this statement means. Elsewhere, Josephus indicates that he was "not of the family of the high priests" (οὐκ ὄντι τῆς τῶν ἀρχιερέων γενεᾶς), *Ant.* 12.387.

[36] 1 Macc does indeed indicate a change in policy around the year 140, when Simon secured his position as high priest and leader of the people, but this change dealt mainly with land. From the time of Simon on, acquiring new land became a goal in a way that it had not been earlier. Note, however, that 2 Macc presents a different picture, with "the land" playing a role in the Maccabean movement from the beginning. See Doron Mendels, *The Land of Israel as a Political Concept in Hasmonean Literature: Recourse to History in Second Century B.C. Claims to the Holy Land* (Tübingen: Mohr/Siebeck, 1987) 49–50.

The king wrote to his whole kingdom that all should be one people, and each should leave behind its customs, and all the gentiles welcomed the speech of the king, and many from Israel were well pleased with his rites (εὐδόκησαν τῇ λατρείᾳ αὐτοῦ), and they sacrificed to idols and profaned the sabbath. And the king sent [orders] . . . to forbid burnt offerings and sacrifices and drink offerings from the sanctuary and to profane sabbaths and festivals to defile sanctuary and priests, to build altars and sacred precincts and idol-temples and to sacrifice swine and common animals and to leave their sons uncircumcised to make their souls detestable in every impurity and profanity so as to forget the law and change all the ordinances (ὥστε ἐπιλαθέσθαι τοῦ νόμου καὶ ἀλλάξαι πάντα τὰ δικαιώματα) and whoever does not do according to the speech of the king will be put to death.

After this decree, the author reports that "many of the people, everyone who forsook the law, joined them and they did evil in the land, they drove Israel into hiding in every place of refuge they had" (1:51–2). Finally, the author relates that the evildoers "erected a desolating sacrilege on the altar of burnt offering" (ᾠκοδόμησεν βδέλυγμα ἐρημώσεως ἐπὶ τὸ θυσιαστήριον, 1:56), built altars throughout Judah, destroyed the "books of the law" (τὰ βιβλία τοῦ νόμου), were violent to Israel (1:58), offered sacrifice on the altar on top of the altar of burnt offering, and put to death circumcised children and their families.[37]

Much of this material fits very well with some of the themes in 1 Macc and is probably more reflective of Maccabean rhetorical aims than Antiochus' policies. For example, the author of 1 Macc fits Antiochus' actions into a biblical model; 1 Macc. attempts to portray foreigners as simply wicked, and so "forming a covenant with them" and "becoming one people" with them is the worst possible scenario for this author and likely hyperbole.[38] 2 Macc, however, emphasizes some of the same details of the decree (such as the

---

[37] Josephus repeats nearly the same list in *Ant.* 12.248–56.

[38] See Daniel R. Schwartz, "The Other in 1 and 2 Maccabees" in *Tolerance and Intolerance in Early Judaism and Christianity*, eds. G. N. Stanton and G. G. Stroumsa (Cambridge: Cambridge University Press, 1998) 30–7, and Seth Schwartz, who points out that there are exceptions to this rule, especially the Romans ("Israel and the Nations Roundabout," 21 n. 19). Joseph Sievers notes the same point: "Judah established good relations with Rome which were kept up by each of his three immediate successors. This demonstrates the Hasmoneans' willingness to cooperate with Gentiles when that seemed to further their goals, although 1 Macc portrays the Hasmoneans and their gentile neighbors as implacable enemies," *The Hasmoneans and Their Supporters: From Mattathias to the Death of John Hyrcanus I* (Atlanta: Scholars Press, 1990) 157.

erection of an altar in the temple, the construction of other altars, the sacrifice of pigs, and the forbidding of circumcision and sabbath observance), which calls for some explanation.

For Bickerman, the decree was the apex of the "Hellenizing" program instigated first by Jason and then by Menelaus.[39] Several authors have shown that such a hypothesis is unlikely; the matters surrounding the gymnasium are a separate affair from Antiochus' actions, and there is no evidence for a grand program of cultural "Hellenizing" on the part of Antiochus.[40] In fact, Bickerman himself argued that the character of the cult in Jerusalem and surrounding areas after Antiochus' decree was more native Syrian than Greek.[41] Tcherikover famously suggested that Antiochus' decree resulted from an open, organized revolt by the Hasidaioi such that "it was not the revolt which came as a response to the persecution, but the persecution which came as a response to the revolt."[42] Tcherikover has not gained a wide following on this point, but Dov Gera seems correct in pointing out that the one-year gap between the quelling of Jason's revolt (169/8 B.C.E.) and the instigation of Antiochus' new measures (167 B.C.E.) is not all that long, and is completely understandable given Antiochus' occupations in other parts of his empire.[43] Thus the new policy in 167 B.C.E., while not a response to an organized rebellion, was a slightly overdue reorganization and attempted pacifying of a rebellious province.[44]

---

[39] *The God of the Maccabees*, 91.

[40] Fergas Millar, "The Background to the Maccabean Revolution: Reflections on Martin Hengel's 'Judaism and Hellenism'" *JJS* 29 (1978) 1–21, and Collins, "Cult and Culture," 52.

[41] *The God of the Maccabees*, 71–3.

[42] *Hellenistic Civilization and the Jews*, 191.

[43] It should not be forgotten that, although our sources portray Judea as the center of world politics, Jerusalem was not a major force in the region. See Gera, *Judaea and Mediterranean Politics*, 223–54, particularly 226–8.

[44] To classify Antiochus' actions as "religious persecution" is thus doubly problematic. While Antiochus' program was "religious" in the sense that it affected cultic worship and "persecution" in that it changed that worship in ways distasteful to some Judeans, such a classification can obscure other aspects of the program. For instance, JoAnn Scurlock has emphasized the constructive side of Antiochus' program, pointing out the positive economic impact of the building of altars (possibly at old cultic sites) in rural Judea, "167 B.C.E.: Hellenism or Reform?" *JSJ* 31 (2000) 125–61. She further suggests that Antiochus' actions may have been specifically directed against Jason and his allies (likely the elite who had become citizen in the *polis* of Jerusalem): "Whatever else it was supposed to accomplish, the re-establishment of high places by Antiochus was certainly *not* designed to appeal to the urban elite of Jerusalem" who benefited from the exclusivity of the Jerusalem temple, 135.

The Maccabees, Part 2: The Family's Origins

Why, then, would the Maccabees choose this time to begin their major maneuvers to take Jerusalem? Schwartz is probably correct that Judas and his followers "exploited the disorder in Jerusalem" to their own ends, but I would argue that the Maccabees are best understood not as Schwartz's "village strongmen," coming to Jerusalem from the outside, but rather as Jerusalem insiders not unlike Jason and Menelaus.[45]

We do not have much information on Mattathias, but scholars often present the little we do possess in somewhat misleading ways. The entry for "Maccabean Revolt" in one of the standard reference works in the field can serve as an example. The author writes:

> Shortly afterward, Jerusalem was again taken by force . . . The Jewish population reacted in three ways to these measures: some reluctantly acquiesced; some preferred martyrdom rather than obey the king's orders; and some resorted to armed resistance. Among those who resorted to arms were Mattathias and his sons. When Mattathias killed the officer who came to his village, Modin, to force pagan rites on the inhabitants, a guerilla warfare [sic] began (about 166 B.C.E.). Shortly afterward, Mattathias died and the leadership of the rebels was given to his son Judas.[46]

Aside from the questionable outline of the three possible reactions to Antiochus' edict,[47] this description implies that Mattathias was just a pious villager in Modein who leapt into battle against invading pagans. This depiction of events obscures key points in the way the ancient sources describe Mattathias—he, like the Oniads and Menelaus, was closely associated with Jerusalem and (again like the others) he was a priest, but of the line of Joarib.

1 Macc 2:1 introduces him as follows: "In those days Mattathias . . . a priest of the sons of Joarib arose from Jerusalem and arrived in Modein" (ἐν ταῖς ἡμέραις ἐκείναις ἀνέστη Ματταθιας . . . ἱερεὺς τῶν υἱῶν Ιωαριβ ἀπὸ Ιερουσαλημ καὶ ἐκάθισεν ἐν Μωδεϊν). Josephus concurs,

---

Thus whether Antiochus' actions amount to religious persecution of Judeans depends on which Judeans we mean.

[45] "A Note on the Social Type and Political Ideology of the Hasmonean Family," 309.

[46] Uriel Rappaport, s.v. "Maccabean Revolt," *The Anchor Bible Dictionary* (New York: Doubleday, 1992) 4.434.

[47] For a much more nuanced and plausible list of possible reactions, see Sievers, *The Hasmoneans and Their Supporters*, 21–26.

describing Mattathias as "a man living in Modai, a village of Judaea . . . a priest of the division of Joarib and a Jerusalemite" (ἦν τις οἰκῶν ἐν Μωδαῒ κώμῃ τῆς Ἰουδαίας, ὄνομα Ματταθίας ἱερεὺς ἐξ ἐφημερίδος Ἰωάριβος Ἱεροσολυμίτης, *Ant.* 12.265).[48] In spite of these clear statements, there is a tendency among scholars to portray Mattathias as a rural priest untainted by "Hellenized" Jerusalem.[49] Samuel Eddy's comments on this point are refreshing:

> The evidence is that in 167 B.C.E. the Hasmoneans were not humble, rural priests, but a family on the rise. They lived in Jerusalem and owned an estate near Modein. A royal messenger is made to address Mattathias at Modein as "leading man, great and distinguished in this place."[50]

There is, of course, no strong evidence that Mattathias owned "an estate,"[51] but Eddy's reading highlights the fact that the sources are silent on the nature of Mattathias' dwelling in Modein, and what little information we have on Mattathias' status suggests that it was quite high.[52] Most scholars assume, without good reason, that Mattathias was a non-affluent, pious villager.

---

[48] Here I follow the Greek text of the Loeb edition; Niese prints Ἰώαβος. If Josephus is dependant upon 1 Macc for this point, he has altered the wording to a high degree. The report of the origins of "Matthias" (Ματθίας) in *Jewish War* 1.36 states that he was "a son of Asamonaios, one of the priests from a village called Modein" (υἱὸς Ἀσαμωναίου τῶν ἱερέων εἷς ἀπὸ κώμεις Μωδεεὶν ὄνομα). Curiously, Matthias' actions in the context of this account seem to take place in Jerusalem and not Modein.

[49] So, to name but one example, Doron Mendels, *The Rise and Fall of Jewish Nationalism* (Grand Rapids: William B. Eerdmans Publishing Co., 1997) 126. Those who at least acknowledge the Jerusalem connection often attempt to minimize it. See, e.g. Seth Schwartz, *Imperialism and Jewish Society, 200 B.C.E. to 640 C.E.* (Princeton: Princeton University Press, 2001) 33. There is some evidence of an ancestral connection to Modein since 1 Macc 2:70 locates the family burial ground there ("he was buried in the tomb of his fathers at Modein"), so also 1 Macc. 9:19 ("Then Jonathan and Simon took their brother Judas and buried him in the tomb of their fathers at Modein"), but this references hardly sustain the contention that the Maccabees were primarily rural folk.

[50] *The King is Dead: Studies in the Near Eastern Resistance to Hellenism 334–31 B.C.* (Lincoln, Neb.: University of Nebraska Press, 1961) 215. The quotation is from 1 Macc 2:17.

[51] It should be noted, though, that the ownership of a large burial ground may support Eddy's reading; see Shimon Applebaum, *Judaea in Hellenistic and Roman Times* (Leiden: Brill, 1989) 38. Later in the Maccabean period, Simon the Hasmonean was wealthy enough to fund mercenaries with his own money (1 Macc 14:32).

[52] On this point, see also Schwartz, "A Note on the Social Type and Political Ideology of the Hasmonean Family," 307.

Even if we regard the material about Mattathias as suspect (indeed, he is not even mentioned in 2 Macc),[53] 2 Macc places Judas' origins in Jerusalem as well. The first we hear of Judas is that he fled from Jerusalem before Antiochus IV's major decree:

> When this man [Apollonius] appeared in Jerusalem pretending to be peaceful . . . he put to the sword all those coming out for the spectacle, then ran into the city with his armed men and killed a great number. But Judas the Maccabean, with about nine others, got away to the wilderness . . ." (5:25–7).[54]

In fact, Modein plays almost no role in 2 Macc.; the town only appears as a campsite for Judas and his force in 13:14. Thus, all three of our major sources for the Maccabeans connect the earliest fighters with Jerusalem.

Also, 1 Macc connects Mattathias to the priestly line of Joarib (Ἰωαριβ). This line rises from relative obscurity to the highest position in priestly lists. The name Joarib or Yoiarib occurs five times as a clan name in the Hebrew Bible (Neh 11:10, 12:6, and 12:19; 1 Chron 9:10 and 24:7).[55] Though not listed among the priests in Ezra 2:36 and Neh 7:39, Yoiarib is found in Neh 11:10 among the priests living in Jerusalem. In Neh 12:6, Yoiarib is named as a priest who went up to Jerusalem with Zerubbabel. In 1 Chron 24:7, it is David himself who makes Yoiarib the head of the first of the twenty-four divisions of priests, pushing the former first position, Jedaiah, to second.[56] This notice is the last we hear of Joarib until the Maccabees rise to power.

---

[53] The whole Mattathias episode has the feeling of legend. Given the close parallels with and overt reference to Phineas, it is surprising that the normally hypercritical Gera seems wholly credulous of the Mattathias tale in its details, *Judea and Mediterranean Politics*, 230.

[54] The quotation continues ". . . he and those with him lived in the mountains the way wild animals do, they continued feeding on grass as food, in order not to share in the defilement" (πρὸς τὸ μὴ μετασχεῖν τοῦ μολυσμοῦ, 5:27). If the decree of Antiochus (6:1–11) had not yet taken place, it is unclear what "defilement" Judas wished to avoid.

[55] There is a Yoiarib mentioned in Ezra 8:16; he is a "man of insight" summoned by Ezra along with Elnathan (τῷ Ιωαριβ καὶ τῷ Ελναθαν συνίοντας). It is unclear who this figure is.

[56] Also noteworthy for comparison in this regard is the Hakkoz family. The descendants of Hakkoz are listed in Ezra 2:61–2 as priests who "could not prove their families or their descent, whether they were from Israel . . . and were excluded from the priesthood as unclean" (so also Neh 7:63 and 1 Esdras 5:58). Already in the book of Nehemiah, however, Meremoth, a son of Uriah and a priest of the line of Hakkoz seems to be an important figure in the rebuilding of the temple

The family of Mattathias and Judas was, like the Tobiads, a family that was gaining, over a long period of time, a higher degree of
prestige than it initially had in the early Persian era.[57] The Tobiads
acquired a notable degree of power a century before the Maccabees,
but Judas and his family were able to succeed where Hyrcanus failed,
in that they actually did gain control of Jerusalem and held on to
power for some eighty years.[58]

THE MACCABEES, PART 3: THE MOTIVATIONS

Just because the Maccabees and these other families share similar
histories does not show that the Maccabees acted for the same reasons
as these families. The Maccabees' motives are generally supposed to
be quite different from those of the Tobiads, Jason, and Menelaus,
who took the initiative and bribed regional powers to improve their
own status. The Maccabees, so the argument goes, were *reacting* to
oppression with military force *against* a regional power on behalf of
"the people," and only later did they get entangled in political matters.[59] I shall argue that a more compelling case can be made that,
as Schwartz phrases it, the Maccabees' "main concern at all periods was their own advancement."[60]

The typical explanation of the Maccabees' early actions is that
the "revolt" began with Mattathias the old villager, full of the zeal
of Phineas, hostile to foreigners, reacting to the prospect of urban
Hellenizing religious practices in his village.[61] The discussion of

---

and fortifications (Neh 3:4, 3:21, 10:5, and 12:3), and by the time of 1 Chron.
24:10, Hakkoz was included among the legitimate sons of Aaron (through Zadok
and Ahimelech). We next hear of the family name Hakkoz as an ally of the
Maccabees in 1 Macc 8:17; Eupolemus, the ambassador to Rome, is son of John
son of Hakkoz.

[57] For the rise of the Tobiad family, see note 16 above.

[58] In fact, there may have been some significant overlap in the composition of
the armies of the later Tobiads and the armies of Jason and the Maccabees. For
a discussion, see Bezalel Bar-Kochva, *Judas Maccabeus: The Jewish Struggle Against the
Seleucids* (Cambridge: Cambridge University Press, 1989) 82–8.

[59] Such a view is certainly the overt rhetoric of the Maccabean literature. For
the most recent scholarly incarnation of the view, see Gera, *Judaea and Mediterranean
Politics*, 223.

[60] "A Note on the Social Type and Political Ideology of the Hasmonean Family,"
309.

[61] The notion that the Maccabees were hostile to foreigners is part of the rhetoric
of 1 Macc, as Seth Schwartz has shown, "Israel and the Nations Roundabout,"
16–38. The reports of the Maccabees alliances with Rome and the Seleucids undercut the author's rhetoric.

Mattathias above has already problematized such a view. In fact, given the shadowy evidence we have, Mattathias is probably not the place to start looking for the Maccabees' motives. Samuel Eddy has pointed out that Mattathias does not come off as terribly important in 1 Macc and Josephus:

> Mattathias died almost as soon as the resistance began . . . his death made no difference at all to the course of events . . . Hence the problem of finding out what motivated Mattathias is not really as important as finding out what intentions the Hasmonean family had and what their contemporaries thought of them . . . they wanted very badly to improve their position in respect to the other priestly families of Judah, or, in other words, to become high priests. This is what actually happened, and there is no reason for thinking that it was not a motive from the beginning. Their piety was tempered with ambition.[62]

This point is worth pressing. After Mattathias' death, Judas led several winning campaigns and then as soon as he gained control of at least part of Jerusalem, he "purified and renewed" the seemingly abandoned temple (1 Macc 4:36). After removing the defiled stones of the gentiles' altar, the priests appointed by Judas[63] even tore down the original altar of burnt offering and replaced it with a newly built one (4:44–7), essentially rebuilt the entire inner sanctuary from scratch and made new "holy vessels" (4:48). Judas then instituted a new festival to commemorate the event (4:58). While Josephus claims that Judas even became high priest, most scholars reject such an idea.[64]

---

[62] *The King is Dead*, 215.

[63] According to Josephus, Judas himself was the only one purifying and rebuilding the sanctuary, *Ant.* 12.317–8.

[64] Josephus is alone amidst the ancient sources in claiming that Judas was a high priest. According to 1 Macc Judas died in battle before Alcimus, the standing high priest, was miraculously struck down in agony, and so there was never a time during Judas' life when the office of high priest was empty (1 Macc 9:18 and 9:56). 2 Macc, however, introduces Alcimus as a man who "had previously been high priest" (προγεγονὼς ἀρχιερεύς, 14:3), who was lobbying with Demetrius ostensibly for the well-being of the Jewish people. At the conclusion of his presentation, Demetrius orders that Nicanor "kill Judas, scatter his men, and install Alcimus as high priest of the great temple" (14:13). Who, if anyone, was high priest after Alcimus' first stint is left unclear. Nicanor's attempts fail, and 2 Macc concludes with Judas alive and well and no word at all on Alcimus. By Josephus' account, however, Judas the Maccabee not only outlived Alcimus, he succeeded him as high priest: "And upon the death of this man [Alcimus], the people gave the high priesthood to Judas" (τελευτήσαντος δὲ τούτου τὴν ἀρχιερωσύνην ὁ λαὸς τῷ Ἰούδᾳ δίδωσιν, *Ant.* 12.414, so also 12.419 and 13.46). Later we hear that Judas "had held the high priesthood for three years when he died" (*Ant.* 12.434). Josephus' information is not entirely consistent, though. In *Ant.* 20.237–9, which is part of a list of all the

Whether or not that is the case, Judas moved beyond simply restoring what was changed under Antiochus.[65] He continued fighting even after the rebuilding of the sanctuary and forged an alliance with Rome (1 Macc 8:1–32). After his death, first Jonathan and then Simon forged more alliances with foreign leaders in order to secure their hold on power in Jerusalem. Jonathan first allied himself with Alexander Epiphanes (also known as Alexander Balas), who claimed to be the son of Antiochus IV. Alexander in turn made Jonathan high priest (1 Macc 10:18–25). When both Philometor and Alexander died and Demetrius II became king of Syria, Jonathan brought riches to Demetrius in Antioch, and Demetrius accordingly confirmed his status as high priest (1 Macc 11:23–9). Then, in exchange for the service of Jewish mercenaries to help quell an attempted coup, Demetrius falsely promised several benefactions for Jonathan. After Demetrius broke his promises, Trypho, the guardian of Antiochus VI, formed an alliance with Jonathan, who at the same time was renewing alliances with Rome, Sparta, and "other places" (12:1–2). Trypho, however, turned on Jonathan and had him killed. Shortly afterward, the *akra*, established under Antiochus IV in 167 B.C.E., finally fell in 141 B.C.E. (13:49–51). Simon confirmed the friendships with Sparta and Rome, sending the latter a gold shield of considerable value (14:24).[66]

---

high priests near the conclusion of the *Antiquities*, Josephus states that after Alcimus had been high priest for three years, "he died; no one succeeded him but the city went on seven years without a high priest. But again the posterity of the sons of the Hasmoneans having been entrusted with the rule of the peoples and having made war on the Macedonians, set up Jonathan as high priest, who ruled over them for seven years." Thus, only 1 Macc excludes the possibility that Judas was high priest. 2 Macc is silent on the question, and Josephus indicates in multiple passages that Judas was high priest, while implying in another passage that he was not. In a typescript he never published himself, Morton Smith considered some of these issues and speculated that the "Books of the Maccabees say nothing of Judas' becoming High Priest, but they say nothing, either, of who served as High Priest at the rededication of the Temple, when the services of a High Priest would probably have been needed. It may be that they were concerned to legitimate the Maccabean claim to the office and therefore preferred to postdate the tenure until it could be justified by appointment by the recognized authority, the King." The typescript was edited by Joseph Sievers and can be found under the title "Were the Maccabees Priests?" in Smith's collected essays edited by S. J. D. Cohen, *Studies in the Cult of Yahweh* (Leiden: Brill, 1996) 1.320–5.

[65] I would argue that in taking these extra steps and in maintaining control of temple activities, Judas reveals some of the ambition at the heart of his program. As Michael Peppard aptly put it in personal conversation, "There is a difference between just wanting the temple to be in a certain condition and wanting to be the one in charge of making it that way."

[66] 1 Macc concludes with a note that Simon's son-in-law (Ptolemy son of Abubus)

This picture of a family gathering an army and acquiring power with the help of shifting political alliances seems very similar to what we saw with the Tobiads, Oniads, and even Menelaus. Seth Schwartz shrewdly describes this phenomenon. He notes that in forming alliances and continuing to wage campaigns after the temple had been retaken Judas

> behaved more like an ambitious courtier than a zealous freedom-fighter. So he was probably not seeking to overthrow the existing system but to advance within it: Judas's strategy of winning concessions from the Seleucids by pestering them militarily had proved successful in the past, and he probably hoped it would continue to work . . .[67]

The Maccabees and their allies fought against the Seleucids while Jason and Menelaus had bribed them, but both actions had the same goal—to gain power in Jerusalem. As stated at the outset, the difference is that the Maccabees clearly cast their actions as a defense of ancestral customs. 1 Macc styles its protagonists as defenders of "the covenant of our fathers" (διαθήκη πατέρων ἡμῶν),[68] and there seems to be little reason to doubt that the movement used such a slogan from early on. As far as we can tell, 2 Macc's "Judaism" (Ἰουδαϊσμός, 2:21, 8:1 and 14:38) is a neologism, but it seems to occupy the same rhetorical position in 2 Macc as does "covenant of our fathers" in 1 Macc. How might this rhetoric function?

"Patrios Politeia" at Athens and "Ioudaismos" in Jerusalem

To my knowledge, no one has looked into the suggestive parallels provided by events in Athens in 411 and 404 b.c.e., at which times appeals to *patrios politeia*, or the "ancestral constitution," became popular.[69] After the devastating failure of the Sicilian expedition in 413

---

murdered Simon and his sons Judas and Mattathias. Simon's other son John Hyrcanus survived an attempt on his life and became high priest (16:11–17).

[67] "A Note on the Social Type and Political Ideology of the Hasmonean Family," 309.

[68] In 1 Macc 2:20 the phrase is parallel to "law and the ordinances" (νόμον καὶ δικαιώματα) in 2:21. Elsewhere, the author uses "holy covenant" (διαθήκης ἁγίας, 1:15).

[69] Doron Mendels has examined the fragments of Hecataeus of Abdera as representative of "a Jewish Patrios Politeia of the Persian Period," but he employs a very static use of that term and does not engage the concept in classical Athens or Judea in the Maccabean era. See his *Identity, Religion, and Historiography: Studies in Hellenistic History* (Sheffield: Sheffield Academic Press, 1998) 334–51. Eddy mentions

B.C.E., Athens was as vulnerable as it had been at any time since the Persian wars. In the wake of this defeat, a party arose and attempted to take power in Athens by appealing to the "ancestral constitution," a situation similar to the Maccabees' move to power with a "traditionalist" rhetoric when Jerusalem was laid low by Antiochus in 169/8 B.C.E. The difference with the Athenian case is that we possess explicit critiques of the use of the rhetoric of ancestral traditions.[70]

Since the inception of democracy in Athens under the guidance of Cleisthenes in 508 B.C.E., Athens had experienced great prosperity, becoming the most powerful state in the Greek world. By the time of the Peace of Nicias (421–413 B.C.E.), however, losses to Sparta and its allies during the course of the Peloponnesian War had seriously damaged the infrastructure and economy of Athens, depleted its manpower, and put the democratic leaders in peril.[71] After the Sicilian disaster, a relatively small group of Athenians, "the Four Hundred," murdered leading supporters of the democracy and attempted to take power under the banner of preserving the ancestral constitution.[72] Although they gained control in Athens for a brief period, the Four Hundred were defeated in 410 B.C.E., but their opposition, the supporters of democracy, had taken up their termi-

---

the events of 404 B.C.E. in a rather different context, *The King is Dead*, 213. He detects parallels between the actions of the Spartans and those of Antiochus IV.

[70] The relevant ancient sources are Thucydides 8.47–98 and the *Athenian Constitution* 29–35, attributed to Aristotle. For more detailed treatments of this episode of Athenian history, see M.I. Finley, *The Use and Abuse of History* (New York: Viking Press, 1975) 34–59; Martin Ostwald, *From Popular Sovereignty to the Sovereignty of Law: Law, Society, and Politics in Fifth-Century Athens* (Berkeley: University of California Press, 1986) 337–411; and Jennifer Tolbert Roberts, *Athens on Trial: The Antidemocratic Tradition in Western Thought* (Princeton: Princeton University Press, 1994) 61–9. For an older view, see Alexander Fuks, *The Ancestral Constitution: Four Studies in Athenian Party Politics at the End of the Fifth Century B.C.* (London: Routledge & Kegan Paul Ltd., 1953).

[71] On the general conditions in Athens at this time, see Donald Kagan, *The Fall of the Athenian Empire* (Ithaca, N.Y.: Cornell University Press, 1987) 1–11 and 110–12.

[72] The *Athenian Constitution* preserves the various platforms in the debate that resulted in the rule of the Four Hundred. One amendment to the proposal for overthrowing the democracy contains an explicit appeal to τοὺς πατρίους νόμους (*Athenian Constitution*, 29.3). Ostwald (contra Fuks) correctly observes that the amendment likely reflects the language of the proposal itself. Thus, those seeking to topple the democracy "presented their proposal of instituting a Council of Four Hundred as a return to the *patrioi nomoi*, presumably as a manifestation of the *patrios politeia*, of Solon, as they saw it," *From Popular Sovereignty*, 370–1. The reign of terror described in Thucydides 8.65–6 mirrors the ferocity of Mattathias' campaign.

nology,[73] and a debate ensued between competing notions of *patrios politeia*. The dispute is most clearly testified in a speech of the contemporary sophist Thrasymachus of Chalcedon, who thought both sides misconstrued and misused the appeal to ancestral tradition. He laments, "There is an uproar over the ancestral constitution (πάτριος πολιτεία), which is in fact easy to understand and which all citizens have in common."[74]

This debate about the ancestral constitution at Athens continued after the fall of the Four Hundred. Thus when another group of Athenians, "the Thirty," attempted to take power after Athens' final surrender to Sparta in 404 B.C.E., Aristotle describes them as "pretending to be administering the ancestral constitution (προσεποιοῦντο διώκειν τὴν πάτριον πολιτείαν). They altered laws "as though restoring and clarifying the constitution (ὡς ἐπανορθοῦντες καὶ ποιοῦντες ἀναμφισβήτητον τὴν πολιτείαν)" when actually they were being extremely innovative.[75] The accusation that the Thirty were "pretending" suggests that the democrats had quite a different idea of the ancestral constitution. Both sides thus laid claim to the ancestral traditions, but as far as we can tell, the "oligarchs," the "democrats," and the "moderates" were proposing new and different forms of life under the guise of ancestral tradition as they tried to take control of a weakened Athenian government.[76] What this Athenian example shows us is that appeals to ancestral traditions need not indicate the stability

---

[73] So Thucydides 8.76.6. See Tolbert Roberts, *Athens on Trial*, 61.

[74] The Greek reads πρῶτον μὲν ἡ πάτριος πολιτεία ταραχὴν αὐτοῖς παρέχει ῥάιστη γνωσθῆναι καὶ κοινοτάτη τοῖς πολίταις οὖσα πᾶσιν, 85B1, *Die Fragmente der Vorsokratiker, griechisch und deutsch*, H. Diels and W. Kranz, eds. (Berlin: Weidmann, 1951–2) 2.321–4, trans. Finley, *The Use and Abuse of History*, 37. See further Ostwald, *From Popular Sovereignty*, 367–8.

[75] *Athenian Constitution* 35.2. The precise order of events in the reign of the Thirty is unclear. For a good discussion of the problems, see Peter Krentz, *The Thirty at Athens* (Ithaca, N.Y.: Cornell University Press, 1982).

[76] Lest we think this debate an artifact of the fifth century, we should note that even a century later in the early Hellenistic period, the terminology/ideology of *patrios politeia* served upstart rulers well. When Demetrius of Phaleron took Athens in 307 B.C.E., he was celebrated as "restoring the ancestral constitution" (ἐκομίσαντο τὴν πάτριον πολιτείαν), Didodorus of Sicily 20.46.3, so also Plutarch, *Demetrius* 10, although the "democracy" Demetrius "restored" was far from that of fifth century Athens. See further Peter Green, *Alexander to Actium: The Historical Evolution of the Hellenistic Age* (Berkeley: University of California Press, 1990) 48–9. There are, of course, many differences between the Athenian cases and that of the Maccabees, but I suspect a similar use of the rhetoric of ancestral traditions was in play as much for the Maccabees as it was for the Athenians.

of the traditions; such appeals can, and in fact often do, point to
the fluidity of the traditions.

I find this situation to be an interesting parallel to the Maccabees'
use of "the covenant of the fathers." In both cases, the rhetoric of
ancestral traditions functions as a means to acquire power and legitimate authority. When Athens was vulnerable, different groups in
the city tried to implement their political views by calling their platforms returns to the ancestral laws. Doing so helped to justify the
sometimes violent suppression of opposing viewpoints. The Maccabees'
appeal to "the covenant of the fathers" allowed them to cast their
own political position as ancestral law and, if the Maccabean literature
is to be believed, legitimated the Maccabees' murder of many of
their own countrymen, scorned as "lawless men who hate their own
nation" (μισοῦντες τὸ ἔθνος αὐτῶν ἄνδρες παράνομοι, 1 Macc. 11:21).[77]

The Athenian example is particularly useful because in that case
we possess the rivaling claims to *patrios politeia* that reveal the term's
ambiguity and hence its usefulness for would-be upstart rulers.[78] The
Maccabean literature, unsurprisingly, does not preserve alternative
viewpoints, but it is very probable that the Maccabees' use of "the
covenant of the fathers" and the like spurred a similar debate, making the definition of Judaism even more of a bone of contention,
thus effecting the rise and proliferation of sectarianism.[79] But that is
a story for another day.

CONCLUSION

I hope I have been able to highlight the many similarities between
the Maccabees and others who struggled for supremacy in Jerusalem.
With Jerusalem in turmoil, a priest goes out of the city and forms
an army, making war on foreigners and fellow Judeans alike in an

---

[77] These particular "lawless men" were not killed, but for examples, see 1 Macc
2:24, 2:44–5, 9:61, and 9:73.

[78] See Tolbert Roberts, *Athens on Trial*, 61–2.

[79] On this point, I differ rather sharply from Hengel, who concludes *Judaism and
Hellenism* with the reflection that the Maccabean episode brought about among Jews
a "fixation" on the law ("the apologetically rigidified understanding of the Torah")
that is opposed to "the universal, eschatological claim of the gospel," 309. The
Maccabees did generate a renewed focus on ancestral traditions, but this focus produced vigorous debates about these ancestral traditions, debates of which Paul and
other early followers of Jesus were very much a part.

attempt to take Jerusalem. Upon his death, his son takes over his military forces and, after taking the city, completely rebuilding the inner sanctuary, and creating a new festival, begins forming alliances with foreign powers.[80] This raising of armed forces, alteration of cultic practice, and cultivation of alliances with foreigners make the Maccabees look less like stubborn defenders of a fixed ancestral law and more like an ambitious family struggling to gain authority in the temple by a variety of strategies. The Maccabees did, however, claim to be preserving ancestral traditions, but these ancestral traditions, this "Judaism," was a part of their power struggle; it functioned as a tool for legitimating these usurpers of the ancestral high priesthood.[81] This "Judaism" was an assertion, and its characteristics were open to debate, a situation not unlike the *patrios politeia* controversy in Athens in the late fifth century B.C.E.

Shaye Cohen focuses on 2 Macc's term "Judaism" (Ἰουδαϊσμός) as a watershed moment in the self understanding of Jews. He writes:

> Even if "Judean" always retained its ethnic meaning, in the Hasmonean period common mode of worship and common way of life became much more important in the new definition of Judean/Jew . . . It was this Hasmonean redefinition of Judaism that permitted Josephus at the end of the first century C.E. to state that the constitution established by Moses was not only a *genos*—a nation, a "birth"—but also "a choice in the manner of life."[82]

John Collins is clearly correct to critique Cohen and argue that there was an established Judean way of life long before 2 Macc introduces the term "Judaism."[83] What needs to be pushed is the way in which these authors construct their particular notion of "Judaism"

---

[80] While Mattathias and Judas have been relatively free of scrutiny in terms of their possible priestly pretensions, the political intrigue associated with the later Maccabees is widely acknowledged, and there has been a good deal of interest in that area since the discovery of the Dead Sea Scrolls. For a review of these discussions, see James C. VanderKam, "People and High Priesthood in Early Maccabean Times" in *The Hebrew Bible and its Interpreters*, eds. W. H. Propp, et al. (Winona Lake, In. Eisenbrauns, 1990) 205–25.

[81] One consequence I hope follows from this treatment of the Maccabean literature is a new angle for understanding the rhetoric of "law" and "Israel" in a variety of authors, from Ezra to the apostle Paul. It would be interesting to treat their claims on the same level as I have treated those of the Maccabees.

[82] *The Beginnings of Jewishness: Boundaries, Varieties, Uncertainties* (Berkeley: University of California Press, 1999) 133–4.

[83] "Cult and Culture," 39.

and "covenant of our fathers" and what work these terms accomplish.[84] The authors of the Maccabean literature had a particular idea of just what the ancestral practices should be (or better, should have been), and the author of 2 Macc called his version of that set of practices "Judaism." There is innovation going on here that tends to be lost when discussions bring in opposing terms like *Jewish* and *Hellenistic, conservative* and *liberal, orthodox* and *reform*.[85] Even adopting 2 Macc's own rhetoric and casting the discussion in terms of Judeans resisting Greek customs obscures the creative aspects of what the authors of the Maccabean literature were doing.[86] I submit that this process of continuous innovation and perpetual "reinvention" of Judaism is easier to see when we read the Maccabees as just another in a line of families contending for power.

This is not to say that we should consider 1 and 2 Macc "mere rhetoric." Far from it. These works are extraordinarily powerful and persuasive, and in the hands of Jospehus, 1 Macc came to be a tool for understanding the Judean conflict with Rome in the late first century C.E. All three documents (1 and 2 Macc and Josephus) have come to be tools for understanding many other conflicts throughout

---

[84] I.e. rather than saying the Maccabees' position was to defend whatever the ancestral traditions were, instead we should say the ancestral traditions were whatever the Maccabees' position was. Such a phrasing does not question the existence or significance of these traditions, it just points out the fact that these traditions are always constructed and defined by certain groups.

[85] Bickermann writes: "The Maccabean movement was, above all, a civil war, a religious struggle between reformers and orthodox (ein Religionskampf zwischen Orthodoxen und Reformisten), *The God of the Maccabees*, 90/*Der Gott der Makkabäer*, 137). Many, including Hengel, have followed Bickerman's terminology, but Bickerman's own analysis elsewhere problematizes these terms. In describing Jubilees, a work often attributed to groups with an outlook similar to that of the Maccabees, he writes: "As it often happens, in order to uphold traditional values, their apologists themselves propose the most radical innovations. The author of the Book of Jubilees outdoes the later talmudic teaching in his severity as to the observance of ritual prescriptions. But to assert the everlasting validity of the Torah, this traditionalist places his own composition beside and even above Scripture, claims for his book a divine origin, and gives precepts which differ widely from those set forth in the Torah," *From Ezra to the Last of the Maccabees: Foundations of Post-biblical Judaism* (New York: Schocken Books, 1962). Bickerman is surely right to highlight the innovative features of "conservative" viewpoints. Martha Himmelfarb has explored this aspect of Bickerman's position further in "Elias Bickerman on Judaism and Hellenism," in *The Jewish Past Revisited: Reflections on Modern Jewish Historians*, eds. D. N. Myers and D.B. Ruderman (New Haven: Yale University Press, 1998) 199–211.

[86] Rajak seems to take this stance in *The Jewish Dialogue with Greece and Rome*, 7. See n. 8 above.

western history. Nor should we say that because the Maccabees'
chief desire was to take power in Jerusalem, their motivations were
not religious. To the contrary, the preceding discussion should highlight the fact that relationships of power, prestige, and politics are
the very substance of religion in antiquity.[87]

[87] I would like to offer thanks to John J. Collins and Diana Swancutt for feed-
back on earlier versions of this paper and to the participants in a lively discussion
of a portion of this paper presented at the Greco-Roman Lunch at Yale University.

THE TORAH BETWEEN ATHENS AND JERUSALEM: JEWISH DIFFERENCE IN ANTIQUITY

Martha Himmelfarb*

In the conclusion to *From Ezra to the Last of the Maccabees*, Elias Bickerman sums up his view of the Jews' encounter with Greek culture:

> Contact with the "enlightened" and universal culture of Hellenism could only be salutary for one who, wrestling as Jacob did with the angel, did not allow himself to be overcome but extorted its blessing, not losing himself in Hellenism, but coming safely away with enhanced strength. Only two peoples of antiquity succeeded in doing so, the Romans and the Jews. The Romans succeeded because they became the rulers even of the Hellenic world. To be sure, they lost much in the process, a good part of their national religion, for instance, whose gods Greek gods supplanted. The Jews succeeded because their knowledge of the oneness of God and of his world rule—in a word, the singular character of their faith—set up an inner barrier against surrender and separated them from the rest of the world.[1]

The essay in which this passage appears was first published in 1947. Many contemporary scholars would reject on both ideological and historical grounds Bickerman's view of Greek civilization as a superior force with which the subject peoples of the hellenistic empires necessarily had to come to terms. Recent scholarship tends to emphasize the continuity of native culture and the relatively limited impact of Hellenism on these peoples.[2] In such a context, the survival of

---

* Princeton Unviersity.

[1] *From Ezra to the Last of the Maccabees: Foundations of Post-Biblical Judaism* (New York: Schocken, 1962). This volume consists of two previously published essays, "The Historical Foundations of Postbiblical Judaism," from *The Jews: Their History, Culture, and Religion* (ed. Louis Finkelstein; New York: Harper and Brothers, 1949), and *The Maccabees: An Account of Their History from the Beginnings to the Fall of the House of the Hasmoneans* (New York: Schocken, 1947). Chapter 7 of "The Historical Foundations" is omitted in *From Ezra*. Bickerman wrote another general treatment of ancient Judaism, *The Jews in the Greek Age* (Cambridge, MA, and London: Harvard University Press, 1988), published after his death. It seems to me that Bickerman's mode of approach to ancient Judaism is clearer in the slimmer *From Ezra*.

[2] For both ideological rejection of the centrality of hellenism for ancient history and emphasis on continuity of the Seleucid empire with the Persian, see, e.g., a work I very much admire, Susan Sherwin-White and Amélie Kuhrt, *From Samarkhand to Sardis: A New Approach to the Seleucid Empire* (Berkeley and Los Angeles: University of California Press, 1993) esp. 1–5, 141–87.

Judaism no longer seems exceptional, and some scholars have played down the hellenization of the Jews as well.[3]

Yet I have come to think that Bickerman was right.[4] Despite the thrust of much recent scholarship, I think there is a great deal to be said for his view of hellenization and the significance of Greek culture, though I will not try to defend that point here. Nor can I offer a thorough evaluation of the encounters of other ancient civilizations with the Greeks, though I hope that some comparisons will make Bickerman's claim about the uniqueness of the Jewish case persuasive. Rather, I am going to take Bickerman's view of the unusual success of the Jewish encounter with Greek culture, a view shared by Arnaldo Momigliano,[5] as my starting point. What I would like to focus on here is how to explain it. As my title indicates, I believe the answer is to be found at least in considerable part in the Torah. That the Torah to a large extent determines the character of ancient Judaism is a claim that surely requires no defense. My point is somewhat different. At the center of Jewish culture stood a single document, available at least in principle to all who could read Hebrew and, by some time in the third century B.C.E., Greek. I want to argue that this fact does a great deal to explain why Jews were able to adapt Greek culture in a variety of ways for their own purposes as no other people of the ancient near east could.

Bickerman's account of the encounter of Judaism and Hellenism runs something like this:[6] Some Jews, impelled by their aversion to idolatry, resisted the hellenistic reform initiated by other Jews and imposed by Antiochus IV and thus saved monotheism and their tra-

---

[3] See, e.g., the quite different approaches of Fergus Millar, "The Background of the Maccabean Revolt: Reflections on Martin Hengel's 'Judaism and Hellenism,'" *JJS* 22 (1978) 1–21, and Louis H. Feldman, *Jew and Gentile in the Ancient World: Attitudes and Interactions from Alexander to Justinian* (Princeton: Princeton University Press, 1993) 3–44.

[4] See Himmelfarb, "Elias Bickerman on Judaism and Hellenism," in *The Jewish Past Revisited: Reflections on Modern Jewish Historians* (ed. David N. Myers and David B. Ruderman; New Haven and London: Yale University Press, 1998), for an appreciation of Bickerman's contribution with attention to the twentieth-century circumstances under which he wrote.

[5] *Alien Wisdom: The Limits of Hellenization* (Cambridge: Cambridge University Press, 1975) 10–11.

[6] As I explain in "Bickerman," 200, I find that Bickerman's views about the dynamics of the encounter of Jewish culture with Greek are expressed most clearly in *From Ezra to the Last of the Maccabees*, and it is thus to this work that I refer rather than *The Jews in the Greek Age*.

ditional way of life.[7] Yet the survival of monotheism, for which the
Maccabees deserve credit, was not enough to ensure the flourishing
of Judaism, for merely to *protect* Judaism from Hellenism would have
led to the loss of the intellectual élite and spiritual "mummification."
The true contribution of the Maccabees was that their victory permitted Jews after the revolt, from their new position of strength, to
adapt Greek ideas so as to transform and strengthen Judaism. Thus
the triumph of the Maccabees enabled Jewish monotheism to flourish
because it permitted the development of a synthesis of Judaism
and Hellenism in which Greek ideas were "fitted into the system of
the Torah."[8]

Thus while Bickerman mentions the Torah, he places the emphasis on monotheism. It is the Jews' "knowledge of the oneness of God
and of his world rule" that motivates their resistance to Antiochus
and ultimately allows the productive encounter of Judaism with
Hellenism.[9] Indeed Bickerman suggests that the centrality of the
Torah is to some extent a result of the impact of Greek rule starting in the third century B.C.E.[10] For example, he sees the Pharisees'
ideal of Torah study for all Jewish men, not only priests or the
wealthy, as a judaization of the Platonic belief in the power of education.[11] Further, in Bickerman's view, the very rise of the Pharisees
is a result of Greek rule, for the Pharisees are the heirs of the scribes,
professionals who began to replace priests as teachers and interpreters
of Torah, to serve the administrative needs of hellenistic rulers.[12]

Yet surely we should not lose sight of the fact that by some time
in the fifth century B.C.E. a different imperial power, Persia, had
made the Torah the constitution of the Jewish people by the hand
of Ezra, the "scribe skilled in the law of Moses" (Ezra 7:6).[13] Indeed,
in order to understand the role of the Torah in the Second Temple
period, we should look back even further, to the publication of the

---

[7] *From Ezra*, 93–135. The claim that Jews were the initiators of the reform is
of course controversial.

[8] *From Ezra*, 153–65, 178–82. "Mummification": 182. "Fitted into the system of
the Torah": 181.

[9] *From Ezra*, 179.

[10] *Ibid.*, 67–71.

[11] *Ibid.*, 160–64.

[12] *Ibid.*, 67–71.

[13] Bickerman himself emphasizes the role of imperial power in establishing the
Torah as the law of the land (*From Ezra*, 9–10).

Book of Deuteronomy in the seventh century B.C.E., well before the
Jews encountered the Greeks. Deuteronomy set forth a program of
reform of which the most notable feature was the prohibition of
sacrifice outside the Jerusalem temple (Deuteronomy 12). By closing
the ancient high places where sacrifices had traditionally been offered,
the reformers hoped to bring an end to the worship of other deities
alongside the Lord. But the reform Deuteronomy envisioned went
beyond the cult. It also mandated reorganization of the judicial system and limits on the power of the king. I shall return to both of
these aspects of the reform.

As far as we know, Deuteronomy is the first book in Israel's history. It repeatedly refers to itself as "this book" (Deut 28:58, 29:26)
or "this book of the Torah" (Deut 28:61; 29:19, 20; 30:10; 31:26).
Its authors give their book authority by presenting it as the words
of Moses.[14] Nor do they simply attach Moses' name to the work and
rest there. Rather, they frame the anonymous legal material that
forms the core of the book and delineates its program of reform
(Deuteronomy 12–26) with speeches in which Moses alludes to the
events of the Exodus, from the redemption in Egypt through the
complaints of the people in the wilderness to the encounters with
enemies as the people Israel stands poised to enter the land of Canaan
(Deuteronomy 1–11 and much of 27–34). Further, the reformers did
not simply produce the book for public reading but arranged to have
it dramatically discovered in the temple in the course of repairs there
(2 Kings 22), as befits an ancient book. A long period of conceal-
ment in the temple served to explain why its central demands had
not been fulfilled without undercutting its authority.

The use of a written document to convey the words of someone
who is absent was clearly a significant innovation in seventh-century
Jerusalem.[15] Thus it is perhaps not surprising that Deuteronomy
shows some anxiety about the power of the written word despite its
attention to writing as a way to remember (Deut 6:9; 11:20; 27:3, 8).
Its use of the speech form is surely not accidental, and the speeches
valiantly attempt to make the past present to the real audience with

---

[14] See the comments of Morton Smith, "Pseudepigraphy in the Israelite Tradition,"
Pseudepigrapha I (ed. Kurt von Fritz; Entretiens sur l'antiquité classique; Geneva:
Fondation Hardt, 1972) 203–08.

[15] See also Jeremiah 36.

expressions such as, "before your eyes," "your eyes have seen," or "you have seen."[16]

Ultimately, however, Deuteronomy cannot really hope to persuade listeners that they were present at the events it describes. Rather, it insists that the covenant with the Lord belongs to them too even though they had not personally experienced the Exodus. It emphasizes the duty to teach children and children's children about the momentous events of the Exodus (Deut 4:9–10, 6:20–25, 11:19, 31:10–13), thus assuring its listeners that the problem of distance from the formative events of the past was by no means a new one. It has Moses proclaim that the covenant is not only with the generation of the wilderness: "Nor is it with you only that I make this sworn covenant, but with him who is not here with us this day as well as with him who stands here with us this day before the Lord our God" (Deut 29:13–14 [29:14–15 Eng.]). Finally, to make sure that its message is available to the entire people, Deuteronomy provides for itself to be read aloud every seven years "before all Israel" when the people assemble in Jerusalem for the festival of booths (Deut 31:10–11). Bickerman points to the contrast between the Torah, which requires that all Jews hear it, and the sacred books of other ancient Mediterranean peoples, which were the private possession of priests, purposely kept from lay people.[17] The Torah as public document, to borrow the phrase of Albert Baumgarten, begins with Deuteronomy.[18]

The other strands that make up the Torah say nothing about a king. Deuteronomy puts a king at the head of the people, but limits his power drastically: he is forbidden to multiply horses, wives, or silver and gold, and he is forbidden to return the people to Egypt (Deut 17:16–17). What is more, Deuteronomy insists that the king enact his acceptance of these limits and indeed his subordination to the laws of Deuteronomy by copying the book himself (Deut

---

[16] "Before your (sing. and pl.) eyes": Deut 1:30, 4:34, 9:17, 29:1 (Eng. 29:2). "Your (sing. and pl.) eyes saw/have seen (perfect or participle)": Deut 3:21; 4:3, 9; 7:19; 10:21; 11:7; 29:2 (Eng. 29:3). "You (pl.) saw/have seen": Deut 1:19, 29:1 (Eng. 29:2).

Moshe Weinfeld, *Deuteronomy and the Deuteronomic School* (Oxford: Clarendon Press, 1972) 171–78, offers several other examples from Deuteronomy itself and the deuteronomic history; for "your eyes see" and "you have seen," 173.

[17] "The Septuagint as a Translation," *Studies in Jewish and Christian History I* (Leiden: Brill, 1976) 198–99.

[18] "The Torah as Public Document in Judaism," *SR* 14 (1985) 17–24.

17:18–19).[19] Thus the "book of the Torah," which contains the
covenant between God and Israel, integrates the king into that
covenant and subordinates him to its regulations for him. Further,
while in one sense Deuteronomy legitimizes the king by including
him in its legislation, in another sense, by subordinating him to the
book itself, it unconsciously prepares for the loss of kingship. It is
surely remarkable that the reformers had a royal patron.

With its emphasis on its form as a book, it is perhaps not surprising that Deuteronomy legislates officials who are forerunners of
the scribe as legal expert. Deuteronomy's provisions for the legal system include judges as an alternative to the usual legal authorities,
the priests.[20] These lay officials, working for an Israelite king rather
than a foreign emperor, could resort to a written text more than a
century and a half before Ezra. Thus the growth of the scribal profession in the hellenistic era had deep roots.

I have noted that Deuteronomy was "discovered" in the temple,
and the Torah was closely linked to that other central institution of
ancient Judaism as long as it stood. Much of the Torah is concerned
with rituals that take place in the temple. By the time Ezra read
the Torah to the people of the Persian province of Judah (Nehemiah
8), the book of the Torah consisted of more than Deuteronomy
alone. One important component was a large corpus of priestly law.[21]
As Bickerman's comments suggest, the publication of priestly law is
a striking innovation. Indeed, it is truly remarkable that priests permitted it, for by offering a public account of the requirements of

---

[19] Moshe Weinfeld argues that Deuteronomy's "law of the king" should be read
as an example of an ancient near eastern genre of the "mirror for kings." He cites
other ancient near eastern texts that place limits on the king and encourage him
to pious behavior, including an Assyrian text roughly contemporary to Deuteronomy.
A colophon to the text has the king say, "I wrote it in tablets . . . and put it in my
palace to my constant reading" (*Deuteronomy 1–11* [AB 5; New York: Doubleday,
1991] 56–57, quotation 56; see also Weinfeld, "'תורה למלך' וא 'מגילת מקדש'"
Shnaton 3 [1978–79] 224–26).

[20] "To the Levitical priests, and to the judge who is in office in those days . . ."
(Deut 17:9); "before the priests and the judges" (Deut 19:17).

[21] In his discussion of the Torah as public document, which also emphasizes the
importance of Deuteronomy, Baumgarten points to the passage in Deuteronomy
about the laws of skin eruptions: "Take heed, in an attack of leprosy, to be very
careful to do according to all that the Levitical priests shall direct you" (Deut 24:8).
This passage, he notes, assumes that the priests' laws known to us from Leviticus
13–14 were not available to all. But once P had been integrated into the Torah
as we know it, those laws, including the laws of skin eruptions, became public.
("Torah," 17).

the cult and other priestly rituals, they opened the door to criticism of their actual practice. The Bible offers one striking example of lay interference in priestly business, Nehemiah's expulsion of Tobiah the Ammonite from the temple chamber in which Eliashib the high priest had installed him (Neh 13:1–9). Presumably Eliashib, who surely felt a chamber in the temple was his to dispose of, was less than delighted with Nehemiah's intrusion into his sphere. Nehemiah invokes Deuteronomy (Neh 13:1, apparently referring to Deut 23:3–5) rather than the laws of P to justify his interference, but the writing down of priestly law could only provide further opportunities for both outsiders and insiders to call priests to account for their failure to live up to their own rules.

The relationship between the Torah and the temple points to another aspect of the centrality of the Torah, its unifying force. Deuteronomy, and thus the Torah, insist that the Jews are permitted only a single temple, the temple in Jerusalem. Several temples existed outside Jerusalem at different times during the Second Temple period, but none ever offered real competition to the Jerusalem temple. As Gideon Bohak points out, the Jews were unusual among ancient Mediterranean peoples in having a single cultic center.[22] Elsewhere among the Greeks as among their subjects, each city had its patron god and its own temple. The Jews had only one god, and that god had only one temple. Bohak argues that the fact that all Jews, whether in Palestine, Egypt, or elsewhere, looked to Jerusalem as the holy city served to unite them. The Torah, a single document acknowledged by all Jews as defining their people's relationship with God, must also have served to bind Jews together. Of course, the opposite side of the unifying function should be noted: the fact of a single cult site and a single authoritative text promotes sectarianism. An Egyptian unhappy with the practices of one temple could find another one, dedicated to the same god or some other. A Jew could not. Thus the many disputes about how the temple should be run and the Torah interpreted.[23]

---

[22] "Theopolis: A Single-Temple Policy and Its Singular Ramifications," *JJS* 50 (1999) 3–16. There were of course other temples in the Second Temple period, but never one that offered real competition to the temple in Jerusalem.

[23] On the temple, Bohak, "Theopolis," 15–16, and Albert I. Baumgarten, *The Flourishing of Jewish Sects in the Maccabean Era: An Interpretation* (Leiden, New York, Köln: Brill, 1997) 69. Surprisingly little has been written about the Torah in this

The Torah contains not only laws, but also stories of Israel's past. Deuteronomy places its legal reforms in the context of the Exodus from Egypt without providing a great deal of detail about the Exodus. It also alludes to the patriarchs, the heroes of Israel's more distant past, but it does not tell their stories. It clearly assumes that those stories were well known to its listeners. In its final form, the Torah includes an elaborate account of Israel's founders and its liberation from Egyptian bondage. The combination of full-scale narrative and laws further strengthens the authority of the Torah, which contains everything a reader needs to know about the covenant; no other source is necessary.

How much did ordinary people actually know about what the Torah contained? In the first century c.e. both Philo and Josephus claim that all Jews were well versed in the Torah. Though this claim is surely propaganda, Baumgarten notes that Juvenal and perhaps Seneca invoke the same stereotype in the course of anti-Jewish comments.[24] Deuteronomy's requirement of a public reading every seven years could hardly insure intimate knowledge. Once the practice of annual or triennial reading of the entire Torah was established, attendance in synagogue on the sabbath would have guaranteed some familiarity with the entire Torah. But this practice appears to have developed considerably later; in the Second Temple period, the Torah was read publicly only in limited doses.[25] Our best evidence for knowledge of the contents of the Torah in the Second Temple period comes from the many texts that draw on it: narratives that develop biblical themes, commentaries, legal works that make use of the Torah either explicitly or implicitly. Obviously this literature is the work of a very small segment of Jewish society, for literacy was extremely restricted. Still, reverence for the Torah was surely not so restricted.

As we have seen, Bickerman understands the centrality of the Torah and the associated rise to prominence of scribes as phenomena of the hellenistic era, the result, to a considerable extent, of

---

regard, perhaps because the point seems obvious. For an interesting discussion of the relationship between literacy and ancient Jewish sectarianism, Baumgarten, *Flourishing*, 114–36.

[24] "Torah," 19–22.

[25] Ismar Elbogen, *Jewish Liturgy: A Comprehensive History* (Philadelphia and Jerusalem: Jewish Publication Society, and New York and Jerusalem: Jewish Theological Seminary of America, 1993) 129–38.

Greek rule.[26] When Bickerman wrote the essays in *From Ezra to the Last of the Maccabees*, the Dead Sea Scrolls had just been discovered, and the non-biblical literary production of the Second Temple period was thought to date almost entirely from the second century B.C.E. and later. Thus there appeared to be a gap of centuries between Ezra and the Jewish literature of the hellenistic era. I suspect that this distribution of evidence is largely responsible for Bickerman's views. With the publication in 1976 of the fragments of *1 Enoch* found among the Dead Sea Scrolls, two important texts, the *Astronomical Book* (*1 Enoch* 72–82) and the *Book of the Watchers* (*1 Enoch* 1–36), were recognized as dating from the third century B.C.E., thus strengthening the case for continuity. The *Book of the Watchers* is particularly important for our purposes. It integrates its account of the descent of the sons of God, which clearly draws on traditions independent of those in Genesis, with Gen 6:1–4's cryptic allusion to the descent (*1 Enoch* 6–8). It presents a view of the way evil entered the world quite at variance from the Torah's, yet feels compelled to take account of Adam, Eve, and the serpent, attempting to neutralize them with a visit to the Garden of Eden that ignores the trespass committed there (*1 Enoch* 32). Further, the *Book of the Watchers* represents its hero Enoch as a scribe (*1 Enoch* 12–16), though he is never shown engaged in interpreting the Torah. Of course there was no Torah in Enoch's day. The third-century date for the *Book of the Watchers* provides an important link between Ezra and Nehemiah in the fifth century and the profusion of works concerned with the Torah in one way or another in the last centuries B.C.E.

I hope that I have succeeded in establishing that the Torah was a central institution for Jews in the hellenistic period. But it is important to understand the Torah's authority in terms appropriate to the era; the fully-developed rabbinic understanding of the Torah, in which not only each letter, but even the crowns on the letters, are viewed as divinely mandated and full of meaning, is nowhere in evidence in the Second Temple period. Texts such as the *Book of Jubilees* and the *Temple Scroll* are not afraid to improve on the version of the Torah that had come down to them. Yet the very act of improving is a kind of recognition of the Torah's special status.

---

[26] Baumgarten suggests that one cause of the growth of literacy he discerns in the Hasmonean period was the needs of administering the new Hasmonean state (*Flourishing*, 122).

Now, finally, I would like to suggest how the status of the Torah
helps to account for the nature of the Jewish encounter with Hellenism.
The Greeks, like the Jews but unlike the other subject peoples of
their empire, had a book, or rather two books, at the center of their
culture. Those books were, of course, the poems of Homer, which
served as the basis of Greek education. Homer was not, as is sometimes
said, the Greeks' Bible; the Greeks had no Bible. A better analogy
is to the place classics once held in British education.[27] Yet despite
the differences, what is important for my purposes is that among
both Jews and Greeks a text (or among the Greeks, two texts) occupied a position of unchallenged cultural authority. Thus one could
acquire Jewish or Greek culture without having been born into it.

The place of the Torah in Jewish culture made it structurally similar to Greek culture. Philosophically minded readers of the Homeric
poems were often appalled by the gods' behavior; some found allegorical exegesis a useful tool for resolving this problem.[28] Their philosophically minded Jewish neighbors could apply the same tool to the
Torah to resolve somewhat different problems. Thus Philo of Alexandria could engage in the same type of intellectual activity as his gentile peers and feel himself as philosophical as they while directing his
attention to the Torah.

In Philo's reading, we find the Torah transformed by Platonism.
But Philo rejects the logical conclusion some members of the Alexandrian Jewish élite drew from Plato, that the spirit of the laws is
superior to their body and that physical observance is therefore
unnecessary for those who understand their meaning. Though the
logic of his position seems to be leading in the same direction as
that of these allegorists, Philo insists on the body of the laws, their
physical observance:

> There are some who, regarding laws in their literal sense in the light
> of symbols of matters belonging to the intellect, are overpunctilious
> about the latter, while treating the former with easy-going neglect. . . . It
> is quite true that the Seventh Day is meant to teach the power of the
> Unoriginate and the non-action of created beings. But let us not for

---

[27] I read this comparison a number of years ago, but I cannot locate the source.
[28] See David Dawson, *Allegorical Readers and Cultural Revision in Ancient Alexandria*
(Berkley, Los Angeles, Oxford: University of California Press, 1992) 23–72, for a
discussion of ancient pagan allegorical exegesis. Dawson emphasizes that allegorical exegesis was only one possible way of dealing with problematic texts (52–72).

this reason abrogate the laws laid down for its observance, and light fires or till the ground or carry loads. . . . It is true that receiving circumcision does indeed portray the excision of pleasure and all passions, and the putting away of the impious conceit, under which the mind supposed that it was capable of begetting by its own power: but let us not on this account repeal the law laid down for circumcising. Why, we shall be ignoring the sanctity of the Temple and a thousand other things, if we are going to pay heed to nothing except what is shewn us by the inner meaning of things. (*On the Migration of Abraham* 89–92)[29]

Philo's attachment to actual practice, the physical enactment of the law shows us Platonism transformed by the Torah.

The Greco-Egyptian Stoic philosopher Chaeremon was a contemporary of Philo who spent a portion of his career in Alexandria in the mid-first century C.E.[30] According to one of the ancient notices he was also a *hierogrammateus*, a type of Egyptian priest expert in hieroglyphs.[31] Among the writings attributed to him is a work on hieroglyphs, together with a history of Egypt and a work on comets; only fragments survive. Several fragments preserve a Stoic interpretation of Egyptian religion,[32] and an allegorical interpretation of the figures of Isis and Osiris and other Egyptian gods transmitted by Porphyry may originate with him.[33]

Among the fragments of Chaeremon's work is an account of the priests of Egypt, which emphasizes their philosophical disposition and their ascetic way of life:

They chose the temples as the place to philosophize. . . . They renounced every employment and human revenues and devoted their whole life to contemplation and vision of the divine. . . . They were always seen near the gods, or rather their statues, either carrying or preceding them in a procession or setting them up with order and dignity. And each of these acts was no empty gesture, but an indication of some allegorical truth. . . . Their diet was frugal and simple, for as to wine, some did not drink it at all and others drank only very little of it. . . . They were not allowed to touch foods or drinks that were produced outside Egypt. . . . they abstained from all kinds of fish, and from

---

[29] F. H. Colson and G. H. Whitaker, trans., *Philo*, vol. 4 (LCL; Cambridge: Harvard University Press, and London: William Heinemann, 1932).

[30] For the testimonia and fragments of his work, Pieter Willem van der Horst, *Chaeremon: Egyptian Priest and Stoic Philosopher* (Leiden: Brill, 1984).

[31] Thus Tzetzes in a scholion on the *Iliad* (van der Horst, *Chaeremon*, Test. 6).

[32] Van der Horst, *Chaeremon*, Frags. 5, 6, 7.

[33] Ibid., Frag. 17D; van der Horst thinks it likely that Chaeremon is the source (*Chaeremon*, 64–65, n. 1).

such quadrupeds as had uncloven hoofs or had toes or had no horns, and also from such birds as were carnivorous. Many of them, however, even entirely abstained from all animals. . . . During this time [of preparation for sacred rites] they abstained from all animal food, from all vegetables and pulse, but above all from sexual intercourse with women, for (needless to say) they never at any time had intercourse with males. . . .[34]

This description of the priests of Egypt clearly belongs to the genre of idealizing descriptions of exotic barbarian sages known from other writers;[35] I think it is safe to assume that it has only a rather tenuous connection to reality. Scholars have long noted similarities of vocabulary and other detail between this passage and Philo's description of the Therapeutae in *On the Contemplative Life*.[36] These men and women according to Philo devote themselves to study and prayer while living a life of celibacy and dietary restraint on the shores of the Mareotic Lake. It is no accident in my view that Philo did not attempt to turn the priests of Jerusalem into philosophers; priests' tasks were clearly spelled out by the Torah, and contemplating the vision of the divine was not one of them. Nor did they become priests on the basis of philosophical inclinations, but rather by mere heredity. Chaeremon could choose those aspects of priestly asceticism that seemed most suitable for his picture, ignoring what he chose and exaggerating as he saw fit. Philo might wish to ignore and exaggerate at many points in his treatises, but there were limits on what was possible for him. There was, after all, a publicly available written text to check him against. It is significant that the way of life of the Therapeutae is one of the few topics not drawn from the Torah that Philo treats. Chaeremon had no Torah to restrain him—or to define his topic for him. The passage that interprets Egyptian gods in philosophical terms treats not a text but well-known myths or sculptural depictions of gods, while the account of the priests never invokes a specific rule associated with a particular temple. This is not surprising. After all Chaeremon's goal was not to illuminate the practices of a specific group of Egyptian priests devoted to a particular god at a certain temple, but rather to rep-

---

[34] Ibid., Frag 10 (6–7); cf. Frag. 11.

[35] Ibid., *Chaeremon*, 56, n. 1 to Frag. 10.

[36] Ibid., and references there. I accept van der Horst's view that the parallels reflect shared vocabulary rather than direct knowledge.

resent the piety and learning of "Egypt"—and there was no single text that could do so.

We know even less about Philo of Byblos, the author of the *Phoenician History* and other works, than about Chaeremon. This Philo probably lived at the end of the first and beginning of the second centuries c.e.[37] The *Phoenician History*, of which fragments are preserved by Eusebius, retells Phoenician myths, turning the gods into human beings who made great discoveries or inventions:

> Hypsouranios settled Tyre and he invented huts made from reeds, and rushes and papyrus. And he quarreled with his brother Ousoos, who first contrived a covering for the body from skins of the animals he was able to capture. . . . When Hypsouranios and Ousoos died, he says, their survivors consecrated staves to them, worshipped the stelai [of Ousoos], and celebrated yearly festivals in their honor.[38]

Philo's approach to myth is that of the early hellenistic writer Euhemerus. Yet not only are Philo's gods human beings; they are Phoenicians. Thus Philo manages to turn the myths into a Phoenician entry in the competitive history so common in the hellenistic period: anything important was done first by the Phoenicians.[39] This feature of his work is noteworthy because there is rather little evidence elsewhere for Phoenician ethnic consciousness.[40]

Philo claimed that the *Phoenician History* was a translation of the work of Sanchuniathon, which, according to Philo, served Hesiod as a source.[41] (Note the swipe at the Greeks here!) For a variety of reasons, including the euhemerism Philo attributes to Sanchuniathon, it is impossible to accept Philo's claim about his relationship to an ancient source. Though his account shows many points of contact with the Ugaritic myths, it is clear that Philo did not draw on them

---

[37] Albert I. Baumgarten, *The* Phoenician History *of Philo of Byblos: A Commentary* (Leiden: Brill, 1981) 32–35.

[38] Baumgarten, *Philo*, 142–43 (808:10,17). The parenthetical reference is to page and line in Felix Jacoby, *Fragmente der Griechischen Historiker*, Part 3 (Leiden: Brill, 1969[2]); Baumgarten reprints the relevant material in his book.

[39] Baumgarten makes these points at various places in his commentary; for a summary, see his conclusions (*Philo*, 265–68).

[40] See the discussion of Fergus Millar, "The Phoenician Cities: A Case-Study of Hellenisation," *Proceedings of the Cambridge Philological Society* 209 (1983) 55–71, on Philo of Byblos, 64–65; *Roman Near East*, 264–95, on Philo of Byblos, 277–79.

[41] Baumgarten, *Philo*, 41–93 (translation of Sanchuniathon); 216–17 (813:11–20), 235–42 (Hesiod).

directly, but rather on sources from much closer to his own time.[42] Like the Greeks before Alexander, the Phoenicians were organized politically into distinct city-states. Part of Philo's project in Baumgarten's view was to transform the local traditions of Tyre and Byblos, to which references can still be discerned in the fragments, including the one quoted above, into a systematic account of Phoenician myth.[43] One reason for Philo's appeal to Sanchuniathon must have been the desire to find a Phoenician equivalent to Homer, a writer of such antiquity that he was understood as the common patrimony of all Greeks.

If Baumgarten's date for Philo of Byblos is correct, Josephus was an older contemporary. Just as Philo of Byblos' *Phoenician History* offered an account of Phoenician mythology for an audience that read Greek, Josephus' *Jewish Antiquities* recounts the history of the Jews from the creation of the world to Josephus' own time for that audience. But Josephus' task was rather different from Philo's, for the main outlines of his story were well established. Like Philo, Josephus drew on a wide range of sources, including documents of the hellenistic era. But for the earliest part of his history, Josephus' primary source was of course the Torah.

The narrative of the life of Abraham in the *Antiquities* offers a good example of Josephus' mode of retelling of the Torah. This is Josephus' version of Abraham's sojourn in Egypt:

> For, seeing that the Egyptians were addicted to a variety of different customs and disparaged one another's practices and were consequently at enmity with one another, Abraham conferred with each party, and, exposing the arguments which they adduced in favour of their particular views, demonstrated that they were idle and contained nothing. Thus gaining their admiration at these meetings as a man of extreme sagacity, gifted not only with high intelligence but with power to convince his hearers on any subject which he undertook to teach, he introduced them to arithmetic and transmitted to them the laws of astronomy. For before the coming of Abraham the Egyptians were ignorant of these sciences, which thus travelled from the Chaldeans into Egypt, whence they passed to the Greeks. (1.166–68)[44]

Josephus' emphasis on his hero's characteristically Greek virtues contributes to his effort to attribute all great discoveries to Jews.

---

[42] Baumgarten, *Philo*, 261–68.
[43] *Ibid.*, esp. 266–68.
[44] All quotations from Josephus are taken from H. St. J. Thackeray, trans., *Josephus*, vol 4 (LCL; Cambridge, MA: Harvard University Press, and London: William Heinemann, 1930).

Even Josephus' retelling of the story of the binding of Isaac, of little use for competitive purposes, incorporates Greek ideas. As Abraham prepares to fulfill God's command by offering his son as a sacrifice, he exhorts him in these words:

> Quit thou now this life not by the common road, but sped by thine own father on thy way to God, the Father of all, through the rites of sacrifice. He, I ween, accounts it not meet for thee to depart life by sickness or war or by any of the calamities that commonly befall mankind, but amid prayers and sacrificial ceremonies would receive thy soul and keep it near to Himself. . . . (1.230–31)

The glory of an early death after great achievement is a Greek idea that appears, for example, in Herodotus' report that Solon considered Kleobis and Biton the happiest of men (*History* 1.31); they died young after the heroic deed of pulling their mother's chariot to the festival of Hera.[45]

But Josephus takes a different approach in his treatment of God's command to Abraham to circumcise himself and his offspring. The presentation of the laws of the Torah in the course of Books 3 and 4 of the *Antiquities* is straightforward with only limited attention to apologetic themes. Thus it is not surprising that when Josephus comes to the command of circumcision, he does not invoke the sorts of philosophical interpretations of the practice Philo of Alexandria alludes to in the passage from *On the Migration of Abraham* quoted above. The explanation he does provide, however, is quite unexpected. Abraham was to circumcise himself and his offspring "to the intent that his posterity should be kept from mixing with others" (1.192). This motive, which cultivated Greeks and Romans were likely to find repugnant, does not appear in the Torah's version of the command in Genesis 17.[46]

---

[45] Louis H. Feldman, *Josephus' Interpretation of the Bible* (Hellenistic Culture and Society; Berkeley, Los Angeles, London: University of California Press, 1998) 278, notes that Abraham emphasizes the parallel between the extraordinary circumstances of Isaac's birth and the extraordinary death he is about to undergo and mentions several Greek and Roman heroes with both an exceptional birth and an exceptional death. Much of the scholarship on the idea of a glorious death in antiquity is ultimately concerned with martyrdom. Thus suicide tends to receive more attention than deaths sent by the gods or inflicted by others. See, e.g., Jan Willem van Henten and Friedrich Avemarie, *Martyrdom and Noble Death: Selected Texts from Graeco-Roman, Jewish, and Christian Antiquity* (London and New York: Routledge, 2002).

[46] Feldman, *Josephus's Interpretation*, also finds the motive for circumcision difficult to explain in light of Josephus' concern elsewhere in the story of Abraham to suggest that dislike of strangers is reprehensible and not characteristic of the Jews

I cannot explain Josephus' introduction of a particularly unhellenic explanation for circumcision. But it is clear that while the authority of the Torah works on him in two rather different ways. While it encourages Josephus to retell its stories in terms appealing to his contemporaries, Jews and gentiles alike, it also requires him to include features that were distasteful by the standards of Greek culture. The importance of practice for both Philo of Alexandria and Josephus in their integration of Greek and Jewish culture stands in contrast to its near absence in Philo of Byblos' *Phoenician History*. The one surviving discussion of a Phoenician cultic practice, child sacrifice, is concerned only with its origins—perhaps the characteristic concern of a euhemerist—not with its relevance in the present.[47]

I hope that I have shown that possession of the Torah permits Philo of Alexandria and Josephus to adapt Greek ideas and values in the service of a new understanding of Jewish tradition, which is, nonetheless, distinctively Jewish. Chaeremon and Philo of Byblos, on the other hand, lack a text that serves to embody their ancestral traditions. Their accounts of Egyptian religion and Phoenician myth are essentially Greek interpretations of those traditions. The only thing distinctively Phoenician about Philo of Byblos' work is his Phoenician patriotism; Chaeremon's admiring account of the priests of Egypt could have come from a Greek author without Egyptian connections since many Greeks viewed Egypt as a repository of ancient wisdom.

This study, then, is the beginning of an argument that the status of the Torah in ancient Judaism accounts in considerable part for the distinctive character of Jewish interaction with Greek culture. To be really persuasive, the argument requires attention to a much wider range of writings. All of the figures I discuss here wrote in the first and early second centuries C.E., at the very end of the Second Temple period and just beyond. A fuller treatment would be attentive to the

---

(245–46, 257). He does discern one possible apologetic theme: by ignoring the fact that circumcision is a sign of the covenant between God and Israel, Josephus eliminates the political implications of the act, turning it into merely a way of guarding against assimilation (254).

After his mention of this motive for circumcision, Josephus goes on to promise that he will elsewhere offer the reason for the practice (1.192), a promise never fulfilled. Thackeray's note to *Antiquities* 1.192 suggests that Josephus is here referring to the projected work on "Customs and Causes" that he mentions in *Antiquities* 4.198 (*Josephus* vol. 4). Perhaps he would have there offered an explanation similar to those Philo mentions.

[47] Baumgarten, *Philo*, 244–45 (814.6–15).

changes that surely took place, among Jews and gentiles, in the four centuries from the coming of Alexander to the destruction of the Second Temple. Further, all of the authors I consider here wrote in Greek. Clearly, it is somewhat easier to show the impact of Greek culture on works written in Greek, though I have no doubt that I could make the case for that impact on Jewish works written in Hebrew or Aramaic such as the *Book of the Watchers*, the *Wisdom of ben Sira*, and *Jubilees*. On the non-Jewish side, little has been preserved in any language but Greek, a fact of some significance. Yet while I must admit to having only scratched the surface of my topic, I feel confident that my results are not uncharacteristic.

"THE JEWISH PHILOSOPHY":
THE PRESENCE OF HELLENISTIC PHILOSOPHY
IN JEWISH EXEGESIS IN THE SECOND TEMPLE PERIOD

Gregory E. Sterling*

The reign of Caligula proved to be nothing short of disastrous for Jews in Jerusalem and in Alexandria. Petronius' response to Caligula's letter ordering the construction and placement of a statue in his honor in the Jerusalem temple, was one of the few bright spots during these otherwise grim years. Philo, who consistently speculated about the motives and inner thoughts of Roman officials, could not resist offering an opinion about Petronius. The Alexandrian suggested that Petronius must have known something about Judaism in advance. He thought that there were several possibilities: "But he had—so it seems—some faint intimations of the Jewish philosophy and religion that he had either learned long ago in his eager pursuit of education or from the time that he began to serve as procurator over the lands in which the Jews are numerous in each city, namely Asia and Syria." An alternative was that he "was so constituted in his soul that by his self-communicating, self-commanding, and self-learning nature (he was drawn) to those things worthy of eager pursuit," (*Legat.* 245).[1] Philo's assessment put the best construction on the circumstances: Petronius was attracted to Judaism. The Judaism that Philo imagined appealed to him was "the Jewish philosophy and religion," a philosophy that he could learn on his own. The three adjectives by which Philo qualified "nature"—αὐτήκοος, αὐτοκέλευστος and αὐτομαθής—recall his description of Isaac, who unlike his father Abraham who acquired virtue by learning and unlike his son Jacob who acquired virtue by practice, acquired virtue by his own nature. Philo consistently used two of these adjectives to describe Isaac's nature.[2] In one text the Torah exegete extended these qualities to

---
* University of Notre Dame.
[1] All translations are my own unless otherwise noted.
[2] Philo uses two of the three adjectives here in his descriptions of Isaac in *Plant.* 168; *Ebr.* 94; *Sobr.* 65; *Somn.* 1.160, 168; *Praem.* 27.

all three ancestors who "made use of the unwritten legislation before
any of the specific laws were written." They were able to do this
because "they were self-communicating and self-learning."[3] Surprisingly,
Philo attributed the same capacities to the Roman governor. Was
this a mere rhetorical device or did the Alexandrian actually think
that the Roman governor could innately understand Judaism? The
answer depends on Philo's understanding of the relationship between
Judaism and philosophy.

Philo was by no means alone in presenting Judaism as a philosophy. His preferred term was "the ancestral philosophy."[4] Josephus
used this phrase in a context similar to the one that we have just
seen in Philo. Citing the legend of the LXX that attributed its origin to Ptolemy Philadelphus, Josephus argued: "surely he would not
have wanted to learn our laws and ancestral philosophy if he despised
and did not greatly admire those who live by them," (*C. Ap.* 2.47).
In another context he used it to explain his *magnum opus*: "For, as I
said, I translated the *Antiquities* from the sacred writings since I am
a priest by descent and familiar with the philosophy in those writings," (*C. Ap.* 1.54). The author of 4 Maccabees used the term in a
retort to a potential interlocutor who emphasized the ethical dimension of Judaism: "You scoff at our philosophy as if living by it (means
that we live) without sound reason." He went on to explain how it
harmonized with reason: "It teaches us moderation so that we control all pleasures and desires; it trains us in courage so that we willingly endure any trouble; it educates us in justice so that we practice
equality in all of our customs; and it teaches us piety so that we
properly honor only the self-existing God."[5]

All of these texts have polemical settings that reflect sensitivity to
the perception of Judaism in the larger world. We might recall that
the earliest Greek impressions of Jews were along similar lines, at
least that is how Theophrastus,[6] Megasthenes,[7] and Clearchus of Soli
presented them.[8] How seriously should we take such claims and

---

[3] Philo, *Abr.* 5–6.
[4] Philo, *Somn.* 2.127; *Mos.* 2.216; *Contempl.* 28; *Legat.* 156.
[5] 4 Macc 5:22–25.
[6] Theophrastus, *De pietate* in Porphyry, *Abst.* 2.26 in M. Stern, *Greek and Latin Authors on Jews and Judaism* (3 vols.; Jerualem: Israel Academy of Sciences and Humanities, 1974) 4 (1:10–12), hereafter abbreviated *GLAJJ*.
[7] Megasthenes in Clement, *Strom.* 1.15.72.5 (*GLAJJ* 14 [1:45–46]).
[8] Clearchus of Soli, *De somno* 1 in Josephus, *C. Ap.* 1.176–83 (*GLAJJ* 15 [1:47–52]).

descriptions? The issue is not whether Hellenistic philosophy made any inroads into Judaism. It had a major impact on the works of Aristobulus, the author of the Wisdom of Solomon, Philo of Alexandria, and the author of 4 Maccabees. It exerted a more limited but still observable influence on a number of other works including Ben Sirach, Pseudo-Aristeas, the *Sibylline Oracles*, Pseudo-Phocylides, and Josephus.[9] The evidence for these documents is well known and need not be repeated. The issue raised by the statements that we have cited above is whether the influence was restricted to elite intellectual circles or whether it had a wider impact on Second Temple Jews. In other words, was there any popular appropriation of Hellenistic philosophy by Second Temple Jews? Is there any evidence that philosophy made its way from elite circles into more widely disseminated forms of instruction that would have influenced a large number of Jews?

In order to answer this question, I propose to examine some of the exegetical traditions in Second Temple Jewish literature. I am assuming that the representations that we have of Jews reading and commenting on their scriptures on the Sabbath day in Philo,[10] Josephus,[11] and the Gospels are accurate.[12] Were there exegetical traditions that were influenced by Hellenistic philosophy in such settings? Unfortunately, most of our evidence comes from elite authors; we have very little evidence from more popular circles and fewer homilies.[13] We can provide some control over the nature of our evidence in two ways. First, we can make an effort to examine traditions from different geographical regions and social contexts. The presupposition is that the greater the geographical spread and the wider the social scale, greater is the chance that the traditions were widely known. Second, we can expand the witnesses in a number of ways. We will include later Jewish texts that draw on earlier traditions.

---

[9] We do not have an adequate comprehensive treatment of the place of Hellenistic philosophy in Second Temple Judaism. For a brief overview with treatments of specific topics in Ben Sira, the Wisdom of Solomon, and Philo see *The Ancestral Philosophy: Hellenistic Philosophy in Second Temple Judaism (Essays of David Winston)* (BJS 331/SPM 4; Providence: Brown Judaic Studies, 2001).

[10] Philo, *Mos.* 2.216; *Spec.* 2.62; *Legat.* 311–12. Cf. also *Dec.* 40; *Praem.* 66.

[11] Josephus, *Ant.* 16.43; *c. Ap.* 2.175.

[12] Luke 4:16–30; Acts 13:13–41, esp. 15.

[13] There are two pseudo-Philonic homilies: *De Sampsone* and *De Jona*. They are both preserved in Armenian. On these see Folker Siegert, *Drei hellenistisch-jüdische Predigten* (2 vols.; WUNT 20, 61; Tübingen: J. C. B. Mohr [Paul Siebeck], 1980, 1992).

We will also include early Christian and pagan authors that drew
on Jewish exegetical traditions. With these provisos, I propose to
explore three areas where Hellenistic philosophy and Jewish thought
shared significant interests: theology, creation, and ethics.

THEOLOGY

Aristotle was the first philosopher to recognize the place of theology
proper within philosophy.[14] In his discussion of causes, the Stagirite
wrote: "So then there are three speculative philosophies: mathemat-
ics, physics, and theology." He explained: "For it is clear that if the
Deity is present anywhere, it is present in such a category and the
most honorable science must deal with the most honorable class."[15]
Discussions of the gods became a commonplace among Hellenistic
philosophers. Artistotle himself offered an important discussion of the
unmoved mover in *Metaphysics Lambda*.[16] Representatives from many
traditions wrote treatises entitled *On the Gods*: Epicurus for Epicureans;[17]
Cleanthes,[18] Chrysippus,[19] and Antipater of Tarsus[20] for Stoics; and
Cicero for Academics.[21] The Stoa, in particular, gave it pride of
place in their curriculum. Although it came last and sometimes never
at all—as Justin Martyr discovered to his chagrin[22]—it was often
considered a presupposition for other discussions, a point which led
Plutarch to criticize Chrysippus for creating a pedagogical and theoretical inconsistency.[23] More importantly for our purposes, the
Platonic, Peripatetic, and Stoic traditions developed a philosophical

---

[14] For a survey of theology within Hellenistic philosophy see Jaap Mansfeld,
"Theology," in *The Cambridge History of Hellenistic Philosophy* (ed. K. Algra, J. Barnes,
J. Mansfeld, and M. Schofield; Cambridge: Cambridge University Press, 1997)
452–78.
[15] Aristotle, *Metaph.* 1026a. Cf. Plato, *Resp.* 379a–b for God as a cause.
[16] Aristotle identified the unmoved mover with God in *Metaph.* 1072b 25–30.
[17] Diogenes Laertius 10.27.
[18] Diogenes Laertius 7.175.
[19] Plutarch, *Stoic rep.* 1052b.
[20] Plutarch, *Stoic rep.* 1051e–f.
[21] *On the Nature of the Gods*, 3 vols.
[22] Justin, *Dial.* 2. In his account of his exploration of various philosophies, Justin
complained that this Stoic teacher never taught him anything about God. He also
found his Pythagorean master's requirement that he learn to control numerous other
fields first problematic.
[23] Plutarch, *Stoic rep.* 1035a–d.

monotheism.[24] A number of Jewish authors also made theology in the proper sense a field for reflection. Pseudo-Aristeas considered theology to be the beginning point of philosophy.[25] Philo made εὐσέβεια "the queen of the virtues."[26] Josephus began his epitome of the law with a discussion about God.[27] It is therefore appropriate to ask whether Hellenistic philosophy influenced the Jewish understanding of God.

Identification

The conquests of Alexander and the culture that sprang from them shrank the Mediterranean and Near Eastern worlds. Greeks came to know people in the East and Easterners came to know people in the West in ways that were not previously possible. It was natural to compare conceptions of the divine. One of the ways in which philosophy influenced this process was to posit a supreme being with many names. For example, Cleanthes began his *Hymn to Zeus* with these words:

> Most eminent of the immortals, with many names, forever almighty, Zeus, guide of nature, director of all things by law, Hail! For to address you is the proper duty of all mortals; for we are your offspring, since only we, of all the mortal creatures that live and move on the earth have received God's image.[28]

The reference to "many names" refers to the strategy of collapsing the identities of numerous deities into one.[29] Dio Chrysostom described the practice in his oration to the citizens of Rhodes: "Some say that Apollo, Helius, and Dionysius are the same—and you think this—and many even combine all gods together into one force and power so that it makes no difference whether we honor this one or that one."[30]

---

[24] For an introduction see Michael Frede, "Monotheism and Pagan Philosophy in Later Antiquity," in *Pagan Monotheism in Late Antiquity* (ed. Polymnia Athanassiadi and Michael Frede; Oxford: Clarendon, 1999) 41–67, esp. 41–57.

[25] Pseudo-Aristeas 234–35.

[26] Philo, *Decal.* 119; *Spec.* 4.135; *Virt.* 95; *QG* 2.38. Cf. also *Spec.* 4.147. For a full treatment see my "'The Queen of the Virtues': εὐσέβεια in Philo of Alexandria," in *Piety in the Ancient World* (ed. L. Michael White forthcoming).

[27] Josephus, *C. Ap.* 2.190–98.

[28] Ll. 1–5 translated from the edition of A. A. Long and D. N. Sedley, *Hellenistic Philosophers*, 2 vols. (New York: Cambridge University Press, 1987) 2:326–327.

[29] See also Diogenes Laertius 7.135, 147.

[30] Dio Chrysostom 31.11.

Some Jewish authors held a similar concept. Pseudo-Aristeas expressed it succinctly when Aristeas appealed to Ptolemy to release his Jewish prisoners: "the (same) God who appointed them their Law prospers your kingdom . . . These people worship God the overseer and creator of all, whom all people worship including ourselves."[31] Philo of Alexandria was more sophisticated. He was convinced that the Platonic conception of the divine was similar to the Jewish conception of God. He wrote: "For what comes to the adherent of the most esteemed philosophy, comes to the Jews through their laws and customs, namely the knowledge of the highest and most ancient Cause of all and the rejection of the deception of created gods."[32] Like Chaeremon of Alexandria, Plutarch of Chaeronea, and Numenius of Apamea, Philo used allegory as a means of combining Hellenistic philosophy with sacred texts of the East. All thought that the same Deity stood behind Eastern and Western traditions.[33]

How could pious Jews explain such a stance? Was there any textual warrant for such a position? There is one distinct possibility. The LXX translators rendered the prohibition אלהים לא־תקלל of Exodus 22:27 by θεοὺς οὐ κακολογήσεις, "You will not speak badly of Gods," preserving the plural deliberately.[34] This at least is how the text was understood by later Jews. Philo thought that Moses prohibited Jews from "blaspheming with an unbridled tongue those whom others considered gods so that they would not be moved to utter what is not appropriate against the One who truly exists."[35] Josephus had a similar opinion: "Our legislator expressly forbade us to blaspheme those considered gods among others on behalf of the appellation 'God.'"[36] While neither make an explicit connection between the identification of Israel's ancestral Deity with the deities

---

[31] Pseudo-Aristeas 15–16. It is worth remembering that the letter attributes this statement to a pagan. Erich Gruen warned against pushing this too far (*Heritage and Hellenism: The Reinvention of Jewish Tradition* [Hellenistic Culture and Society 30; Berkeley/Los Angeles/London: University of California Press, 1998] 215–16).

[32] *Virt.* 65. Cf. also *Spec.* 2.164–67. Later Christian authors expressed the same view, e.g., Clement, *Strom.* 1.5.28; Augustine, *Civ.* 8.12.

[33] For details see my "Platonizing Moses: Philo and Middle Platonism," *SPhA* 5 (1993) 96–111.

[34] The most important treatment of this text is P. W. van der Horst, "'Thou shalt not revile the gods': The LXX translation of Ex. 22:28 (27), its background and influence," *SPhA* 5 (1993) 1–8.

[35] Philo, *Spec.* 1.53. Cf. also *Mos.* 2.203–05 and *QE* 2.5.

[36] Josephus, *C. Ap.* 2.237. Cf. also *Ant.* 4.207.

of others and the prohibition of cursing foreign deities, the two are conceptually related, i.e., the identification explains the prohibition. Whether Second Temple Jews used this reasoning or not, the understanding of Exodus 27:27 and the statements of identification point to Jewish efforts to relate to the deities of other people.

Anthropomorphisms

This general conception led to specific practices and constructs. Hellenistic philosophers regularly critiqued Greek religion.[37] One of the easiest targets was the crude anthropomorphic depictions of Greek gods in the epic tradition.[38] The Stoa formed a noteworthy exception to the typical practice by using allegory as a technique to interpret the Homeric texts.[39] Whether the anthropomorphisms were rejected or reinterpreted, they could not stand.

This sensitivity posed a problem for Jews since early Hebrew authors often used anthropomorphisms—although not to the same degree that Greek epic did—to depict the Deity. One of the first sustained reactions to the practice was the LXX which regularly replaced offensive expressions with less problematic phrases.[40] So, for example, the phrase "and his heart was saddened" (Gen. 6:6) became "And God took it to heart that he had made the man upon the earth" (καὶ ἐνεθυμήθη ὁ θεος; ὅτι ἐποίησεν τὸν ἄνθρωπον ἐπὶ τῆς γῆς). The avoidance of metamevlomai or a synonym with reference to God is striking. This is not a singular occurrence but a regular pattern in the Pentateuch of the LXX,[41] although it is not consistently maintained in the LXX as a whole.[42] The effort was expanded in the

---

[37] For a survey see Harold W. Attridge, "The Philosophical Critique of Religion under the Early Empire," *ANRW* II.16.1 (1978) 45–78.

[38] For a criticism see Pliny, *Nat.* 2.5.17; Lucian, *Dialogues of the Gods.*

[39] The most important representatives are Heraclitus and Cornutus. For a recent treatment see David Dawson, *Allegorical Readers and Cultural Revision in Ancient Alexandria* (Berkeley/Los Angeles/Oxford: University of California Press, 1992) 23–72. For a critique of the consensus see A. A. Long, "Stoic Readings of Homer," in *Homer's Ancient Readers: The Hermeneutics of Greek Epic's Earliest Exegetes* (ed. Robert Lamberton and John J. Keaney; Princeton: Princeton University Press, 1992) 41–66.

[40] For a detailed treatment see Charles T. Fritsch, *The Anti-Anthropomorphisms of the Greek Pentateuch* (Princeton Oriental Texts 10; Princeton: Princeton University Press, 1943).

[41] נחם appears in Gen 6:6, 7 and Exod 32:12, 14. The LXX never gives a Greek equivalent.

[42] E.g., 1 Sam 15:35 (compare 15:29!); Jer 18:8, 10; Amos 7:3, 6; Jonah 3:9, 10; 4:2; 1 Chron 21:15.

second century B.C.E. by Aristobulus who attempted to explain the anthropomorphisms through allegory on the basis of philosophy. He offered a rationale for his reinterpretations of phrases relating to God such as "hand,"[43] "standing,"[44] "descend,"[45] and "voice,"[46] in these words: "For it is agreed by all philosophers that it is necessary to hold holy views about God, which our *hairesis* does especially well."[47] The anti-anthropomorphic practice continued. Philo of Alexandria preserved a number of anti-anthropomorphic traditions that Thomas Tobin has explored. Tobin demonstrated that there are a number of pre-Philonic anti-anthropomorphic exegetical traditions that range from the second through the first centuries B.C.E. reflecting first Stoic and then Platonic concerns.[48] The effort to address anthropomorphic conceptions of God thus extended throughout the entirety of the Alexandrian Jewish community's literary production from the LXX to Philo. It is also worth remembering that when later Jewish authors explicitly turned to philosophy they shared the same concern over anthropomorphisms. The most famous example is Saadia Gaon (882–942) who adamantly rejected literal anthropomorphic readings. He wrote: "Consequently for all divine attributes pertaining to either substance or accident that are encountered in the books of the prophets it is necessary to find in the language of Scripture nonanthropomorphic meanings that would be in keeping with the requirements of reason."[49] Saadia's concern with reason explains the basis for his concern, a concern that he shared with earlier Jewish exegetes who, like him, were influenced by Greek philosophy.

Transcendence

There are other conceptions. Jews were intrigued by some of the statements of transcendence that Greek poets made. At some point

---

[43] F 2.2 (Eusebius, *Praep. Ev.* 8.10.7–9).

[44] F 2.2 (Eusebius, *Praep. Ev.* 8.10.9–12).

[45] F 2.2 (Eusebius, *Praep. Ev.* 8.10.12–17).

[46] F 4.3 (Eusebius, *Praep. Ev.* 13.13.3–8).

[47] F 4 (Eusebius, *Praep. Ev.* 13.12.8).

[48] Thomas H. Tobin, *The Creation of Man: Philo and the History of Interpretation* (CBQMS 14; Washington, D.C.: The Catholic Biblical Association of America, 1983) 36–55.

[49] Saadia Gaon, *The Book of Beliefs and Opinions* 2.8 (Samuel Rosenblatt, *Saadia Gaon*, The Book of Beliefs and Opinions [New Haven: Yale University Press, 1948] 111–12).

in the first century B.C.E. or the first century C.E., a Jewish author collected or composed a number of lines of dramatic poetry attributed to the great dramatists that celebrated the transcendent God and arranged them in a γνωμολογία.[50] In particular, the author found lines from Aeschylus, Sophocles, and Euripides or Philemon that postulated a divine being who existed apart from mortals, one in very truth, and who was unseen.[51] The same effort took place in contexts that were explicitly philosophical in nature. One of the most intriguing translations in the LXX from a philosophical perspective is that of Exodus 3:14 where אהיה אשר אהיה became "I am who it is I am" (ἐγώ εἰμι ὁ ὤν). The suggestiveness of this rendition was fully exploited after Platonism recreated itself in the form that we know as Middle Platonism. The transformation took place in Alexandria in the first century B.C.E. The possibility of combining the Torah's ἐγώ εἰμι ὁ ὤν with Plato's τὸ ὂν ἀεί was not lost on Philo. He situated God in the realm of being rather than becoming: "Of the virtues, the existence of God is truly according to being since only God exists in the state of being." He then clinched his argument with the biblical citation: "for this reason he speaks about him as adequately as possible, ἐγώ εἰμι ὁ ὤν."[52] The same play appeared later in the work of Numenius of Apamea who may have known of the connection through the works of Philo. He wrote: "the Self-Existent (ὁ μέν γε ὤν) plants the seed of every soul in everything that has a share in him."[53] For both Philo and Numenius the transcendent God of the Hebrew Bible was identified with the ultimate reality of Platonism.

CREATION TRADITIONS

A second area of common interest to Hellenistic philosophy and Second Temple Jews was creation. The most important text from the Hellenistic philosophical tradition for our purposes was Plato's

---

[50] For the texts see Albert-Marie Denis, *Fragmenta psudepigraphorum graeca* (Leiden: E. J. Brill, 1970) 161–74. For an English translation with notes see Harold Attridge, "Fragments of Pseudo-Greek Poets (third to Second Century B.C.)," *OTP* 2:821–30.

[51] See frgs. 4, 5, 9 respectively (*OTP* 2:824–25, 825–26, 827–28). Clement attributes frg. 9 to Euripides (*Protrepticus* 6.68.3) while Pseudo-Justin cites Philemon as the author (*De monarchia* 2).

[52] *Det.* 160.

[53] F 13. For details see Sterling, "Platonizing Moses," 109–10.

Timaeus. Raphael captured the significance of the treatise in *The School of Athens* when he painted Plato holding the *Timaeus* in his left hand and extending his right hand with the index finger pointed to the intelligible world. As with other significant texts, the understanding of the *Timaeus* was contested.

Two Creations

One of the central debates was whether there was a literal creation or not. Plato asked: "What is that which always exists (τί τὸ ὂν ἀεί) and has no becoming (γένεσιν δὲ οὐκ ἔχον)? What is that which is always becoming (καὶ τί τὸ γιγνόμενον μὲν ἀεί) and never in the state of being (ὂν δὲ οὐδέποτε)?" His answer was epistemological: "the former is grasped by intellection with reason, always existing in the same state (ἀεὶ κατὰ ταὐτὰ ὄν); the latter is opined by opinion with unreasoning sense-perception, coming into existence and perishing but never truly existing (γιγνόμενον καὶ ἀπολλύμενον, ὄντως δὲ οὐδέποτε ὄν)." Shortly after this he asked "whether the cosmos always was (πότερον ἦν ἀεί), having no beginning (γενέσεως ἀρξὴν ἔχων οὐδεμίαν), or became (ἢ γέγονεν), having begun from a certain beginning." He answered: "it became (γέγονεν)."[54] The debate was whether an actual creation took place or not. The majority opinion among the Old Academy and the later Middle Platonists was that it did: the sense-perceptible world was dependent on the intelligible world.[55]

The Platonic concept of creation made its way into Judaism in the late Second Temple period after the rise of Middle Platonism made it an attractive option. Philo attests at least two versions in his *On the Creation of the Cosmos*. In the first version, he drew the divide between the intelligible and sense-perceptible worlds after day one and before the second through the sixth days on the basis of the shift from the cardinal number "one" to the ordinal numbers "second . . . third . . . fourth . . . fifth . . . sixth."[56] In a brief—at least compared to his treatment of the hebdomad—commentary on "one" he wrote: "For it contains the exquisite intelligible cosmos as the treatise on it states." He explained how by using the metaphysical

---

[54] Plato, *Tim.* 27d–28b.

[55] For details see my "*Creatio temporalis, aeterna, vel continua?* An Analysis of the Thought of Philo of Alexandria," *SPhA* 4 (1992) 15–41, esp. 21–32.

[56] Philo, *Opif.* 15–16, 35.

categories of the monad (= the intelligible cosmos) and the dyad (= the sense-perceptible cosmos): "For God, being God, assumed that a beautiful copy would never come into existence apart from a beautiful pattern nor would anything among the sense-perceptibles be without blemish which was not shaped with respect to an archetype and intelligible Idea." He then applied this to the cosmos: "When he wanted to create this sense-perceptible cosmos, he first shaped the intelligible so that he could use the incorporeal and most divine model to make the corporeal (cosmos), a younger copy of the older, containing as many sense-perceptible kinds as there are intelligible kinds in the model."[57] Philo appears to sustain this scheme until we reach Genesis 2:4 where he shifts the line of separation between the intelligible world and the sense-perceptible world to the two creation stories. In this second version the two accounts of creation correspond to the two worlds: the creation of the intelligible world is reported in Genesis 1 and the creation of the sense-perceptible world is related in Genesis 2.[58] The presence of multiple and conflicting traditions suggests that one or both are pre-Philonic.[59] Philo is unconcerned with the tension that the two schemes create within a single treatise; his concern is to make the ontological distinction.

Surprisingly, the apocalyptic seer of *2 Enoch* shared the perspective of two worlds. The seer presented the act of creation in these words: "And I thought up the idea of establishing a foundation, to create a visible creation."[60] The use of an architectural image for the creation of the sense-perceptible world is quite striking.[61] Philo introduced his Platonic cosmology with the famous image: "When a city is founded." After he described the role of an architect he made his point: "We must think much the same things about God. When

---

[57] Philo, *Opif.* 15–16.

[58] Philo, *Opif.* 129–30.

[59] The most important treatment of these traditions is Tobin, *The Creation of Man*, esp. 123–24, 129–30, 167–72. The most important recent treatments that offer a different reading of the text are Valentin Nikiprowetzky, "Problèmes du 'recit de la creation' chez Philon d'Alexandrie," *REJ* 124 (1965) 271–306; repr. in *Études philoniennes* (Patrimoines Judaïsme; Paris: Les Éditions du Cerf, 1996) 45–78, esp. 61–62 and David T. Runia, *Philo of Alexandria*, On the Creation of the Cosmos according to Moses (Philo of Alexandria Commentary Series 1; Leiden: E. J. Brill, 2001) 19–20 and 309–13.

[60] *2 Enoch* 24.5 (J and A [*OTP* 1.142–43]).

[61] For a more thorough treatment see my "Recherché or Representative? What is the Relationship between Philo's Treatises and Greek-speaking Judaism?," *SPhA* 11 (1999) 8–10.

he decided to create the megalopolis, he first had its forms in mind from which he constituted the noetic cosmos and then made the sense-perceptible cosmos by using it for a model."[62] The image is repeated several centuries later in a saying attributed to Rabbi Hoshaya at the outset of *Genesis Rabbah*: "(In the cited verse) the Torah speaks, 'I was the work-plan of the Holy One, blessed be he.' In the accepted practice of the world, when a mortal king builds a palace, he does not build it out of his own head, but he follows a work-plan." Hoshaya continues, "And (the one who supplies) the work-plan does not build out of his own head, but he has designs and diagrams, so as to know how to situate the rooms and the doorways." He concluded: "Thus the Holy One, blessed be he, consulted the Torah when he created the world." He clinched his conclusion with two citations: "So the Torah stated, 'By means of "the beginning" (that is to say, the Torah) did God create . . .' (Gen 1:1). And the word for 'beginning' refers only to the Torah, as Scripture says, 'The Lord made me as the beginning of his way' (Prov 8:22)."[63] The similarity between the imagery of Hoshaya and Philo has led to a debate over whether Hoshaya drew from Philo and whether the later rabbi used Platonic categories.[64] The presence of the same image in Philo, *2 Enoch*, and Hoshaya suggests that the image may have been part of a tradition. The reference in *2 Enoch* is not purely coincidental: on two other occasions the author speaks of bringing the visible from the invisible.[65]

The apocalyptic seer has one other striking similarity with Philo in his account of creation. Martha Himmelfarb has pointed out that *2 Enoch*, like Philo, sets off day one of creation.[66] The apocalyptic seer uses Genesis 1:3–5 as a means of explaining how God spanned

---

[62] Philo, *Opif.* 17–19.

[63] *Gen. Rab.* 1:1 (Jacob Neusner, *Genesis Rabbah, The Judaic Commentary to the Book of Genesis (A New American Translation)* [3 vols.; BJS 104–06; Atlanta: Scholars Press, 1985] 1:1–2).

[64] E. E. Urbach, *The Sages: Their Concepts and Beliefs* (2 vols.; Jerusalem: Magnes Press, 1987) 1:198–202, accentuated the difference between the two. David T. Runia, on the other hand, has repeatedly argued that Hoshaya drew his imagery from Philo via Origen. See his "Polis and Megalopolis: Philo and the Founding of Alexandria," *Mnemosyne* 42 (1989) 110–12; idem, *Philo in Early Christian Literature* (CRINT 3.3; Assen: Van Gorcum/Minneapolis: Fortress, 1993) 14; and idem, *Philo of Alexandria, On the Creation of the Cosmos according to Moses*, 154–55.

[65] *2 Enoch* 24.2 (J); 48.5 (A).

[66] Martha Himmelfarb, *Ascent to Heaven in Jewish and Christian Apocalypses* (New York/Oxford: Oxford University Press, 1993) 84–86.

the gap between the invisible and the visible. The apocalyptic author does so by means of two intermediary figures, Adoil (identified with light) and Arkhas (identified with darkness). The two represent the highest and lowest principles from which everything else was formed.[67] Although the account uses a mythological cosmogony, it associates the attempt to bridge the invisible world in which God moved prior to creation with the world of creation by developing elements in the account of day one in Genesis 1. In this way *2 Enoch* appears to reflect the exegetical tradition attested in Philo that day one represents the intelligible world.

There is another possible witness to the same tradition. It is widely recognized that John 1:1–5 drew from Genesis 1:1–5. Most recognize the influence of Jewish exegetical traditions on these verses. What strikes me about the first two strophes of the prologue to the Fourth Gospel (vv. 1–2 and 3–5) is that they use day one of creation to describe the eternal Logos and his role as God's agent in creation.[68] In particular, they connect the Logos with light and life set over against darkness. The use of "light," "darkness," and the conflict between them could easily stem from a reading of Genesis 1:1–5; however, the association of the Logos with these and the addition of "life" suggest that the author is working with an exegetical tradition. In his account of creation on day one, Philo recounted the seven components of the intelligible cosmos, all drawn from

---

[67] *2 Enoch* 25:5 and 26:3 (J and A for both).

[68] The analyses of the hymn underlying the prologue are numerous. Although it is now dated, see the summary in Raymond Brown, *The Gospel according to John* (2 vols.; AB 29 and 29A; Garden City: Doubleday, 1966–70) 1:21–23. It is unimportant for our purposes to solve this other than to note that the interpretation of Genesis 1:1–5 in John 1:1–5 is set off in an unambiguous way. There are two strophes. Each uses staircase or climactic parallelism in which the last noun or phrase of one clause becomes the first in the next clause.

First Strophe
ἐν ἀρχῇ ἦν ὁ λόγος,
καὶ ὁ λόγος ἦν πρὸς τὸν θεόν,
καὶ θεὸς ἦν ὁ λόγος.
οὗτος ἦν ἐν ἀρχῇ πρὸς τὸν θεόν.

Second Strophe
πάντα δι᾽ αὐτοῦ ἐγένετο,
καὶ χωρὶς αὐτοῦ ἐγένετο οὐδὲ ἕν.
ὃ γέγονεν ἐν αὐτῷ ζωὴ ἦν,
καὶ ἡ ζωὴ ἦν τὸ φῶς τῶν ἀνθρώπων·
καὶ τὸ φῶς ἐν τῇ σκοτίᾳ φαίνει,
καὶ ἡ σκοτία αὐτὸ οὐ κατέλαβεν.

Genesis 1:1–3: heaven, earth, air (= darkness), the void (= abyss), water, *pneuma*, and light. Of the latter two he said: "he judged *pneuma* and light worthy of special privilege. For he named the former '*pneuma* of God' because the *pneuma* is most life-giving—and God is the cause of life, while with respect to light he says that it is exceptionally beautiful." He explained: "For the intelligible is brighter and more radiant than the visible to the same extent, I suppose, that the sun is than darkness, day than night, and mind, the ruler of the entire soul, than the body." He added: "That invisible and intelligible light came into existence as an image of the divine Logos who interpreted its genesis."[69] Following his exegesis of light, Philo turned to darkness: "after the shining out of intelligible light which came into existence before the sun, the opponent, darkness, withdrew." He understood evening and dawn to be barriers that God put between light and darkness as a way of keeping two perpetual antagonists separated: "For God separated them from one another with a wall and kept them apart knowing their opposite natures and the conflict that arises from their natures."[70] The similarities between the Fourth Gospel and Philo are noteworthy.[71] The chief difference is that the Fourth Gospel conceived of the shining and conflict in temporal rather than eternal terms. I suggest that the author of the prologue knew a Jewish exegetical tradition that drew a distinction between the eternal world of the Logos and the sense-perceptible world of humanity based on the shift from the cardinal to the ordinal numbers in Genesis one, but altered it to fit the contingencies required by the identification of Jesus with the Logos.

The Instrument of Creation

This leads us to a consideration of the instrument of creation, the Logos. The expression καὶ εἶπεν ὁ θεὸς in Genesis 1 led to an exegetical tradition that identified God's instrument with an intermediate being. The tradition began as early as the second century B.C.E. with Aristobulus who wrote: "For it is necessary to take the divine voice not as a spoken word, but as creative acts, just as Moses said in his

---

[69] Philo, *Opif.* 29–31. For details see Runia, *Philo of Alexandria*, On the Creation of the Cosmos according to Moses, 163–73.

[70] Philo, *Opif.* 32–33.

[71] The most helpful treatment of the similarities is Thomas H. Tobin, "The Prologue of John and Hellenistic Jewish Speculation," *CBQ* 52 (1990) 252–69.

legislation that the entire creation of the cosmos consisted of God's words (θεοῦ λόγους). For he repeats in each case, 'and God said, and it became.'"[72] This statement set up an extended citation from Pseudo-Orpheus *On the Holy Logos* (Κατὰ τὸν Ἱερὸν Λόγον).[73] The juxtaposition of the exegesis of the Genesis statements with the pseudo-Orphic material might make us wonder whether the word is hypostacized in Aristobulus; however, I cannot see any evidence that it was.[74] Second Temple Jewish interpreters regularly referred to the account of Genesis 1 as creation by word without necessarily implying a hypostasis.[75]

The turn towards hypostacization came with the rise of Middle Platonism. Plato did not posit a Logos; however, he did have second principles. For example, he made the Good a second principle in *Republic* 6, the One in the *Parmenides*, the Demiurge or World Soul in the *Timaeus*, and the principles of unlimited (indeterminate potentiality) and limit (precise numbers) in the *Philebus*. Later Middle Platonists elevated God or the Supreme Principle to such a transcendent level that they found it necessary to posit an intermediary metaphysical principle. They gave this intermediary a number of names, including "the Idea,"[76] "the heavenly Mind,"[77] "the demiurgic God,"[78] and the "Logos." The Logos appears as early as Antiochus of Ascalon[79] and Eudorus,[80] who are among the earliest known representatives of Middle Platonism. Later Platonists such as Plutarch used the Logos for the immanent (not the transcendent) aspect of God's relationship to the cosmos and humanity. In his allegorical interpretation of the Isis-Osiris myth, Plutarch identified Isis with the

---

[72] Aristobulus F 4 (Eusebius, *PE* 13.12.3).

[73] Aristobulus, F 4 (Eusebius, *PE* 13.12.4–5).

[74] So Nikolaus Walter, *Der Thoraausleger Aristobulus: Untersuchungen zu seinen Fragmenten und zu pseudepigraphischen Resten der jüdisch-hellenistischen Literatur* (TU 86; Berlin: Akademie Verlag, 1964) 81, who is followed by Carl R. Holladay, *Fragments from Hellenistic Jewish Authors, Volume III: Aristobulus* (SBLTT 39/SBLPS 13; Atlanta: Scholars Press, 1995) 219 n. 93.

[75] *Jub.* 12:4; *Wis* 9:1; *Sib. Or.* 3.20; *2 Bar.* 14:17; 21:4; *T. Ab.* A 9:6. There is a biblical basis for this in Ps 33 (32):6. For an early Christian example see Hebrews 11:3.

[76] Timaeus of Locri, *On the Nature of the World and the Soul* 7.

[77] Alcinous, *Didaskalios* 10.3.

[78] Numenius F 12 ll. 1–3.

[79] See Cicero, *Acad. Post.* 28–29.

[80] The evidence is Philonic, i.e., if it can be assumed that the two shared a common view. See John Dillon, *The Middle Platonists: 80 B.C. to A.D. 220* (Ithaca: Cornell University Press, 1977) 128.

receptacle, Osiris with the Logos, and their offspring Horus with the sense-perceptible cosmos, brought about by the imposition of order and reason on the receptacle.[81] Philo belongs to the same tradition, only he used the Logos for both the immanent and the transcendent aspect of God's relationship to the cosmos. Did he have a biblical basis for the Logos? The key passage in *On the Creation of the World* is Genesis 1:26–27. Did he draw on the refrain καὶ εἶπεν ὁ θεός ("and God said")? Unfortunately, we do not have an extant Philonic commentary on that phrase. The only evidence that we have is the frequency of the Genesis refrain, the prominence of the Logos in Philo, and the suitability of the match. Most reasonably assume that his selection of Logos is tied to the Genesis refrain.[82] The same may be said for the use of Logos in the prologue of the Fourth Gospel. Virtually all commentators agree that the use goes back to Genesis 1, although there is no explicit evidence for this.

Creation of Humanity

We are more fortunate in the accounts of the creation of humanity. We will begin with Philo. In his comments on Genesis 2:7, the Torah commentator wrote: "Through this statement he indicates that there is an enormous difference between the *anthropos* who has now been molded and the *anthropos* in the image of God who previously came into being." Philo distinguished between the heavenly *anthropos* of Genesis 1:26–27 and the earthly *anthropos* of Genesis 2:7 by using the two creation accounts as the line of demarcation between the intelligible and the sense-perceptible worlds. After contrasting the two, the exegete returned to the *anthropos* of Genesis 2:7: "It says that the construction of the sense-perceptible and individual human being is a compound of earthly substance and the divine spirit (ἔκ τε γεώδους οὐσίας καὶ πνεύματος θείου)." He explained the dual nature: "For the body came into existence when the Craftsperson took dust (χοῦν) and molded (διαπλάσαντος) a human form out of it; the soul (ψυχήν), however, did not come from anything made but from the Father and Ruler of all." He continued, "For what he breathed in (ἐνεφύσησεν) was nothing other than the divine spirit (πνεῦμα θεῖον)." The result is that the human being "is simultane-

---

[81] Plutarch, *Mor.* 369.
[82] So Runia, *Philo of Alexandria*, On the Creation of the Cosmos according to Moses, 143.

ously mortal and immortal: mortal with respect to the body, immortal with respect to the mind."[83] Philo made a sharp distinction between Genesis 2:7a which refers to the mortal nature of humanity and 2:7b which presents our immortal nature.[84] He has moved from his earlier Platonic distinction between the two *anthropoi* of Genesis 1:26–27 and 2:7 to a Stoic interpretation of the inbreathed *pneuma* with which he associated the image of God.[85]

Similar understandings of the creation of humanity are found in a variety of texts. One of the most interesting occurs in the *Hellenistic Synagogue Prayers*, a collection of Jewish prayers edited by Christians that have a large number of conceptual parallels with Philo.[86] One example must suffice. In a prayer that reflects on creation, the Jewish liturgist wrote the following reflections on Genesis 1:27:

> You have appointed him a cosmos out of the cosmos. Out of the four elements you molded a body for him, but you prepared a soul for him out of non-being. You freely gave him five-fold sense-perception and set a mind as a charioteer over his sense-perceptions.[87]

---

[83] Philo, *Opif.* 134–35.

[84] For similar statements see *Opif.* 144; *Leg.* 1.33; *Det.* 83; *Her.* 55–57; *Spec.* 1.171; 4.123.

[85] For the texts setting out the Stoic understanding of *pneuma* see Long and Sedley, *The Hellenistic Philosophers*, 28L, 46A, 47H-T, 48C, 53E, G-H, 55F–G. Philo knows the technical Stoic discussions: 47P (= *Leg.* 2.22–23); 47Q (= *Deus* 35–36); 47R (= *QG* 2.4). For recent treatments with bibliography of the Stoic view see A. A. Long, *Hellenistic Philosophy: Stoics, Epicureans, Sceptics* (Berkeley: University of California Press, 1986²) 147–78, esp. 152–58 and R. B. Todd, "Monism and Immanence: The Foundations of Stoic Physics," *The Stoics* (ed. J. Rist; Berkeley: University of California Press, 1978) 148–55. For Philo's use of this Stoicizing exegetical tradition see Tobin, *The Creation of Man*, 77–87.

[86] K. Kohler was the first to point out that the prayers in the *Apostolic Constitutions* are similar to the first six prayers in the Benedictions ("Über die Ursprünge und Grundformen der synagogalen Liturgie: Eine Studie," *MGWJ* n. F. 1 [1893] 441–51, 489–97). W. Bousset made the same observation, apparently independently ("Eine jüdische Gebetssammlung in siebenten Buch der apostolischen Konstitutionen," *Nachrichten von der Königlichen Gesellschaft der Wissenschaften zu Göttingen, Philologische-historiche Klasse 1915* [1916] 438–85). The relationship between the Jewish and Christian elements in these prayers has long been debated. Erwin R. Goodenough, *By Light, Light: The Mystic Gospel of Hellenistic Judaism* (New Haven: Yale University Press, 1935) 306–36, argued for extensive parallels between Philo and later Jewish liturgists. David A. Fiensy, *Prayers Alleged to be Jewish: An Examination of the* Constitutiones Apostolorum (BJS 65; Chico, CA: Scholars Press, 1985), took a minimalist stance. For a more balanced approach see Pieter van der Horst, "The Greek Synagogue Prayers in the Apostolic Constitutions, book VII," in *From Qumran to Cairo: Studies in the History of Prayer* (Jerusalem: Orhot, 1999) 19–46.

[87] P 3 (*AC* 7.34.6 [20–21]. There is a similar description in P 12 (*AC* 8.12.16–17 [36–40]).

Like Philo, the prayer drew a contrast between the corporeal origin of the body and the incorporeal origin of the soul.[88] The reference to "non-being" may be an early non-technical formulation that later Christians used to articulate a theory of *creatio ex nihilo* or could be a Christian emendation. The last two lines are an open allusion to Plato's charioteer in the *Phaedrus*, an allusion Philo himself makes repeatedly.[89]

2 Enoch shared a similar view. In an ethical warning against insulting another, the author wrote: "The Lord with his own two hands created humanity; and in a facsimile of his own face. Small and great the LORD created."[90] This is clearly an interpretation of Genesis 2:7 where God "breathed into his face the breath of life." The author apparently knew an exegetical tradition which connected the image of God in Genesis 1:27 to the inbreathing of Genesis 2:7. This is the same Stoicizing interpretation that we found in Philo.

A final example comes from an earlier century. In 1 Corinthians 15:44–49 Paul argued against the Corinthians' understanding of creation traditions. Genesis 2:7 had apparently become the focal point of a controversy between the apostle and the community. Paul paraphrased the text, but reversed clauses c and b. Genesis 2:7 reads: "God fashioned the human as dust from the ground and breathed into his face a breath of life and the human became a living being." Paul recast this as: "The first human Adam became a living being (clause c), the last Adam a life-giving spirit (clause b)." He explained: "The spiritual is not first, but the natural, then the spiritual" (1 Cor 15:45–46). For Paul the natural is Adam and the spiritual is Christ, an understanding governed by an eschatological perspective. The apostle goes on to provide a midrash on Genesis 2:7 in which he identified classes of people with ὁ χοϊκός *anthropos*, "the clay-made man," and ὁ ἐπουράνιος *anthropos*, "the heavenly man" (1 Corinth. 15:48). He concluded with a reference to the image that we carry of both of these *anthropoi*, a reference to the language of Genesis 1:27 and 5:1–3.

There are a number of items that strike me about this text. Why does Paul engage in a polemic about order? What is the relation-

---

[88] For the specific language of line two see e.g., Philo, *Opif.* 146; *Decal.* 31; *Spec.* 1.294; *Aet.* 29; 4 Macc 12:13.

[89] Philo, *Leg.* 1.73; 3.118, 128, 132, 134, 136, 223–24; *Sac.* 45, 49; *Agr.* 72–73; *Migr.* 67.

[90] *2 Enoch* 44.1–2 (A). The quote is from 1.

ship between Genesis 2:7 which is the basis for his comments and
Genesis 1:26–27 which he slips in at the end? The simplest expla-
nation is that Paul is countering a view of the Corinthians. They
appear to have identified the spiritual or heavenly with the *anthropos*
of Genesis 1:26–27 and the natural or earthly with the *anthropos* of
Genesis 2:7, the same distinction that we have already found in
Philo. It was probably this type of Platonizing exegesis that led the
Corinthians to devalue corruptible body and deny the resurrection.[91]

ETHICS

Jewish faith and Hellenistic philosophy converged in another related
area. The goal of Hellenistic philosophy was the attainment of happiness (εὐδαιμονία). The question raised by Socrates, "who is happy
and who is not,"[92] became the goal of philosophy for Aristotle.[93]
Hellenistic philosophical schools followed this lead: the Academics,
Peripatetics, Epicureans, Cynics, and Stoics all made εὐδαιμονία the
telos of philosophy. One of the results was that ethics became a central concern. This is evident in the place of ethics within each of
the Hellenistic schools. Xenocrates (*fl.* 339–314 B.C.E.), the second
scholiarch of the Academy, is credited with the threefold division of
philosophy: physics, ethics, and logic.[94] While various traditions questioned this tripartite structure,[95] it was generally accepted.[96] The placement of ethics within this scheme varied: in some traditions it was
one of the three (Platonists and Peripatetics); in others it was the
heart of philosophy which the other branches supported (Epicureans
and Stoics); in still others it alone was the tradition (Cynics); in all
traditions it was important.

The schools formulated the *summum bonum* of ethics differently.[97]
Most of them assigned a theological dimension to ethics in either
the explicit formulation of the *summum bonum* or in the way that it
functioned within their system. The former is evident among the

---

[91] For details see my "'Wisdom among the Perfect': Creation Traditions in
Alexandrian Judaism and Corinthian Christianity," *NovT* 37 (1995) 355–84.
[92] Plato, *Gorg.* 472c.
[93] Aristotle, *Eth. nic.* 1.4.2 (1095a18–20); 1.7.1–16 (1097b1–1098a20).
[94] F 1 Heinze.
[95] Sextus Empiricus, *Outlines of Pyrrhonism* 11.12–13; *Against the Mathematicians* 7.2–23.
[96] Seneca *Ep.* 89.9; Diogenes Laertius 7.39–41.
[97] Cf. Carneades' catalogue in Cicero, *Fin.* 5.16–20.

Pythagoreans who defined it as "following God"[98] and the Middle Platonists who held it to be "likeness to God."[99] The latter is true of the Cynics and Stoics who held that the aim of ethics should be "to live harmoniously with nature," although they articulated this in different ways.[100] The Epicureans thought that pleasure, defined as tranquility, was the goal.[101]

Natural Law

Given the importance of ethics, it is not hard to see why Clearchus was interested in Jewish ethics or why Jews would be interested in Hellenistic moral philosophy. They found a number of elements attractive. The first, and perhaps most important, was the Jewish effort to identify Mosaic legislation with natural law. There are a significant number of texts from a broad chronological and geographical spectrum that make this identification. Within Alexandria (or perhaps Egypt) we could mention the *Testaments of the Twelve Patriarchs* (assuming that there was an early Jewish recension),[102] the *Third Sibylline Oracle*,[103] the Wisdom of Solomon,[104] and Philo.[105] The final author has given the fullest expression to this understanding. He prefaced his Exposition of the Law with a treatise *On the Creation of the World*. At the outset he explained why Moses prefaced the law with an account of creation: "The beginning, as I said, is most impressive: it contains an account of the creation of the world since the world is in harmony with the law and the law with the world. The lawful person is at once a citizen of the world, guiding his affairs by the will of nature by which the entire world is governed."[106]

---

[98] Iamblichus, *VP* 137.

[99] Eudorus in Stobaeus 2.7.3 following Plato, *Theaet.* 176a–b and Philo, *Fug.* 63, where he cites *Theaet.* 176a–b. Cf. also the citations of the formula without an explicit reference to Plato in Philo, *Opif.* 144; *Decal.* 73; *Spec.* 4.188; *Virt.* 8, 168.

[100] Arius Didymus in Stobaeus 2.75.11–76.15.

[101] Epicurus, *Ep. Men.* in Diogenes Laertius 10.128.

[102] *T. Naph.* 3.2–4. Cf. also *T. Reu.* 4.11 and *T. Jud.* 11.1 that mention reason as an arbiter and *T. Reu.* and *T. Jud.* 20.1–2 that mention conscience.

[103] *Sib. Or.* 3.244–47, 757–59. Cf. also 3.594–600.

[104] Wis 6:4.

[105] E.g., *Opif.* 3, 145; *Mos.* 2.48–49; *Praem.* 23; *Contempl.* 2.

[106] *Opif.* 3. The specific relation between the Mosaic law and the law of nature in Philonic thought is a matter of some dispute. The most recent treatments are Hindy Najman, "A Written Copy of the Law of Nature: An Unthinkable Paradox?," *SPhA* 15 (2003) 54–63 and John W. Martens, *One God, One Law: Philo of Alexandria*

The association of Torah and natural law extended beyond Alexandria and Egypt. The author of 4 Maccabees has a formulation that is similar to Philo's: "believing that God has established the law, we know that the creator of the cosmos legislates in keeping with our nature."[107] Josephus assigned an interpretation to Genesis one that is so strikingly similar to that of Philo in *On the Creation of the World* that it is a good indication that the historian knew the philosopher's work.[108] Josephus promised to expand on this line of inquiry in his *Customs and Causes* which either he did not write or it has been lost.[109] The identification of Torah and natural law even made its law into Jewish liturgy. The later *Hellenistic Synagogue Prayers* repeatedly mention the implanted law.[110] They even go beyond Philo by providing explicit statements about the relationship between the natural and written laws:

> And when humans had corrupted the natural law,
> And at one time had in fact esteemed the creation as occurring without cause,
> And at another time honored it more than is right
> By comparing it to you, the God of the cosmos,
> You did not permit them to wander astray
> But delivered your holy servant Moses
> And gave through him the written law
> As an aid to the natural law.[111]

Virtues and Vices

A similar phenomenon took place in texts that transformed Torah legislation into Greek virtues and vices. The practice was again commonplace: *The Testaments of the Twelve Patriarchs*, Pseudo-Phocylides, Philo, Josephus, and *4 Maccabees* are the best—but by no means the only—exempla. Some of these texts present the virtues or vices with-

---

on the Mosaic and Greco-Roman Law (Ancient Mediterranean and Medieval Texts and Contexts; Leiden: E. J. Brill, 2003).

[107] 4 Macc 5:25. Cf. also 1:16–17; 6:18.

[108] In particular see *Ant.* 1.24. For details see my "Philo and Greek-speaking Judaism," 27–29.

[109] Josephus, *A.J.* 1.18–26, esp. 24–26. For the lost work see also 4.198; 20.268.

[110] *Apos. Con.* 7.26.3 (P 1.45 in *OTP* 2:677); 7.33.3 (P 2.8–10 in *OTP* 2:677–78); 8.12.18 (P 12.43 in *OTP* 2:692).

[111] *Apos. Con.* 8.12.25 (P 12.68–69 in *OTP* 2:693). Cf. also *Apos. Con.* 8.9.8 (P 11.3 in *OTP* 2:689).

out any appeal to Mosaic legislation, e.g., Pseudo-Phocylides;[112] while others present a harmony between the two. In 4 Maccabees the law educates reason but "reason is the governor of the virtues and the autocrat of the vices."[113] For Philo, the virtues are already present in Torah legislation. This is why he can use the virtues as a means for organizing Torah legislation in a series of appendices to his Exposition of the Law known as *On the Virtues*) in the same way that he used the Decalogue to structure the Torah in *On Special Laws*.

Conclusions

We could multiply such examples, but these are sufficient to illustrate the nature of the evidence. What can we conclude? There are more texts that betray the influence of Hellenistic philosophy in the area of ethics than in Jewish speculations about God or creation. This is hardly surprising given the emphasis on ethics in both Hellenistic philosophy and in Second Temple Judaism. There are a sufficient number of texts reflecting Platonizing and Stoicizing interpretations of Genesis 1 and 2 that we can say that these interpretations were widely disseminated geographically and temporally. The evidence of exegetical traditions on the nature of God that reflect philosophical influences are not as impressive; however, even here it is possible to make a case. It could be buttressed quite easily if we included texts that did not have an exegetical base, especially some of the poetic material.

The impact of these traditions on Jewish thought is difficult to assess from this point in time. It appears that there were sophisticated exegetical traditions influenced by Hellenistic philosophy that enjoyed wide circulation. Most who heard them knew them and must have thought of them as interpretations or, more naively, as the meaning of the text. It is doubtful that any but the elite who had been trained in philosophy recognized the philosophical thought in exegetical traditions. At the same time, the presence of Hellenistic philosophy in exegetical traditions that touched on the central con-

---

[112] For a thorough treatment see Walter T. Wilson, *The Mysteries of Righteousness: The Literary Composition and Genre of the Sentences of Pseudo-Phocylides* (TSAJ 40; Tübingen: J. C. B. Mohr [Paul Siebeck] 1994).

[113] 4 Macc 1:30.

cepts in Judaism suggests that we should take the influence of
Hellenistic philosophy seriously. Perhaps someone who attended a
Greek-speaking synagogue would have discovered that there was
more than polemics involved in Philo's description of the Sabbath:
"...Jews practice their ancestral philosophy every seventh day by
devoting that time to the study and contemplation of the principles
of nature." Why? "For what else are our places of prayer than schools
of prudence, courage, moderation, justice, piety, holiness, and every
virtue by which obligations to humans and God are understood and
successfully practiced?"[114]

---

[114] Philo, *Mos.* 2.216. Cf. Josephus, *C. Ap.* 2.171.

"'TALKING THEIR WAY INTO EMPIRE': JEWS, CHRISTIANS, AND PAGANS DEBATE RESURRECTION OF THE BODY"

Claudia Setzer*

In her book on the development of Christian discourse, Averil Cameron talks about the mysterious process by which "Christians, the quintessential outsiders, as they appeared to men like Nero, Pliny, Suetonius, and Tacitus, talked and wrote themselves into a position where they spoke and wrote the rhetoric of empire."[1] Surprisingly, one early Christian talks his way in using the belief in resurrection of the body, possibly the strangest Christian tenet to pagan ears. Here I will look at two quite different debates in the Roman Empire that employ the concept of resurrection. Both groups that profess the belief are uneasy in their social standing, poised between the need to assert a separate, distinctive identity and the need to survive and accommodate the surrounding Greco-Roman society.

The first argument I will consider is the early rabbinic attack on Epicureanism, an attack that is partially about the belief in resurrection. The second is the debate over resurrection between certain Christian apologists, here represented by Athenagoras, and some pagan intellectuals. While one conflict is cloaked in legal language and the other in elegant rhetoric, both show signs of intense feeling and high stakes.

Put simply, in the rabbinic-Epicurean struggle, the threat comes from sameness, so the rabbis exploit difference. For the Christian-pagan struggle, the threat comes from difference, so the apologists exploit sameness. Curiously, resurrection belief is essential in both arguments, where it functions in similar ways, and trails the same ideas in its wake.

An idea that often drew lines of demarcation between groups, belief in resurrection determined who was in and out of a commu-

---

* Manhattan College.
[1] *Christianity and the Rhetoric of Empire* (Berkeley: University of California, 1991) 14.

nity, such that by the second century, it is a criterion for belonging to a variety of Jewish and Christian groups. According to Josephus, Acts, and *Avot of Rabbi Nathan*, the Pharisees are the earliest group identified by this doctrine. The *mehayeh hametim*, "he who raises the dead" benediction appears associated with God's power in the Mishnah, where it is referred to in an abbreviation, (*mehayeh hametim* or the *gevurot*) as if everyone recognizes this prayer. At an early stage it is thus part of the liturgy, which is perhaps the ultimate expression of who is in and who is out.[2] Paul, in 1 Cor 15:16, hangs the whole Christian enterprise on the belief, "If there is no resurrection (for believers), then Christ has not been raised." The second century apologist Justin, who can tolerate a range of belief on other matters, asserts that resurrection deniers may call themselves Christians, but are not (*Dial.* 80.3–4).

While a survey of its development is not practical here, several points about resurrection belief are significant. First, it does not show a steady, detour-free unfolding over time. It took shape in different times and places, in confrontation with other cultures, in response to events, and as a result of internal developments. Streams of belief in resurrection of the body and immortality of the soul ran side by side and mingled. One did not replace the other over time. Second, it is too simple to say Jews believed in one and Greeks in the other. The conceptions vary according to the type of literature and more than one idea may appear in the same document. Third, the mention of afterlife often tells only half the story and does not spell out all the ramifications. The details of how afterlife will be experienced, translation to an astral body, resurrection of the body or the like are sacrificed to make another point, such as recompense for the righteous. Last, resurrection is not an isolated concept, but part of a shifting constellation of ideas. Many ideas appear in tandem with it, the assertion of a powerful God, ultimate reward and punishment, correct interpretation of Scripture, and the legitimacy of those who hold the belief. It functions as shorthand for this constellation of ideas.

For the people who held this belief it would be a shorthand that reassured them of the continuing power of the God of Israel and scripture's story, as well as their own eventual vindication. For the

---

[2] The final form and arrangement of the liturgy is fixed much later, but the blessing itself is recognizable in the Mishnah.

local Roman bureaucrat and his deputies, it might be an innocuous belief, and could be packaged to sound like Greco-Roman ideas of immortality of the soul.

RESURRECTION AS SYMBOL AND STRATEGY IN
EARLY JEWISH GROUPS

Why is the belief in resurrection so essential that the rabbis read its deniers out of Israel and the world to come in the lists in the Mishnah and Tosefta, and reject them implicitly in the rejection of Epicureanism? Sociologist Anthony Cohen's work on symbols in modern constructions of community may suggest some reasons why resurrection functioned so effectively as a symbol for early Jewish (and Christian) groups. Like other symbols, resurrection condenses a worldview.[3] Other beliefs, such as the belief in God's power, his involvement in human affairs, the primacy of the Torah, the crucial role of those who interpret the Torah correctly, the legitimacy of those who preach resurrection, and a belief in ultimate justice, adhere to it, and often appear alongside it.

Cohen argues that the most effective symbols of community are imprecise, capturing a variety of subjective meanings and individual interpretations.[4] Our references do not delineate when and how resurrection will unfold, and a people reciting their belief in it may hold varying views. Yet the proclamation or denial of the belief draws boundaries. The statements in the Mishnah and Tosefta are most explicit that belief in resurrection puts one within the bounds of community and rejection of it puts one outside, and forfeits him the next world, a privilege extended to "all Israel." Cohen notes that symbolic boundaries are increasingly important as structural bases of community weaken. In the wake of the destruction of the Temple in 70, two failed revolts in Palestine, and the re-assertion of Roman hegemony, political, class, and even ethnic boundaries are less reliable. Being a priest no longer carried any advantages. The sects dissipated and even non-Jews could be found in the synagogues. The lack of clear boundaries hence renders symbolic ones more pressing.

---

[3] Cohen uses the term "condensation symbols" to refer to a mnemonic that evokes an emotional response, often draws on a mythic past, and sums up a set of values, *The Symbolic Construction of Community* (London: Tavistock, 1985).

[4] Cohen, *Symbolic Construction*, 21.

Resurrection belief is linked to the legitimacy of those who preach it. The rabbis attempt to assert their authority in the process of pronouncing on who will merit the next world. The belief carries authority because it is recognizable to a significant number of Jews as shorthand for their cultural values, and is part of an effective strategy to solve some of the problems created by their subjection to Rome. Re-establishing Jewish control of the land was impossible for the near future.

Much of the Mishnah is theoretical and reads "as if" the rabbis hold the reins of civil power. *M.San.* 10.1–3 stands out because it moves everything to the next world. The concept of afterlife is apparently so well fused into the culture that the rabbis assume their right to pronounce on who merits one. The anomaly of this mishnah and the relatively small amount of space afforded it suggests that by now resurrection is either so universally accepted that it needs no defense, or is of minor importance. Its presence in the liturgy suggests the former.

For the moment, belief in resurrection meant its adherents could live in the world as it is. Symbolic forms, says Cohen, can reconcile the gap between beliefs and reality, "massage away the tension" between what is and what ought to be. Jews could retain the idea of God and his power, with its corollary, the gift of the Torah, but reconcile it with the situation of Roman domination and their experience of suffering. They had an answer to problems of injustice and theodicy. God has not abandoned the Jews, but the final resolution of injustice and vindication of the righteous has been delayed. Resurrection becomes part of a powerful strategy that retains elements of God's power, justice, the Torah, authenticity, and, not incidentally, the legitimacy of those who preach it. Those who deny both resurrection and Torah as well as those who deny a providential God, therefore, cannot be absorbed into the community.

The Rabbis and the Epicureans[5]

In the earliest rabbinic literature, a peculiar mishnah provides evidence that the belief in resurrection distinguished groups and underscored legitimacy:

---

[5] Portions of my discussion on the rabbinic material appear in my article, "Resurrection as Symbol and Strategy," *JAAR* 69 (2001) 65–101.

All Israel has a share in the world to come, as it is said, *Thy people shall all be righteous, they shall inherit the land forever; the branch of my planting, the work of my hands that I may be glorified* (Isa 60:21). And these are the ones who have no portion in the world to come: he who says there is no resurrection of the dead [to be derived from the Torah],[6] the Torah does not come from heaven, and an Epicurean. R. Akiva says, Also, he who reads heretical books, and he who whispers over a wound and says, *I will put none of the diseases on you that I put on the Egyptians, for I am the Lord who heals you* (Ex 15:26). Abba Saul says, Also he who pronounces the Divine name as it is spelled out (Sanhedrin 10.1).

This mishnah is peculiar in its inclusion of transgressions that are transgressions of belief and imposing a penalty that cannot be carried out in this world. With the exception of the mishnayot in 10:1–3 and the beginning of mishnah 4, *Sanhedrin* is about capital cases surrounding violation of laws of Sabbath, sexual behavior, murder, and sorcery. The rabbinic legislation puts forth rules of evidence, testimony of witnesses, and penalties to be handed out. Our mishnah stands out in contrast: it legislates belief. It identifies as crimes the denial of two articles of faith, resurrection of the dead and the divine origin of the Torah, and professing an alternate belief system, Epicureanism. These transgressions are not punishable by the methods discussed elsewhere in Sanhedrin, nor by excommunication, but by denial of life in the next world.

Who are these three groups whose transgression is so great that their punishment extends to eternity? First, there are those who say there is no resurrection from the dead. Whether these people rejected afterlife completely or accepted some notion of immortality of the soul is not clear, but their punishment is eternal loss of the next world. Denying the next world to people who do not believe in it may not be as absurd as it seems. David Kraemer has shown that the rabbis' mourning and burial practices and their teaching indicate they believed the dead remained sentient beings for some period after death.[7] So from the rabbinic perspective, a denier might confront his/her horrifying loss of the next world soon after death.

---

[6] The phrase, "to be derived from the Torah" is probably an interpolation, possibly added under the influence of the Gemara, which contains numerous proofs of resurrection from the Torah.

[7] David Kraemer, *The Meanings of Death in Rabbinic Judaism* (New York: Routledge, 2000) 12–13, 39.

Denial of this tenet is sufficiently threatening to the rabbinic enterprise that they call down the severest of punishments. The second
group, who say "the Torah is not from Heaven," are equally threatening in that they strike at the core value of the Torah as divine
revelation, and thus implicitly reject the importance of the rabbis
who interpret it. Seth Schwartz has suggested that it may be the act
of actually pronouncing these beliefs out loud that qualifies them as
a form of idolatry.

The final one denounced is the Epicurean. Although other religions and philosophical systems were known to the rabbis, and
Stoicism was more mainstream, the rabbis attack the Epicureans by
name. In *m. Avot* 2.4, for example, "R. Eleazar said: Be eager to
study the Torah; know what to answer an Epicurean; know before
whom you toil, who your Employer is, and who will pay you the
reward of your labor." Judah Goldin presents a different reading
based on a number of manuscripts from the Cairo Geniza as well
as *Avot of Rabbi Nathan*: "Be diligent to learn how to answer an Epicurean, know in whose presence you are toiling, and faithful is your
ba'al berit (one who made the covenant)."[8] Not only is this reading
preferable on stylistic grounds, but it also clarifies the element of
Epicureanism that the Rabbis would find so objectionable, the denial
of Providence, a God who attends to human activity, and rewards
and punishes accordingly. More cryptically, *Sifre Numbers* 112 comments on Num 15:31, "'and his commandment he has broken'—
this is an Epicurean."

While the term "Epicurean" becomes a general term of abuse in
rabbinic and other literature, as Goldin notes, it only appears twice
in the mishnah and does not seem to be an over-used epithet for
any kind opponent. Nor is the manuscript tradition confused.[9] A
recent thesis by Jenny Labendz shows the evolution of the term from
its specific use as "Epicurean" in Tannaitic materials to more general terms of abuse in later rabbinic materials.[10] In the early mate-

---

[8] Judah Goldin, "A Philosophical Session in a Tannaite Academy," *Essays in
Greco-Roman and Related Talmudic Literature* ed. H. Fischel, (New York: Ktav, 1977)
369–70.

[9] J. Goldin, "Tannaite Academy," 370–71.

[10] Labendz argues that the later Amoraim take their understanding of Epicurean
from the Sifre passage and use it to mean one who does not respect Torah scholars, while the Talmudic editors broaden it further by conflating it with a term based
on the Aramaic root *pqr* "to be irreverent," "'Know What to Answer the Epicurean':

rials, however, we are entitled to assume that the word means what it says.[11]

The Epicureans, while never achieving the respectability of the Stoics, achieved considerable popularity. The digest of references to Epicureans by John Ferguson confirms Henry Fischel's observation that the second and early third century saw an upsurge in the popularity of Epicureanism as well as anti-Epicurean rhetoric.[12] The second-century inscription of Diogenes of Oenoanda in the second century further attests to their visibility outside the academies.[13]

What made the Epicureans so threatening to the rabbis? Which of their fundamental assertions would be as serious as the first two in the mishnah? Surely Epicurus' theory of atomism or sense impressions is not the problem. Doubtless it is the Epicurean argument against Providence. While they were often accused of atheism, Epicureans recognized the existence of the gods and even promoted cultic practice. These gods, however, do not reward or punish, and have no stake in human behavior.[14] In fragment 18 of the inscription of Diogenes, as reconstructed by Smith, it says "[Let us not think the gods are capable of examining people who are unjust] and base and [noble] and just. [Otherwise the] greatest disturbances [will

---

A Diachronic Study of the *Apikoros* in Rabbinic Literature," Jewish Theological Seminary of America, April 16, 2002.

[11] A. Wasserstein suggests that it means Sadducees, and that anti-Sadducean and anti-Epicurean propaganda were mixed. While similar complaints are lodged against the Sadducees, the rabbis do not hesitate to attack them by name. Furthermore, by the time of the Mishnah the Sadducees are no longer around, while the Epicureans are. Wasserstein's argument requires the addition of another step in the process. See review of Fischel, *Rabbinic Literature and Greco-Roman Philosophy*, *JJS* 25 (1974) 456–60.

[12] John Ferguson, "Epicureanism under the Roman Empire," *ANRW* II 36.4, 2257–2327. See also Henry Fischel, *Rabbinic Literature and Greco-Roman Philosophy*, 2. While some of Fischel's work has not been accepted on the level of formal parallelism, for example his contention that the famous story of the four who entered *pardes* in *b. Hag.* 14b is an anti-Epicurean polemic, he has contributed to the general appreciation of parallelism between Talmudic and Greco-Roman literatures. For recent work on the *pardes* story, see Alon Goshen-Gottstein, "Four Entered Paradise Revisited," *HTR* 88 (1995) 69–133, and on Elisha ben Abuyah in particular, see *The Sinner and the Amnesiac* (Stanford: Stanford University, 2000).

[13] *Diogenes of Oinoanda: The Epicurean Inscription*, ed. Martin Ferguson Smith (Naples: Bibliopolis, 1993).

[14] Epicureans were exceptional, even among philosophers. See Myrto Dragona-Monachou, who argues that some version of providence was held by every other philosophy that believed in God or gods, "Divine Providence in the Philosophy of the Empire," *ANRW* II 36.7, 4418–4490.

be created in our souls.][15] In fragment 19, a similar argument appears, "let us reverence the gods [rightly] both at festivals and on [unhallowed occasions, both] publicly [and privately] and let us observe the customs [of our fathers in relation to them; and let not the imperishable beings be falsely accused at all] by us [in our vain fear that they are responsible for all misfortunes], bringing [sufferings to us] and [contriving burdensome obligations] for themselves."[16]

Such ideas undercut the entire rabbinic system where God creates and sustains the universe, rewards and punishes human beings for their deeds. Fischel argues that the Epicureans effectively "depersonalized the Universe." The rabbis' frequent complaint against their opponents, that they say *lyt din wlyt dayan*, "there is no judgment and no judge," argues Fischel, is an anti-Epicurean statement, a point even Fischel's critics concede.[17]

The phrase that denied divine justice is often combined with a denial of the next world, as in the early targum, *Targum Neofiti* I on Gen 4:8, "There is no judgment and no Judge; and there is no Other World; There is no bestowal of recompense for the just; and there is no reckoning for the wicked." Resurrection is implicit here, and appears explicitly in the later Palestinian Talmud, *ayn matan skar wayn tehiyat hametim*, "there is no giving of reward and there is no resurrection from the dead" (*y. Hag.* 2:1, 77b).

In the Tosefta, denial of resurrection and denial of Torah are listed with Epicureanism as transgressions that earn permanent punishment. Three types of recompense await: eternal life, eternal punishment, and temporary punishment. I have condensed the text to include the relevant material:

> The House of Shammai says, "There are three groups, one for eternal life, one *for shame and everlasting contempt* (Dan 12:2)—these are those who are completely evil. An intermediate group go down to Gehenna and scream and come up again and are healed . . . but heretics, apostates, traitors, Epicureans, those who deny the Torah, those who separate from the ways of the community, those who deny the resurrection of the dead, and whoever both sinned and caused the public to sin— for example Jeroboam and Ahab—and those who sent their arrows against the land of the living and stretched out their hands against the

---

[15] Smith, *Epicurean Inscription*, 376.
[16] Ibid.
[17] Wasserstein, review of Fischel, *Rabbinic Literature*, 459.

lofty habitation, Gehenna is locked behind them, and they are judged therein for all generations . . . (*t.San.* 13.3–5).

As in the mishnah in Sanhedrin, those who deny a providential God and deny resurrection of the dead undercut the authority of the rabbis and are placed beyond divine mercy.

A second factor may have made Epicureans threatening to the earliest rabbis, namely their congeniality to rabbinic ideals. Like the rabbis, Epicureans promoted the ideal of the philosopher/sage, the moderate, disciplined life, the joy of study, the cultivation of a community of learners, and the cult of friendship, and the unity of body and soul. In a general way, the rabbis may have experienced competition with the Epicureans, a group who outwardly shared some of their ethics and way of life, but who dangerously denied the root of the rabbinic system, a just God who attends to human beings.

These Epicureans are Jews. The first two groups in the Mishnah, the Torah-deniers and the resurrection-deniers, would not be of much interest if they were not Jews. Furthermore, the list of people condemned in the Tosefta is of people who were part of the Jewish community but whose relationship to it is now fractured, "heretics, apostates, traitors, Epicureans, those who deny the Torah, those who separate from the ways of the community, those who deny the resurrection of the dead, and whoever both sinned and caused the public to sin, for example Jereboam and Ahab." These last two are viewed by the Deuteronomist as Israelites who compromised the worship of Yahweh. These Epicureans, then, are likely Jews attracted to and perhaps professing a form of Epicureanism.

Seth Schwartz' recent book, *Imperialism and Jewish Society*, argues for the pervasiveness of pagan culture, including local cults and competing philosophical schools in the urban centers of Israel, where the rabbis were concentrated. Between 100 and 350 C.E. Jewish Palestine was virtually the same as any other Roman imperial province, and rabbinic influence was slight in the face of pagan religiosity. He cites as evidence the prominence of pagan iconography, images of gods and goddesses on coins and other archaeological finds, funerary and other inscriptions that departed little from Greco-Roman norms, and rabbinic accounts of the public life of Palestinian cities that show the cities dominated by images and shrines of the gods.[18]

---

[18] Seth Schwartz, *Imperialism and Jewish Society* (Princeton: Princeton University, 2001) 136–61. Schwartz' conclusion is that the rabbis limited themselves to prohibiting acts of worship towards pagan fetishes.

If pagan religiosity is so prevalent, so too is an awareness of pagan philosophical ethics and worldviews.[19] It stands to reason that some Jews would be attracted to the popular Epicureanism. Some impulses were like the rabbinic ones, the elevation of study, the cultivation of right actions, and the avoidance of excess. The performance of Jewish cultic acts would still be admissible to an Epicurean Jew, as the Diogenes inscription shows. The Epicurean, however, differs in the denial that God is interested in human behavior, or that he rewards or punishes in this life or the next. Such a position is a natural reaction to theodicy, analogous to people today who call themselves "Jewish atheists." Whether such a person would call himself a Jew, an Epicurean, an Epicurean Jew, or a Jewish Epicurean, we cannot know.

Be that as it may, the rabbis understandably felt the need to underscore their differences with these Jews, who might resemble them closely in practice and ethics, but who thoroughly undercut their own authority and agenda. The rabbis underscore difference, perhaps exaggeratedly so, and in the Mishnah read these groups out of the body "all Israel," who by definition have a share in the world to come. Epicureans, they tell us, do not belong to Israel.

In both the Mishnah and the Tosefta, the rabbis link resurrection, a correct understanding of Torah, and an affirmation of God's power in the world to dispense ultimate justice. Denial of justice is behind "Epicurean" claims in the targums that "there is no justice and no judge." In the Tosefta, a motley list of opponents is excluded, whose only common trait is a non-acceptance of rabbinic principles and authority. The rabbis promote their own legitimacy as the correct interpreters of Torah and based on these categories, they pronounce on the fate of their opponents.

---

[19] In another example, Azzan Yadin has suggested Rabban Gamaliel's response to the challenge concerning his presence in the bath house of Aphrodite, "I did not enter her territory; she entered mine" (m. 'Abod. Zar. 3:4) may be read as a response to a saying of Plotinus. This reading depends on this Rabban Gamaliel being the son of Rabbi Judah, or a later reality projected onto the earlier Gamaliel. If so, this reading shows a knowledge of some philosophies and respect for their aniconic traditions in the patriarchate, "Rabban Gamaliel in Aphrodite's Bath and the Question of Pagan Monotheism," talk given at the Jewish Theological Seminary, New York City, March 13, 2003.

ATHENAGORAS AND THE PAGANS

We possess a great deal more material to view the second debate over resurrection, between Christian apologists and pagans. The full flowering of an articulate resurrection apologetic appears in the mid-second century, in Justin, especially in a work attributed to him, *On the Resurrection*. He adds quantity and specificity to arguments from nature that have been scattered in earlier documents, uses for the first time the actual expression "resurrection of the flesh," and painstakingly proves it from Scripture. The leap in intensity in the defense of resurrection and material continuity in Christian circles accompanied second century developments, particularly the emergence of alternative understandings of the resurrection of Jesus and of believers among Gnostic and other groups, the pagan intellectual challenge, and the increasing possibility of martyrdom.

Two decades after Justin, Athenagoras promotes the Christian belief in bodily resurrection in two ways, using it as a weapon of defense against widespread charges against Christians in one work, while defending the doctrine itself in the other. Like Justin, he recommends Christianity to the emperor as compatible with the philosopher's search for truth. His *Plea on Behalf of the Christians*, addressed to the emperor Marcus Aurelius and his heir apparent Commodus, is dated around 176, and *On the Resurrection*, promised at the end of *Plea*, is dated some years later. The second work is considered pseudonymous by some, but for our purposes, actual authorship is not as significant as dating, and it fits well with other second century texts.[20]

In general, subjects throughout the empire could appeal to the emperor if they were mistreated by local officials. Athenagoras sets out to disprove three well-known charges against Christians: atheism, cannibalism (especially Thyestean feasts), and sexual excess (especially incest). Steeped in Greco-Roman rhetoric, he applies many of the rhetorical strategies identified by Chaim Perelman and Lucie

---

[20] For questions of dating see R. Grant, "Athenagoras or Pseudo-Athenagoras," *HTR* 47 (1954) 121–9; W. Schoedel, *Athenagoras: Legatio and De Resurrectione* (Oxford: Oxford University, 1972) who consider it pseudonymous, and L. Barnard, "The Authenticity of Athenagoras' *De Resurrectione*," *Studia Patristica* 15 (1984) 39–49; B. Pouderon, "L'Authenticité du Traité *Sur La Résurrection* Attribué à l'Apologiste Athénagore," *VC* 40 (1986) 226–40, who consider it authentic.

Olbrechts-Tyteca.[21] Part of his approach is associative, appealing to the idea that the Christians and the emperor are on the same side and agree on premises and values. He invokes the example of the pagan martyrs, Pythagoras, Heraclitus, and Socrates, who, like Christian martyrs, were champions of virtue persecuted for their devotion to the truth. He employs the "loci of quality" which praises the unique and uncommon,[22] against the vulgar and popular. Only the "stupid crowds" oppose Christians (3.3), as they opposed the pagan heroes. Similarly, the Christians are, like the Stoic Emperor, "servants of reason" (35.4). He further associates Christians and the emperor by noting that they are on the same side against those who believe in the exploits of the gods (32). He appeals to sameness and erases difference when making his case to the emperor and the pagan world at large.

Resurrection comes into play in the second strategy, of quasi-logical arguments (which imitate formal mathematical arguments using non-mathematical elements), where a thesis is disproven by showing it is incompatible with another thesis. Even more effective to cancel out a thesis, says Perelman, is to show it incompatible with a bundle of facts.[23] Because Christians believe in resurrection and expect to live again, they must live impeccable lives. They cannot be guilty of the three charges against them. The charge of cannibalism is particularly absurd in light of the belief in resurrection, "What man who believes in resurrection would offer himself to be a grave for bodies slated to arise? For it is impossible at the same time to believe that bodies will arise and then eat them as though they will not arise, or to think that the earth will give back its dead and then suppose that those whom a man had buried within himself will not demand back their bodies" (36.1).

The charge of murder is refuted even more effectively because Athenagoras shows it incompatible with several facts. Christians renounce attending spectacles where people are killed, forbid abortion, and do not expose babies (35.4–6). Any kind of wrong-doing is refuted by Christian belief in resurrection (31.3–4; 33.1; 35.6; 36.1–2).

---

[21] Chaim Perelman and Lucie Olbrechts-Tyteca, *The New Rhetoric* (Notre Dame: University of Notre Dame, 1969) and Perelman, *The Realm of Rhetoric* (Notre Dame: University of Notre Dame, 1982).

[22] Perelman and Olbrechts-Tyteca, *New Rhetoric*, 75.

[23] Perelman, *Realm*, 24.

In explaining resurrection Athenagoras revises it for Stoic ears, "...since we believe that when we let go of this life we shall live another life better than that here, a heavenly one, not earthly, so that with God and with his help remain unchanging and impassive (*apathies*) in soul *as though we were not in body*, even if we have one, but heavenly spirit..." (31.4). Athenagoras not only invokes the Stoic virtue of *apatheia*, passionlessness, but also blurs the distinction between spiritual immortality and physical resurrection.

Athenagoras assumes that Christian belief in resurrection is a given, something "everyone knows" about Christians. He does not need to prove it, nor does he let on that there are Christian groups out there who reject it. He knows that his pagan accusers, whether informers, or mere critics, reject it, and takes the offensive against them at many points, mounting *ad personam* attacks that condemn their morals (33.2–3; 35.4,6). He suggests that it is their lack of belief that they will be called to account that gives them license. Resurrection belief is not at issue, but becomes one of his arsenal of weapons to defend Christians against their accusers, a rejoinder to other charges against them.

On the Resurrection

In this document, Athenagoras argues vigorously for resurrection of the body against its detractors. Like *Plea*, it is an apologetic to outsiders (1.5; 11.1; 19.2), but it is also an in-house document, written to other Christians (1.5; 19.1), some of whom reject the belief in bodily resurrection, and some of whom need help in defending their belief. The arguments of those who reject resurrection are audible behind Athenagoras' rejoinders. Called "our opponents" or "our disputants," these are people admired for their wisdom. Athenagoras suggests they are some kind of intelligentsia carried along by the masses, "this [understanding of resurrection] seems to have greatly upset some people whom others marvel at for their wisdom, because for some reason I do not know, they regarded the doubts of the crowd as strong arguments" (3.3). Athenagoras himself, Pouderon suggests, belongs to a Christian intellectual elite, a school movement independent of the churches.[24]

---

[24] See Bernard Pouderon, "Réflexions sur la Formation d'une Élite intellectuelle chrétienne au II Siècle: Les Écoles' d'Athènes, de Rome, et d'Alexandrie, *Les*

Athenagoras makes familiar arguments for resurrection, evincing the same values that appear in resurrection arguments in Paul, Justin, the Pharisees, and the rabbis; God's power, ultimate justice, the unity of a human being, and the meaningfulness of life in the face of persecution. Newer, more precise arguments emerge, answering charges raised by others. The overwhelming argument for resurrection, in Athenagoras' view, is an argument from authority,[25] from the conviction of God's power and providence, evidenced by creation itself, ". . . as to power, the creation of our bodies shows that God's power suffices for their resurrection . . . such a power can unite what has been dissolved, can raise up what has fallen, can restore the dead to life, and can change the corruptible into incorruption" (*Res.* 2.3; 3.1, 3). God's power also answers the problem of chain consumption, when someone is devoured by an animal, which is in turn eaten by another animal, ". . . the same God and the same wisdom and power can also separate out what has been torn apart and devoured by numerous animals of every kind" (3.3; 5.1).

Indeed, Athenagoras identifies the proof for God's power from creation as one of the three primary arguments that confirm resurrection, the one from which all others arise (18.1). He cites the same proof as Justin, the slogan that the pagan Celsus mocks, "What is impossible with men is possible with God" (9.2). God's power in creation is also demonstrated from natural phenomena, or as the rhetoricians put it, from the structure of reality. A model suffices to establish a rule. Athenagoras asks who, for example, could imagine a drop of semen contains within it the beginnings of a whole person, made of flesh and bone? Who could imagine, looking at a child, the stages of development that will transform him (17.1–2)?

The second familiar argument Athenagoras makes is the argument from justice. Since justice is clearly not accomplished in this life, resurrection is necessary (18.2). Death alone cannot satisfy the thirst for ultimate justice. One death is too good for some evil-doers (*Res.* 19.7) and for such people insensibility would be a boon. But justice is the natural desire and goal of human life, as natural as the desire for food and offspring (*Res.* 14.4; 18.4).

Apologistes Chrétiens et la Culture Grecque (ed. B. Pouderon et J. Doré; Paris : Beauchesne, 1998) 237–69.

[25] The argument from God's authorship is the ultimate argument from authority, Perelman and Olbrechts-Tyteca, *New Rhetoric*, 305–10.

The third argument comes out of the first and second. Because God in his power creates the human as a composite, and because humans long for justice, for justice to prevail God must judge the entire human being. Justice will only happen if the body and soul are reunited. Whether a person lived a life of virtue or sin, that life was lived by the body and soul together, so justice demands they be punished together (*Res.* 13.2; 21–22). The same argument appears in Justin and in rabbinic literature (*Lev. Rab.* 4.8). Athenagoras asks, "Where is justice if when it is the body which first experiences passions and then draws the soul along to experience them and share the deeds to which the body is driven, yet the soul alone is judged (21.4)?" To judge the composite human being, God must reunite the soul and body, so must effect resurrection (18.4).

Both this and the preceding two arguments, then, argue from justice, but also use the rhetorical device of argument by definition. A human being is by definition both body and soul, destined by God's creation to be above the animals and to long for justice, so a human's very nature requires bodily resurrection, "a just appraiser does not assign the same destiny to beings whose nature is not the same" (*Res.* 10.4).

Resurrection as Symbol and Strategy

Examining Athenagoras' *Plea on Behalf of the Christians* and *On the Resurrection* through the lens of rhetorical criticism yields a picture of debates over bodily resurrection in his time, including arguments from pagans and other Christians. By this time, belief in resurrection is widely recognized as part of being a Christian. Although Athenagoras does not explicitly "read in" or "read out" of the community on the basis of belief in resurrection, he does so implicitly by linking belief in resurrection to Christian identity. In *Plea* he does not explain it to the emperor, nor make the case for its Christian provenance. Furthermore, belief in resurrection drew refutations and ridicule from the pagan world. Many of these are answered by Athenagoras' counter-arguments. For example, the argument that dissociates humans from other animals and extends resurrection to them alone is a response to the pagan argument that humans no more merit resurrection than animals. The claim that the nature of humanity is body and soul is a response to those who say the soul

alone is judged. Paradoxically, the quality and quantity of the arguments show that Christianity is being presented and taken seriously
as a philosophy, that it is in the process of "talking its way into
empire." By now, the fault lines over bodily resurrection within the
Christian community, visible as early as Paul and Justin, have deep-
ened. A set of arguments against resurrection have grown up around
the issue, so that Christians promoting resurrection need increasingly
sophisticated arguments to make their case.

In Athenagoras' thought, as for the rabbis, resurrection is a useful symbol, serving as shorthand for the same ideas: God's power,
ultimate justice, the unity of the human being, and the legitimacy
of those who hold it. It is elastic and abstract, even presentable to
a Stoic emperor. Athenagoras does not use the idea to draw boundaries, because they have already been drawn by others. In *Res.* he
frequently mentions "opponents" and "disputants" (4.4; 5.1; 8.2; 9.1),
saying those who argue against resurrection are ignorant of God's
power and wisdom (5.1). Anyone would agree with him "who is not
half-beast" (8.5). The opinions of unbelievers are absurd and false
(11.1) while those who share Christian faith, but reject resurrection,
ignore their own presuppositions (19.1–2). Clearly, Athenagoras faces
opposition from within and without.

In *Plea* the boundaries are also drawn by others. Athenagoras uses
resurrection differently here, defending Christians slandered by informers (31.1–2; 32.1) who accuse Christians of atheism, cannibalism, and
incest. Belief in resurrection provides proof that they are not guilty
of these charges, since fear of judgment motivates them to a disciplined, abstemious life (34.1–3) and certainly forbids cannibalism
(36.1) for how could one being destined to arise consume another
also destined to arise?

Athenagoras creates a liaison when he tries to incorporate Christians
on the same side as the emperor, the side of wisdom, "you whose
wisdom is greater than that of all the others" (31.3). Christians uphold
justice, and "the laws which you and your ancestors promulgated to
further every form of justice" (34.3). He dissociates the slanderers
from the emperor because they are adulterers, pederasts, and flouters
of justice, however, not only pagan disputants are a threat to the
community. So too are fellow Christians who disbelieve in bodily
resurrection. These people repudiate their own principles (19.1).
Following Christian faith to its logical conclusion necessitates belief
in resurrection.

In making his case to the larger society, Athenagoras emphasizes sameness, and for the moment ignores difference. He draws from the wells of Greco-Roman culture, creating liaisons between it and Christianity. He quotes Plato seven times, Homer eighteen times, and numerous other lines from Greek philosophy and literature. In *Plea* 31.4 he describes bodily resurrection in a way that makes it sound like spiritual immortality, where it partakes of the Stoic virtue of *apatheia* ". . . changeless and passionless in soul as though we were not flesh, though we have it . . ." He links Christians to the heroes of pagan culture, others who pursued virtue but were misunderstood, slandered by some, and rejected by the masses.

Similarly he creates a liaison between two different systems, God's revelation and the dispassionate search for truth in accord with nature. He invokes truth, saying "it is harmony with truth" to say "what is impossible with men is possible with God." He solves the problem of chain consumption using Galen's biology *and* belief in the providence of a powerful God. The body does not digest what is not its proper food (*Res.* 8.1–4) and God has not destined creatures to eat their own kind (*Res.* 5.1–2). The nature of humans created by God as rational beings requires they have a different end from other animals (*Res.* 13.2; 14.4; 24.2). Both God and nature are brought to bear in Athenagoras' argument.

Two pagans who attack Christian belief in resurrection provide a backdrop to Christian arguments. Celsus, writing around 177–180, is a staunch Platonist informed about Jews, Jewish complaints against Christianity, and several kinds of Christianity. Caecilius, whether a historical or fictional character, appears as the representative of intellectual paganism in Minucius Felix's early third century work, *Octavius*. Both pagan witnesses are positioned within Christian refutations of their ideas, testifying to the Christian desire to meet the pagan intellectual challenge directly.

Their objections to resurrection, which lock into their general slurs against Christianity, provide a mirror to Athenagoras and the Christian apologists. To summarize the anti-Christian complaints of these two pagan writers briefly:

1)   Christians are uneducated and lower-class. Resurrection is at worst, ridiculous, and at best, a misunderstanding of classical ideas (*Cels.* 7.28, 32). With their lack of education, Christians could not hope to follow the path of Plato or "men of intelligence" (*Cels.*

7.42–45). Caecilius similarly claims the Christians succeed with low-class illiterates and credulous women (*Oct.* 8.4; 13.4) and despite their lack of schooling, presume to hold forth on matters the philosophers still debate (*Oct.* 5.3–4; 12.7).

2)   Christians are anti-social, disrespectful of the government, customs, values of their society. Celsus links class, lack of education, and lack of patriotism. Their attachment to the body and expectation that it will be raised stems from their being a people "boorish and unclean, destitute of reason and suffer from the disease of sedition" (*Cels.* 8.49). If they enjoy the pleasures of this world, such as marriage and children, they should show honor and perform rites to the gods in charge of these things (*Cels.* 8.55). Similarly, Caecilius says they "spit upon the gods," "jeer at sacred rites" (*Oct.* 8.3–4), denying and mocking with false oaths the very gods that protect and aid the inhabitants of their cities (*Oct.* 8.4).

3)   Christians denigrate life in this world. They throw away the good life provided by traditional religion and the security of the empire, because they believe in the next world. Caecilius says "poor wretches, for whom there is no life hereafter, yet who live not for today" (*Oct.* 12.6). They "have no love for this life, " notes Celsus, "offering their bodies to be tortured and persecuted to no purpose" (*Cels.* 8.54).

4)   Christians are arrogant and immodest. Emblematic of Christian blindness to their own place in society is their blindness to their place in the universe. Visualizing a final conflagration, they assume that they alone will survive (*Cels.* 5.14). They rate themselves higher than the stars, exclaims Caecilius, pronouncing destruction for them, but "for themselves, creatures born to perish, the promise of eternity!" (*Oct.* 11.3).

5)   Resurrection belief offends reason and logic. Celsus, though he seems to believe in reward and punishment after death (*Cels.* 8.49), cannot stomach the idea of the return of the body. Who has ever returned from the dead (*Cels.* 2.55) and how could the body, once dissolved, return to its original state (*Cels.* 5.14)? Like Celsus, Caecilius asks for evidence of one person who has ever come back (*Oct.* 11.8).

6)   Resurrection contradicts God's power and dignity. Celsus' talk of God and what befits him is confusing only if we hold to an image

of all pagans as polytheists. Robert Wilken observed some years ago that many pagan intellectuals were monotheists.[26] A recent work argues that no sharp clash between pagan polytheists and Christian monotheists took place, but rather a widespread trend towards monotheism in late antiquity was shared by Christians and pagans.[27] God's power and dignity weigh against the possibility of resurrection, argue these two pagan writers. Since the nature of the flesh is impermanence, God could not raise up a dissolved body without violating reason and the laws of the universe, namely his own nature and laws. ". . . For he himself is the reason of everything that exists; therefore he is not able to do anything contrary to reason or to his own character" (*Cels.* 5.14). Caecilius puts forth the query as to why God allows suffering and injustice in this life but will raise up and reward the righteous in the next: "Where is the God who will succor you in the next life, but in this life cannot?" (*Oct.* 12.2–4).

7)   The flesh is impermanent and inferior. By nature bodies change over time and return to their original state. As matter, they cannot take on permanence (*Cels.* 4.60–61). Celsus does accept some kind of afterlife, but relies on the essential dichotomy of the body and soul, "the soul is God's work, but the nature of the body is different" (*Cels.* 4.58). The human being "is bound to the body, weighed down by the passions before being purified" (*Cels.* 8.53).

Pagan disgust at Christian preaching of resurrection of the body is propelled by a set of convictions about God as reason, and spirit, and by an attitude towards the body as inferior matter. Resurrection is just one of the more dramatic and disdainful examples of Christian credulity, ignorance, arrogance, and mistaken understandings of God and nature.

---

[26] Robert Wilken, *The Christians as the Pagans Saw Them* (New Haven: Yale, 1984) 106.

[27] Polymnia Athanassiadi and Michael Frede, *Pagan Monotheism in Late Antiquity* (Oxford: Clarendon, 1999). Frede cites Platonists, Peripatetics, and Stoics, who espouse the idea of one God who guides the universe, while accepting the existence of other gods and divine beings, "Monotheism and Pagan Philosophy in Later Antiquity," 41–67.

Conclusions

The rabbis and the Christian apologists differ considerably in their methods. The most glaring difference is in language. The rabbis choose to write in Hebrew, not Greek, as does the one clear example of Jewish apologetic, *Against Contra Apion*, or more general promotions of Judaism like Philo or *Joseph and Asenath*. The choice of Hebrew implies a text *primarily* aimed at insiders or people they hope will be insiders. The form the rabbis choose is legal, even if it is utterly unenforceable and utopian. There is little scope for flights on the glory of the body or God's dignity, although interestingly, the verse from Isa 60:21 cited in *m. San.* 10.1, which begins "All Israel" is about the wonder of God's creation. Any "heroes" the rabbis cite are representatives of the rabbinic-Pharisaic tradition. Athenagoras, on the other hand, writes in Greek, ably wielding the forms of Greco-Roman rhetoric. His heroes are the heroes of pagan tradition: Pythagoras, Socrates, Plato. He delicately avoids mentioning Jesus or the early Christian martyrs.

But the problems the tannaim and the apologists face are similar. Both are struggling to gain purchase in an unsympathetic, shifting environment. This image seems particularly apt if we take Seth Schwartz' book to heart about the essentially pagan environment the rabbis inhabit and their relative marginality. They live under the political umbrella of the Roman empire and therefore must compete with the pervasive prestige of Greco-Roman intellectual traditions.

Both use the strategy of dividing themselves from the vulgar masses. Athenagoras cleverly solves the problem of the intelligentsia's attacks on Christians by saying they must have been carried away by the masses. Anti-Epicurean polemic referred to Epicureans as vulgar and uncultured. Epicurus is called an ignoramus by some because he disdained the traditional curriculum, used his own style of Greek, and claimed to be self-taught. Epicureans are called vulgar by some because they are anti-social and anti-culture, even atheists with respect to local gods, coming in for the same censure as early Christians. Whether or not the charge of vulgarity is part of the freight that the rabbis put on the heavily-loaded word "Epicurean," it is quite clear that it stands for a fundamental ignorance about God and the nature of his workings in the world.

Both the rabbis and the apologists are writing for insiders, and also for people half-in and half-out of the community. No Gentile pagans are reading the Mishnah, but it partially has in view Jews drawn to Gentile pagan intellectualism. Witness the charge in *Avot*, "Know what to answer an Epicurean," not, as Goldin notes, "Beware" or "Avoid" the Epicurean.[28] Gentile pagans are probably not reading Athenagoras directly either, (except for the *Plea* directed to the emperor) but he is telling some Christians "know what to answer a resurrection denier."

Athenagoras and other Christian apologists are trying to deflect persecution. He answers outright three specific charges against Christians in *Plea*, answers others implicitly in *Plea* and *Res.* (for example, the charge that Christians are unlettered and ignorant he answers with his citation of pagan intellectual heroes and the use of rhetoric) and ignores others. He massages away the dissonance between Christians and the Empire by highlighting sameness.

Whether the rabbis felt physically endangered by the nearness of Epicureans, Torah-deniers and resurrection-deniers is less certain. In some circles, Epicureans are considered unsafe. But if Schwartz is right that the rabbis preside over a splintered Judaism and enjoy little intellectual prestige, the "Epicureans," represent primarily an ideological danger and threaten annihilation of rabbinic values, while holding considerable appeal as a cult of learners preaching a disciplined life. As such, the rabbis are confronted by sameness and similarity, and so highlight their core differences.

In both debates, belief in resurrection is a crucial piece of the argument. Certain values—God's power, ultimate justice, a correct understanding of Scripture, the legitimacy of the group that professes it, the unity of the human being—consistently adhere to it in a number of communities and literatures. Both groups are both talking their way into empire as well as holding empire at arm's length, the apologists doing more of the first and the rabbis doing more of the second. Both find the idea of resurrection useful as shorthand for their core values, and a touchstone for who is in and out of the community.[29]

---

[28] Goldin, "Tannaite Academy," 371.
[29] Thanks to Aryeh Cohen, Martin Goodman, Richard Kalmin, Seth Schwartz, and Burton Visotzky for providing bibliography and helping to clarify certain points.

JEWS AND JUDAISM IN THE MEDITERRANEAN DIASPORA IN THE LATE-ROMAN PERIOD: THE LIMITATIONS OF EVIDENCE

Martin Goodman*

Modern interpretations of the nature of Judaism in the Mediterranean diaspora in the late-Roman period have been based mainly on the evaluation of archeological and epigraphic data. Such interpretations are mostly quite possible, but all involve eisegesis and (often undeclared) assumptions which are here systematically questioned. In particular, evidence customarily used to reconstruct a picture of a liberal diaspora Judaism is scrutinized to see how much of it in fact may have been produced by pagan polytheists who revered the Jewish God. The evidence from Sardis is treated as a test case. In the final section a decrease in the variety within Judaism, and a decline in the numbers of pagan polytheists worshipping the Jewish God, are postulated for the period after 388 c.e., when Roman emperors began to attack pagan shrines and to give state support to the Jewish patriarchs.

No one doubts that the population of the Mediterranean core of the Roman Empire at its height, from the first to the fifth century c.e., contained a large proportion of Jews. Estimates of their number vary quite widely,[1] but that they constituted a group of sufficient size to exercise considerable influence over Mediterranean society is generally agreed. What elicits much less agreement is the nature of their Judaism in the centuries which followed the destruction of the Temple in Jerusalem by the Romans in 70 c.e.

It will be evident from the title of this article that I believe it to be helpful to study diaspora Judaism in this period separately from religion of Jews in the land of Israel. This separation is desirable despite the similar geographical and economic constraints on Jewish communities in all parts of the Mediterranean world, despite the

---

* University of Oxford.
[1] Cf. S. W. Baron, *A Social and Religious History of the Jews*, 2nd ed. (New York: Columbia University Press, 1952) vol. 1, 167–171, 370–372.

comparative ease of transport between such communities in the first
century c.e. because of the *pax Romana* and extensive inter-regional
trade,[2] and despite the common obeisance of all Mediterranean Jews
to the same Torah by which God bound Israel in covenant on
Mount Sinai.[3] Despite all this, the special role of Israel as a holy
land necessarily influenced religious behaviour, and may well have
caused the religious outlook of Jews who lived there to be different
from that of diaspora Jews. In Jews' religious geography, the centre
of the world, the core of purity, lay in the Holy of Holies in the
Temple in Jerusalem. The rest of the world was relegated to spheres
of decreasing purity in a series of concentric circles, from the Temple
to the city of Jerusalem to the boundaries of the land of Israel and
thence to the diaspora.[4]

The probability that diaspora Judaism in the Mediterranean world
differed from that of Jews in the homeland is strengthened by the
fact that most evidence about Judaism in this period happens to
derive either from the land of Israel or from the Jews of Mesopotamia
who, since they lived outside the Roman empire, had little contact
with the western diaspora. This same fact means that disagreement
about the nature of Judaism in the Mediterranean diaspora begins
from uncertainty about how much, if at all, to rely on the rabbinic
evidence from late antiquity: some scholars assume that all Jews followed rabbinic norms until proved otherwise, others that none did
until shown to have done so.[5]

Both views are possible, but I should confess that my own preference is for skepticism about the applicability of rabbinic evidence
outside the immediate circles for which it was composed.[6] The preser-

---

[2] Cf. K. Hopkins, "Taxes and trade in the Roman Empire (200 b.c.–a.d. 400),"
Journal of Roman Studies 70 (1980) 101–125.

[3] E. P. Sanders, *Paul and Palestinian Judaism: a Comparison of Patterns of Religion*,
(London: SCM, 1977); *Idem, Judaism: Practice and Belief: 63 b.c.e.–66 c.e.* (London:
SCM, 1992).

[4] Cf. M. Goodman, *The Ruling Class of Judaea: The Origins of the Jewish Revolt Against
Rome, a.d. 66–70* (Cambridge: Cambridge University Press, 1987) 106.

[5] Contrast the assumption by Schiffman, *Who was a Jew?* (New York: Ktav, 1985),
that rabbinic discussions in the land of Israel were capable of bringing about the
split between Judaism and Christianity to the assertion by Kraabel, "Impact of the
Discovery of the Sardis Synagogue" in *Sardis from Prehistoric to Roman Times*, ed.
G. M. A. Hanfmann (Cambridge, MA: Harvard University Press, 1983) 178–193,
that rabbis had no influence at all in Asia Minor.

[6] Cf. M. Goodman, *State and Society in Roman Galilee, a.d. 132–212* (Totowa, N.J.:
Rowman and Allanheld, 1983) 5–14.

vation of so much rabbinic literature by Jews of later generations encourages the impression that the rabbis predominated in Jewish society of the time when the literature was composed, but it is in principle not justified to take the survival of material as evidence of its original importance. Rabbinic texts from late antiquity are extant only because their contents interested enough Jews through the medieval to the early modern period for them to be continuously copied and eventually printed. In contrast, Jewish texts written in Greek were totally ignored by the later rabbinic tradition, which operated primarily in Hebrew and Aramaic. Thus it is entirely possible that diaspora Jews composed just as many literary works in Greek after 70 c.e. as before that date, but that all such literature has disappeared simply because the religious traditions which eventually triumphed had no interest in their preservation: on the one hand, the rabbis, who only preserved writing in Semitic languages, and on the other, the Christian Church, which treasured and appropriated Jewish texts written in Greek before c. 100 c.e. but which treated later Jewish compositions as the product of an alien faith.[7]

The possibility of a misleading bias in the preservation of the evidence is not the only factor which complicates the use of rabbinic texts. The rabbis took it for granted that their view of the world was normative for all Israel, but such a view can quite well persist regardless of reality. It is entirely possible, even if in the final analysis unprovable, that, even within the communities in which they operated, the rabbis were sometimes met with indifference.[8] If rabbinic literature can be used only with care to reconstruct the religious outlook of Jews in the land of Israel where it was composed, it will be all the more difficult to use it to understand the Judaism of Alexandria, Antioch, Sardis, Rome.

For some scholars the non-rabbinic nature of (some) diaspora Judaism in late antiquity is simply taken for granted,[9] and over the past few decades many attempts have been made to construct a picture of an alternative Judaism based on different kinds of evidence.[10] Such

---

[7] Cf. G. Vermes and M. Goodman, "La littérature juive intertestamentaire à la lumière d'un siècle de recherches et de découvertes" in *Etudes sur le Judaisme Hellénistique*, eds. R. Kuntzmann and J. Schlosser (Paris: Editions du CERF, 1984) 19–39.

[8] M. Goodman, *State and Society in Roman Galilee*, 93–111.

[9] E.g. A. T. Kraabel, "Impact of the Discovery of the Sardis Synagogue," 178.

[10] E.g. E. R. Goodenough, *Jewish Symbols in the Greco-Roman Period*, 13 vols. (Princeton: Princeton University Press, 1953–1968); Kraabel, *idem*, 188–90.

attempts are encouraged by the abundance of non-rabbinic material found in the diaspora. So, for instance, in the corpus of Jewish
inscriptions from the diaspora the proportional increase in documents
dated after 70 c.e. is quite striking,[11] and not simply part of any
general increase in epigraphic evidence in the late-Roman period.
Archeological evidence is similarly much more abundant than in earlier times, especially from excavations of buildings at Dura-Europos,
Sardis and elsewhere, and from investigation of Jewish catacombs at
Rome.[12] These material remains are supplemented by a considerable corpus of comments about Jews by pagan and (more especially)
Christian writers.[13] Of these, the most illuminating are often the
Roman laws about Jews, which repay close study.[14]

This non-rabbinic evidence has been used in the past to produce
dramatically disparate pictures of diaspora Judaism. In earlier generations the standard stereotype, molded perhaps by a Christian perspective and the assumption that right-thinking Jews ought really to
have joined the Church, portrayed diaspora Judaism as the religion
of small, embattled groups who adopted syncretistic ideas in order
to ingratiate themselves with their gentile neighbours.[15] A more recent
stereotype reverses many of these judgments. It is now commonly
claimed that diaspora Judaism was the religion of prosperous, self-
confident, outgoing people, who were fully accepted as Jews by their
gentile neighbours, unconcerned by surrounding idolatry, uninclined
to syncretise, and keen to proselytise.[16]

It is worth stressing that this revised picture is almost entirely, and
quite overtly, dependent on analysis of archeological evidence and

[11] J.B. Frey, *Corpus Inscriptionum Judaicarum* (vol. 1 rev. New York: Ktav, 1975;
vol. 2 Rome: Pointifico Istituto di archaeologia christiana, 1936).

[12] E. Schürer, *The History of the Jewish People in the Age of Jesus Christ*, vol. 3.1, rev.
and eds. G. Vermes, F. Millar and M. Goodman (Edinburgh: T. and T. Clark,
1986) 1–176.

[13] M. Stern, *Greek and Latin Authors on Jews and Judaism*, 3 vols. (Jerusalem: Israel
Academy of the Sciences, 1974–86); J. Juster, *Les Juifs dans l'Empire romain: leur condition juridique, économique et sociale*, 2 vols. (Paris: Geuthner, 1914) 1: 43–76.

[14] A. Linder, *The Jews in Roman Imperial Legislation* (Detroit: Wayne State University,
1987).

[15] Cf. the critique in A. T. Kraabel, "The Disappearance of the 'God-Fearer,'"
Numen 28: 113–126 (1982).

[16] P. R. Trebilco, *Jewish Communities in Asia Minor* (Cambridge: Cambridge University
Press, 1991).

inscriptions, and especially the material from Sardis.[17] It is claimed, for instance, that the size of the Sardis synagogue, its position at the centre of the city, and the presence in it of inscriptions set up by gentile Godworshippers show the important role of Jews in the civic community and the acceptance of that role by their gentile neighbours.[18] Such an interpretation is of course possible, but it is hardly necessary. The great synagogue of Alexandria was also huge, according to Tosefta Sukkah 4:6, but this fact can hardly have signified good relations with the local Greeks since the Jews and Greeks of Alexandria were more of less openly hostile to each other throughout the first and early second centuries C.E.[19] It is quite possible that in both Alexandria and Sardis the erection of a large, prominent synagogue may have signified bravado by an embattled minority in a hostile environment. Similarly, gentile Godworshippers who gave money to Jewish institutions may have done so for a variety of reasons, without approving of either Judaism or Jews: so, for instance, if Jews were indeed rich and powerful, it might have seemed sensible for a gentile politician to donate money to their synagogue, regardless of his real view about them or their religion.[20] From the point of view of a polytheist, the term *theosebes* ("God-worshipper") was sufficiently anodyne for any pagan to accept it as a title.

I raise these other possible interpretations not to advocate them but simply to show the vulnerability of archeological and epigraphic material of this kind to imaginative exegesis. In the rest of this paper I intend to sketch more fully the limitations of the evidence for Judaism in the Mediterranean diaspora in the period, with an epilogue to suggest why and how the radical uncertainty which I shall advocate in interpreting the remains from earlier periods may be inappropriate in the fifth century C.E. and after.

Radical uncertainty in interpreting Jewish-type material down to c. 390 C.E. is based on two factors which in principle bear no relation to each other. First, there may have been much variety within

---

[17] Kraabel, "The Disappearance of the 'God-Fearer'"; *Idem*, "Impact of the Discovery of the Sardis Synagogue."

[18] Trebilco, *Jewish Communities in Asia Minor*, 57.

[19] V. A. Tcherikover, A. Fuks and M. Stern, *Corpus Papyrorum Judaicarum*, 3 vols. (Cambridge, MA: Harvard University Press, 1957–64) 1: 48–93.

[20] J. Murphy-O'Connor, "Lots of God-Fearers? 'Theosebeis' in the Aphrodisias Inscription," *Revue Biblique* 99/2 (1992) 418–424.

diaspora Judaism, to the extent that it may be more accurate to talk of Judaisms in the plural.[21] Second, and even allowing for great variety and for different definitions of who was a Jew, some material commonly ascribed to Jews and Judaism may not reflect Jews of any kind, by any definition in antiquity or today. The first issue has been much discussed, and I shall consider it here only briefly. The second issue, which I believe is undeservedly overlooked in much of the scholarly literature, I shall tackle at greater length.

Variety in Diaspora Judaism

Any individual type of Judaism consists of a single religious system, encompassing most aspects of life. Unlike most other ancient cults, Judaism could be contrasted in antiquity not just to other religions but to other cultures in the broad sense: the first use of the term *ioudaismos* (2 Macc. 2:21) specifically compared Judaism to Hellenism, and both gentile and Jewish Greek writers sometimes described the Jewish way of life as a philosophy.[22] Thus, when they viewed their own lifestyles from within their systems, Jewish writers tended to assume that there was only one Judaism. So, for example, to the rabbis Jewish identity was defined in rabbinic terms, in what Sacha Stern has described as a solipsistic sense of Jewishness, to the extent that only adult male rabbinic Jews were thought of as fully part of Israel, and the Judaism of women and children, let alone proselytes and slaves, was left ill-defined.[23]

It is notoriously unwise to rely on a group's self-depiction to produce an accurate picture of that group, but in the study of the late-antique diaspora the non-Jewish evidence, plentiful though it is, is not entirely helpful in balancing out the picture. Greek and Latin pagans after the early second century c.e. seem largely to have fallen into literary clichés when writing about Jews,[24] and little that they

---

[21] Cf. for the first century, J. Neusner, W. S. Green and E. S. Frerichs, *Judaisms and their Messiahs* (Cambridge: Cambridge University Press, 1987).

[22] J. G. Gager, *The Origins of Anti-Semitism: Attitudes Towards Judaism in Pagan and Christian Antiquity* (New York and Oxford: Oxford University Press, 1983).

[23] "Jewish Identity in Early Rabbinic Writings," Unpublished D. Phil. Thesis, Oxford University.

[24] Stern, *Greek and Latin Authors on Jews and Judaism, idem* M. Stern, "The Jews in Greek and Latin Literature" in *The Jewish People in the First Century*, eds. S. Safrai and M. Stern (Assen: Van Gorcum, 1976) vol. 2, 1101–1159.

wrote sheds any light on the Jews of their own day; in any case, they lacked any interest in differentiating between one sort of Jew and another, simply lumping them all together as one despicable *supersitio*.[25]

The evidence of Christian authors about Jews is almost equally unsatisfactory, but for rather different reasons.[26] In the early Church the term "Jew" was generally applied to one of three groups: either to the Israel of the Old Testament (usually on occasions when they disobeyed divine commands, since the positive aspects of Israel's heritage were appropriated by the Christians themselves);[27] or to the Pharisees who opposed Jesus according to the Gospels' narrative, with whom Jews as a whole were often identified;[28] or to Christian literalists, since in the internal debate within the early Church about the correct way to interpret the Old Testament, those who took the biblical commands to apply to themselves were readily attacked by their opponents as Jews.[29] Since in all these cases the terms "Jews" and "Judaism" were more or less terms of abuse, there was no incentive to distinguish between one kind of Jew and another. Those Christians like Hippolytus (c. 170–c. 236 C.E.) who referred to the different sects of Judaism culled their information from earlier sources, which normally described the Judaism of the land of Israel before 70 C.E.[30]

But despite this lack of direct evidence for diversity in the Judaism of the late-Roman diaspora, there remain good grounds for believing variety to be probable. First is the direct evidence of Josephus that one and the same individual could claim the perfect unity of Judaism while also being aware of considerable variety. Thus Josephus

---

[25] Cf. Tacitus, *Hist.* 5.8.2–3; *Ann.* 2.85.

[26] Cf. in general M. Taylor, "The Jews in the Writings of the Early Church Fathers (150–312): Men of Straw or Formidable Rivals?" Unpublished D. Phil. Thesis, Oxford University, 1992.

[27] Cf. M. Simon, *Verus Israel: A Study of the Relations Between Christians and Jews in the Roman Empire* (135–425) (Oxford: Littman Library, 1986).

[28] R. Reuther, *Faith and Fratricide: the theological roots of anti-semitism* (New York: Seabury Press, 1974).

[29] D. P. Efroymson, "Tertullian's Anti-Judaism and its role in his theology," Unpublished PhD Thesis, Temple University, 1976.

[30] Miriam Taylor, "The Jews in the Writings of the Early Church Fathers (150–312)," points out that Simon, *Verus Israel*, may be wrong to assume that because Christian writers came up against real Jews, they therefore described them as they really were. It is almost as easy to impose a stereotype on real people as on imaginary ones.

wrote in *Contra Apionem* 2. 179–180, a work composed in Rome in the nineties C.E., that one remarkable fact about Jews was their unity on all matters of theology and worship: one God, one Law, one Temple. Nor was this a passing remark, since Jewish unity constituted an important element of his proof in *Contra Apionem* of the superiority of Jews over Greeks, whose cults, myths and beliefs he characterized as hopelessly jumbled. But the same Josephus could write in three other works about the three (or sometimes four) distinctive philosophies of the Jews (Pharisees, Sadducees, Essenes, and the "Fourth Philosophy"), whose tenets he was at pains to delineate.[31] It appears that for Josephus these two opinions, which he proffered as part of two different arguments, were quite easily correlated. Variety within Judaism presumably lay in his eyes on a different level from its unity: all Jews accepted the one Torah, even if they disagreed about its significance.

If someone like Josephus could write about diversity within Judaism in his histories of the land of Israel before 70 C.E., it is clearly at least possible that such diversity continued in the late-Roman diaspora. When Josephus was writing he was living in the diaspora in Rome and after the destruction of the Jerusalem Temple, but he wrote about the varied philosophies of Judaism not as a past but as a present fact. The factors which had encouraged a diaspora Jew in the mid-first century like Philo of Alexandria to evolve his curious blend of Platonic philosophy and allegorical exegesis of the Bible[32] were just as potent after the destruction of the Temple as before; indeed, since Philonic types of theology were to become popular among some Christians during the late-Roman period, it was evidently possible for Jews also to continue thinking in such ways.

So far as is known, no authority existed within diaspora Judaism to impose rules of practice and belief. Such a role has often been claimed for the rabbinic patriarch (*nasi*) in the land of Israel whose formal jurisdiction under the auspices of the state over Jews throughout the Roman empire I shall discuss in the epilogue (below).[33] But

---

[31] *B.J.* 2. 119–166; *A.J.* 18. 11–25, *Vita* 10 12.

[32] Cf. S. Sandmel, *Philo of Alexandria: An Introduction* (New York: Oxford University Press, 1979).

[33] Cf. L. I. Levine, "The Jewish Patriarch (*Nasi*) in third century Palestine," *Aufstieg und Niedergang der römischen Welt* 19/2 (1979) 649–88.

I believe not only that the evidence that he has any such authority before the late fourth century is not compelling,[34] but also that there are positive reasons to deny that he had such a role at any earlier date: first, it was contrary to normal Roman practice in the high empire for a single spokesman to be appointed or recognized either for an ethnic group such as Spaniards or Gauls, or for a religious movement such as Mithraists or Isiacs; secondly, the fact that the third-century Christian writer Origen referred to the *nasi* by the title "ethnarch,"[35] whereas fourth-century Roman sources consistently call him "patriarch," suggests that the *nasi* in his time was not a Roman official at all, since the Roman state was normally very careful and precise in the conferring of titles.[36]

If there was no authority to impose uniformity, there was also no incentive to suppress variety. Opinions might vary wildly between one community and another on crucial questions of Jewish status such as the validity of conversions and the status of the offspring of mixed marriages,[37] let alone less public aspects of Judaism, from domestic liturgy and behaviour to philosophical speculation on the hidden meanings of Torah. After 70 C.E. there did not even exist any more the Temple as the symbolic focus of unity to which all Jews could show their solidarity by contributing their annual offerings, as the Jews of Asia Minor had done in the mid first century B.C.E.[38] Nor was there any more a high priest to act as ruler and leader of the nation, as Josephus had claimed he should.[39]

It would be reasonable to expect Judaism in the Mediterranean diaspora to have become more varied after 70 C.E., not less.

---

[34] The only extant inscription from the diaspora which may show the rabbinic patriarch exercising some authority in the diaspora is a text from Stobi in Macedonia, of the second or third century C.E. Cf. M. Hengel, "Die Synagogeninschrift von Stobi," *Zeitschrift für die Neutestamentliche Wissenschaft* 57 (1966) 145–83, but the huge fine payable to the patriarch according to the inscription would have been unenforceable (cf. Schürer, *History of the Jewish People in the Time of Jesus Christ*, 67).

[35] *Ep. Ad Africanum* 20 (14).

[36] Cf. M. Goodman, "The Roman State and the Jewish Patriarch in the Third Century" in *Galilee in Late Antiquity*, ed. L. I. Levine (New York: Jewish Theological Seminary, 1992) 127–139.

[37] Cf. M. Goodman, "Identity and Authority in Ancient Judaism" *Judaism* 39 (1990) 192–201.

[38] Cf. Cicero. *Flac.* 66.

[39] *C. Ap.* 2.193–194; cf. *A.J.* 20.251.

Jews, non-Jews and "Jewish" evidence

Whatever their divergences, one common denominator for all Jews was that each thought of himself or herself as belonging within a system defined as Judaism. Outsiders may have been uncertain whether any particular individual should be considered a Jew, but the individual himself would always know whether he was bound by the covenant between God and Israel.

This was not just a matter of theological logic. I have argued in detail elsewhere[40] that when the emperor Nerva in 96 C.E. reformed the collection of the *fiscus Judaicus*, the special poll tax imposed by the Roman state on all Jews within the empire after the Judean revolt of 66–70 C.E., he exempted Jewish apostates, thereby ensuring that the selection of those liable to the tax should be by religious self-definition: those who professed Judaism (whether native-born or proselytes) were required to pay two dinarii a year towards the temple of Jupiter on the Capitol in Rome. In return for this tax, self-professed Jews were exempted from the normal requirement to take part in the pagan ceremonials of the state.

If this theory is correct, in practice any Jew will have been quite clear about the distinction between himself and the gentiles. Conversely, non-Jews who were interested in worshipping the Jewish God would be entirely clear that their devotion to this divinity did not in itself make them into Jews unless they also wished to embrace the (or a) whole system of Judaism (including exclusive monotheism) and, as a corollary, to pay the *fiscus Judaicus* to Rome.

The best evidence up to now that some polytheistic gentiles were indeed interested in worshipping the Jewish God has emerged only comparatively recently, with the publication in 1987 of a long inscription from Aphrodisias in Caria, in modern Turkey.[41] This inscription, tentatively dated by its editors to the early third century C.E.,[42] contains a long list of names of donors to a Jewish institution whose precise nature is obscure. The names on side A and at the top of side B of the list are most distinctively Jewish and include three indi-

---

[40] M. Goodman, "Nerva, the *fiscus Judaicus* and Jewish identity" *Journal of Roman Studies* 79 (1989) 40–44.

[41] J. Reynolds and R. Tannenbaum, *Jews and God-Fearers at Aphrodisias*, Cambridge Philological Society, supplementary volume, 7 (Cambridge: Cambridge Philological Society, 1987).

[42] Ibid., 19–22.

viduals specifically designated as *proselytos*.[43] In contrast, on side B, under a separate heading entitled "and these [are] the god-reverers,"[44] are found fifty-three non-Jewish names, of whom the first nine are described as *bouleutes*, city councillor.[45]

It is clear that these latter individuals were gentiles honoured by the Jewish community in Aphrodisias. It is likely that they were polytheists, since all city councillors could normally expect to take part in civic cults, unless, like Jews, they were specifically exempt.[46] It is also likely that the appearance of their names on the list reflected their interest in Judaism and not just in Jews in their locality: the inscription starts with an invocation to the helping God (*theos boethos*),[47] and their designation as "God-reverers" (*theosebeis*) suggests that they were devoted in some way to the Jewish God.

Over the past twenty years or so the problem of these pious gentiles, usually designated as "Godfearers"[48] has attracted a huge literature,[49] but I believe that more can and should be said. Most scholars have been primarily interested in the role of Godfearers in the Acts of the Apostles as the recipients of Christian mission in the interlude between the rejection of the Gospel by the Jews and the full-blooded mission to the gentiles.[50] The scholars who have approached the topic primarily through the epigraphic evidence, including the Aphrodisias inscription, have tended to portray such gentiles from the Jewish point of view, describing them as on the fringes of Judaism, "of but not in."[51]

I do not doubt that ancient Christians and Jews may indeed have taken such a view of gentiles, but I wonder whether these depictions also reflect the self-perception of the gentiles themselves. City councillors in Aphrodisias who became Godfearers did so voluntarily, presumably because they found religious meaning in the act. They could have become full proselytes and part of the covenant if they had wanted to do so, as the open designation of individuals as proselytes

[43] A, lines 13, 17, 22.
[44] B, line 34.
[45] B, lines 34–38.
[46] Cf. Reynolds and Tannenbaum, *Jews and God-Fearers at Aphrodisias*, 58.
[47] A, line 1.
[48] Cf. Acts of the Apostles 10:2, 22; 13:16, 26.
[49] E.g. F. Siegert, "Gottesfürchtigen und Sympathisanten" *Journal for the Study of Judaism* 4 (1973) 109–64.
[50] Cf. critique by Kraabel, "The Disappearance of the 'God-Fearer'".
[51] Reynolds and Tannenbaum, *Jews and God-Fearers at Aphrodisias*, 88.

at Aphrodisias shows,[52] but since they chose not to, it may be that worshipping the Jewish God as a gentile had a meaning for them as polytheists quite different from that experienced by those who entered the exclusive covenant of Judaism.

For a pagan polytheist there were many reasons to worship the Jewish God. The main reasons, as with any deity, lay in his power: he was the Lord of the Universe, the highest god (*theos hypsistos*).[53] A deity's power could be divined from his activity in the world: as Josephus put it, in a curious reversal of the arguments of later theologians, only God could have created the irregularities of the heavenly bodies.[54] The aura of the divinity was not necessarily diminished by the destruction of the Jerusalem Temple in 70 C.E., for pagans could presumably accept (if they wished to) the claim addressed to them by Josephus that the outcome of the Jewish revolt had been God's will,[55] since it was through God's support alone that the Romans held their empire.[56] The lack of a single cult centre might even have been a positive attraction to polytheists, who devoted themselves in increasing numbers in the high Roman empire to divinities such as Isis, Mithras or Jupiter Dolichenus, who had been displaced from their actual or alleged place of origin;[57] it may be that lack of local roots made more plausible each god's claims to universal significance. It is likely also that knowledge of the existence of Jewish communities throughout much of the Empire, full of initiates devoted to God to such an extent that his laws shaped their entire lives, would encourage interested polytheists to believe that this must be a divinity worth cultivation. Large public temples dedicated by non-initiates to divinities like Isis to whom initiates were also known to be devoted are found in many cities in the Roman empire.[58]

How would such a polytheist convinced of God's power normally be expected to worship? It can be said immediately that it would not be at all obvious to carry out part, but not all, of the lifestyle of a full Jewish initiate, as in the standard picture of Godfearers as

---

[52] If there was indeed a prohibition by the Roman state on conversion to Judaism, it seems to have been blatantly ignored by some, cf. Ibid., 43–44.

[53] Cf. Trebilco, *Jewish Communities in Asia Minor*, 127–44, 163 64.

[54] *A.J.* 1.155–156.

[55] Cf. *B.J.* 6.250.

[56] *B.J.* 2.390.

[57] Cf. M. J. Vermaseren, *Mithras, the Secret God* (London: Chatto and Windus, 1963).

[58] Cf. R. E. Witt, *Isis in the Graeco-Roman World* (London: Thames and Hudson, 1971).

gentiles who chose to follow an arbitrary selection of some of the injunctions of the Torah.[59] Of course, a polytheist *might* behave in such a way, perhaps keeping the sabbath but not the dietary laws or the requirement to circumcise sons,[60] but if such behaviour was intended to mark devotion to the Jewish God, rather than just imitation of attractive Jewish customs, it suggests an individual on the way to becoming a Jew[61] rather than a pagan polytheist simply honouring a powerful divinity. At any rate, for most pagans there might seem to be no religious advantage in listening to synagogue services run by Jews: they might hope to derive some philosophical insights from readings from the Bible,[62] but it would not be very uplifting to listen to catalogues of legal injunctions which, as non-Jews, they believed did not apply to them.

The standard way for ancient polytheists to worship a divinity was through offerings on altars. This form of worship, hallowed by antiquity, was still widespread and popular in the second and third centuries C.E., as numerous inscriptions attest.[63] Among such inscriptions are some which are more plausibly ascribed to gentiles devoted to the Jewish God. An inscription on a small altar from Pamphylia dated to the first or second century C.E. and published in 1992 reads: "For the truthful god who is not made with hands (in fulfillment of) a vow;[64] since the most striking aspect of the Jewish God in the eyes of outsiders was the remarkable fact that he has no image, it is most likely that the inscription was addressed to him. Similarly, an altar of the second century C.E. from Pergamon, with an inscription which reads at the top: "God, Lord, who is One for ever," and on the bottom: "Zopyros [dedicated] to the Lord the altar and the support with the lamp," is most plausibly ascribed to a pagan worshipper of the Jewish God.[65]

---

[59] E.g. Siegert, "Gottesfürchtigen und Sympathisanten"; Reynolds and Tannenbaum, *Jews and God-Fearers at Aphrodisias*, 65.

[60] Cf. Juvenal, *Satires* 14. 96–99.

[61] Cf. Juvenal, *Satires* 14. 96–106.

[62] Cf. J. G. Gager, *The Origins of Anti-Semitism*, 75–76.

[63] R. Lane Fox, *Pagans and Christians in the Mediterranean World from the Second Century* A.D. *to the Conversion of Constantine* (Harmondsworth: Viking, 1986) 69–72.

[64] P. W. van der Horst, "A New Altar of a Godfearer," *JJS* 43 (1992) 32–37.

[65] B. Lifshitz, *Donateurs et fondateurs dans les synagogues juives*, Cahiers de la Revue Biblique, supplementary volume 7 (Paris: Gabalda, 1967) no. 12; cf. E. Bickerman, "The Altars of Gentiles" in *idem, Studies in Jewish and Christian History*, part 2 (Leiden: Brill, 1980) 341–42.

The general attitude of Jews to such gentiles' worship can only be suggested through the logic of a somewhat complex argument, as follows. There is good evidence in Palestinian rabbinic texts, from the Tosefta[66] and Sifra,[67] both probably redacted in the third century C.E., to the Jerusalem Talmud,[68] redacted probably in the late fourth century, that some rabbis sometimes assumed that gentiles (unlike Jews) were permitted to make offerings to God outside Jerusalem; the debate in the Jerusalem Talmud text was only over whether Jews should allow themselves to help gentiles to do this. Such approval by rabbis quoted in these texts is particularly significant because in these same texts can also be found strong disapproval of gentiles' worship of other gods; the prohibition of alien worship (*avodah zarah*) was a consistent element in the so-called Noachide laws considered by the rabbis to be incumbent on all humans, gentiles as much as Jews, and first attested in the Tosefta.[69] Unlike these rabbis, some Jews in the diaspora apparently did not object to the pagan practices of gentile God-worshippers, for they honoured gentile city-councillors who almost certainly took part in civic cults,[70] so it will have been comparatively easy for them to accept the much less obviously objectionable practices of gentiles who made offerings not to idols but to the Jewish God.

If gentiles did regularly make such offerings, what would one expect the archeological evidence to look like from the buildings in which they worshipped? First, and most obvious, there could be no cult statue: pagans knew that what distinguished the Jewish God from other deities was the lack of any image.[71] To indicate the Jewishness of the divinity, therefore, one might expect characteristic Jewish iconography on mosaics or wall paintings: as the reliefs on the Arch of Titus in Rome demonstrate, pagans were aware of such Jewish images as the candelabra (*menorah*) and incense shovels of the Jerusalem Temple. One might also expect to find in the shrines of such gentiles fragments of Hebrew words and letters, since, regardless of its

---

[66] *Zevakhim* 13:1, which refers even to Samaritans.
[67] 83c., ed. Weiss.
[68] *y. Megillah* 1.13, 72b (ed. Krotoschin).
[69] *Avodah Zarah* 8:4; cf. D. Novak, *The Image of the Non-Jew in Judaism: A Historical and Constructive Study of the Noachide Laws* (New York and Toronto: Edwin Mellen, 1983) 3–4, 107–48.
[70] See sup.
[71] Cf. Varro, *apud* Augustine, *De Civitate Dei* 4.31.

incomprehensibility, the divinity's special language might be thought to have an intrinsic power, as can be seen from the use of Hebrew in non-Jewish magical papyri. In all other respects the building might be expected to look like any other pagan temple—a fact, however, of dubious advantage in identification, since such temples varied greatly in plan from one place to another and from one shrine to another.

Such gentile worshippers would not necessarily have any collective name for themselves, any more than (for example) worshippers of Apollo or Jupiter Dolichenus did. Since they were not Jews (or, as they might think of it, 'initiates of the Jewish God'), their worship of the divinity formed only one part of their religious lives, let alone their political and social identity; Jews, Christians, Mithraists and Isiaci were unusual in ancient religious history in their adoption of a group name to describe themselves.[72] Nor did such gentiles necessarily espouse common myths or uniform rituals: each shrine might quite well follow its own local rules, as was common in ancient paganism.[73]

This variation and anonymity will, of course, make such gentiles difficult to identify in the surviving evidence from late antiquity. Nonetheless, it is not just an entirely theoretical hypothesis that such people may have existed, nor that they may have set up altars and special buildings.

In 407 C.E. the emperors Theodosius, Arcadius and Honourius issued a law against a 'new crime of superstition', which has 'claimed the unheard name of heaven-worshippers (*caelicolae*),'[74] ordering that their buildings (*aedificia*), 'which contain meetings of some new dogma,' should be vindicated to the churches, i.e. confiscated.[75] The evidence about the *caelicolae*, found in this law, in another similar law issued in 409 C.E., and in a few remarks by Latin patristic writers,[76] is

---

[72] Cf. J. A. North, "The Development of Religious Pluralism" in *The Jews among Pagans and Christians in the Roman Empire*, eds. J. Lieu, J. North and T. Rajak (London: Routledge, 1992) 174–93.

[73] Cf. Lane Fox, *Pagans and Christians in the Mediterranean World*, 64–101.

[74] The assertion by the emperor in each reference to the *caelicolae* that he has never heard of them before (cf. Linder, *The Jews in Roman Imperial Legislation*, 256) may show only his ignorance or their adoption of a new name, and not necessarily that they were a new religious phenomenon.

[75] *Codex Justinianus* 1.9.12.

[76] Cf. Juster, *Les Juifs dans l'Empire romain*, vol. 1, 175, n. 3.

strangely ignored in the standard modern discussions of Godfearers,[77] but it seems very likely that the term describes individuals of the same type as those called *theosebeis* ("God-worshippers") in Greek. In the law of 409 C.E. the emperors moved straight from condemning the *caelicolae* to condemning those who dare to convert Christians to Judaism.[78] The *caelicolae* were included in the heading of a title of the Theodosian Code along with Jews and Samaritans; despite this link with Jews, they seem to have been pagan polytheists.[79] The term *caelicolae* ("heaven-worshippers") seems to be a direct analogue to the Hebrew *yir'ei shamayim* ("heaven-fearers") used in rabbinic texts of the third to fifth century C.E. to refer to gentiles who respect the Jewish God.[80] At any rate, if the *caelicolae* were indeed pagans who revered the Jewish God, the most significant datum to emerge from the Roman legal texts is the fact that they possessed buildings for worship,[81] in which case modern scholars might be thought to have every reason to hunt for evidence of such buildings in the archeological remains of the late-Roman period.

It is time to make explicit the relevance of such questions to the study of Jews and Judaism in the late-Roman diaspora. How much evidence customarily ascribed by scholars to Jews and used to reconstruct "Judaisms" might actually reflect gentiles of the kind, who may have worshipped the Jewish God without any contact at all with Jews? I stress the word "might." My aim is not to estimate the most

---

[77] E.g. Siegert, "Gottesfürchtigen und Sympathisanten;" contrast Linder, *The Jews in Roman Imperial Legislation.*

[78] *Codex Theodosianus* 16.8.19.

[79] Linder (*The Jews in Roman Imperial Legislation I*, 257) takes the *caelicolae* to be Christian renegades, oddly translating "*nisi ad . . . venerationem . . . Christianam conversi fuerint*" as "unless they *return* to . . . the Christian veneration." This interpretation seems to go back to Juster (*Les Juifs dans l'Empire romain*, vol. 1, 175, n. 3). Juster was (rightly) keen to counter claims by previous scholars that *caelicolae* were Jews, but he did so by a misinterpretation of *Codex Theodosianus* 16.5.43. He took *quamvis Christianos esse se simulent* ("although they pretend that they are Christians") at the end of that decree to refer to all previously mentioned groups, which included the *caelicolae*. But this is not plausible, since another group mentioned previously in the same law were the *gentiles* ("pagans"), who by definition did not claim to be Christian. The words at the end of the decree ("pretend to be Christians") most obviously refer to the group mentioned in the final sentence of the law, immediately preceding this phrase—that is, the Donatists, who were indeed a Christian heresy. The Christian writer Philastrius (*Haer.* 15, CSEL 38, 6–7) thought that the *caelicolae* were Jews, who worshipped with sacrifices the goddess Caelestis, who personified the heavens.

[80] Reynolds and Tannenbaum, *Jews and God-Fearers at Aphrodisias*, 52–53.

[81] *Codex Theodosianus* 16.8.19.

plausible explanation of the surviving archeological and epigraphic evidence, but to illustrate the fragility of the scholarly assumptions which lie behind attempts to describe diaspora Judaism in the Mediterranean region. I shall concentrate on just one, celebrated, case study: the late-Roman "synagogue" at Sardis.

POSSIBLE RE-INTERPRETATIONS OF THE EVIDENCE

It will be recalled that the modern re-evaluation of diaspora, and especially Asia Minor, Judaism has been based to a considerable extent on the alleged implications of the huge building at Sardis which the excavators identified as a synagogue (see above). The building is a large basilica built originally in the early Roman period as part of the gymnasium complex in the centre of the city. The basilica was identified as a synagogue in its later phases on account of the discovery of fragmentary Hebrew inscriptions and the iconography of its decoration.[82] Numerous mosaic depictions of candelabra (*menorot*) were discovered, and fragments of one actual, stone *menorah*. The mosaics included pictures of a ram's horn (*shofar*) and other objects which have been discovered in a number of synagogue sites in the land of Israel.[83] There were also two small fragments of Hebrew inscriptions, one beyond clear decipherment, one reading *shalom* ("peace").

Since the building has been firmly decreed by the excavators in 1962 to be a synagogue on the basis of these finds, when the first inscriptions came to be published in 1964 the framework was already taken for granted.[84] The mosaic inscription of a certain Aurelius Olympios from the tribe of the Leontii,[85] unique among Jewish inscriptions according to its editor,[86] was nonetheless presumed to be Jewish simply because is was known to come from what was believe to be a synagogue. A rough graffito incised on the neck of a jar found in a shop outside the building to the south, with the name "Jacob"

---

[82] Cf. D. G. Mitten, "The Synagogue" in Report of the Fifth Campaign at Sardis (1962), *Bulletin of the American Schools of Oriental Research* 179 (1963) 40.

[83] L. I. Levine, *The Synagogue in Late Antiquity* (Philadelphia: American Schools of Oriental Research, 1987) 185.

[84] L. Robert, *Nouvelles inscriptions de Sardes* (Paris: Librarie d'Amérique et d'Orient, 1964) 37.

[85] Ibid., no. 6.

[86] Ibid., 46.

and four other letters (πρου), was reconstructed to read "Jacob the elder" and ascribed to a "councillor of the Jewish community" mainly because a Jewish community could be expected to have such officials and because a shop next to a prominent Jewish public building was likely to be owned by a Jew.[87]

All such interpretations may be entirely correct, but it may be worthwhile to consider briefly other, quite different, ways of explaining the same evidence. What factors might encourage the belief that the Sardis building might not have been a Jewish synagogue at all, but might rather have housed a cult of gentile, polytheist God-worshippers?

Negative reasons to suggest that the building might not have been a synagogue are easily enumerated. First, it is many times bigger than any other synagogue yet identified.[88] Secondly, its size might seem to militate against its usefulness as a synagogue where the main focus of ritual was to hear the Law read and explained: in a throng of over a thousand people, the reader might sometimes be hard to hear. Third, the plan of the building is unparalleled among ancient synagogues.[89] Fourth, the huge marble table in the centre of the hall is unique in Jewish buildings and the edifice lacks the stone benches standard in synagogues elsewhere.[90] Fifth, at least one donor to the building came from outside Sardis (from nearby Hypaepa),[91] which was odd for a communal synagogue intended for the use of Jews who lived close enough to come regularly to hear the Law read. Sixth, and in contrast to donors' names in synagogues elsewhere, the mosaic inscriptions in Sardis do not apparently stress rank, honour and prestige, within the Jewish community; instead, they emphasize civic status, and in particular, for those who could boast it, the rank of *bouleutes*, city councillor.[92] None of the inscriptions refers to Jews, Israel, Hebrews, synagogues, or anything else specifically Jewish.

Positive reasons to suggest that the building might have been a place for God-worshippers to reverence the Jewish God are rather

---

[87] Ibid., 57, on no. 22.
[88] A. R. Seager, "The Synagogue and the Jewish Community: The Building" in *Sardis from Prehistoric to Roman Times*, ed. G. M. A. Hanfmann (Cambridge, MA: Harvard University Press, 1983) 177.
[89] Ibid.
[90] Ibid.
[91] Trebilco, *Jewish Communities in Asia Minor*, 46.
[92] Robert, *Nouvelles inscriptions de Sardes*, 54–57.

less numerous, but not negligible. First is the designation on the mosaics of six donors as *theosebeis*, "God-worshippers;"[93] none has a Jewish name and, in the light of the proximity of Sardis to Aphrodisias, it is much more plausible that the *theosebeis* here, as at Aphrodisias, were gentiles.[94] The Jewish iconography (such as the *shofar*) will then have been taken over by these non-Jews as symbolic representations of their cult of the Jewish God. Such appropriation of the images of other faiths was common in late antiquity: Christians sometimes used Jewish images,[95] just as Jews sometimes used pagan symbols,[96] so it should not surprise if the pagans who revered the Jewish God borrowed Jewish motifs.

Whoever the worshippers were in the building in its last phase, they seem to have kept a scroll of the law, or something similar, in the formal niche designated by the archeologists as the "Torah shrine." The evidence lies in the discovery around the niche of a marble inscription with the word *nomophylakion* ("guarding-place of [the] law"?),[97] and in the probable depiction of Torah scrolls in the form of two stylized spirals.[98] Such appurtenances of worship might seem too obviously appropriate to Jewish synagogue liturgy for any other explanation to be worth considering, but in fact even Torah scrolls might have a function in pagan worship. There is good evidence that non-Jews sometimes treated Jews' veneration for their scrolls as the direct equivalent of pagan veneration of idols:[99] when a soldier burnt a Torah scroll in first-century C.E. Judea, the Roman governor had him publicly executed,[100] and in the triumph held by Titus and Vespasian in Rome to celebrate the suppression of the Jewish revolt, the procession of booty contained, after the impressive loot from the Temple itself, a scroll of the Jewish law.[101] It would be easy for pagans to imagine that the scroll of the law embodied the divinity—and for those who worshipped the divinity to keep, in

---

[93] Ibid., 39–45; Trebilco, *Jewish Communities in Asia Minor*, 158–59.

[94] Cf. ibid., 159.

[95] Cf. Goodenough, *Jewish Symbols in the Greco-Roman Period*, vol. 2, 13.

[96] Ibid., *passim*.

[97] Kraabel, "Impact of the Discovery of the Sardis Synagogue," 189.

[98] Y. Shiloh, "Torah Scrolls and the Menorah Plaque from Sardis", *Israel Exploration Journal* 18 (1968) 54–57.

[99] Cf. M. Goodman, "Sacred Scripture and 'defiling the hands'", *Journal of Theological Studies* 41 (1990) 99–107.

[100] *B.J.* 2.229–231.

[101] Ibid., 7.150.

a wall oriented towards Jerusalem, a special copy of the scroll as the central focus of their worship, even if they did not actually read it, let alone understand the meaning of its contents.

Nor need the presence of a Hebrew inscription in the building signify that this was a synagogue: a word like "*shalom*"[102] is just the sort of word non-Jews enthusiastic about the Jewish God might employ as a sort of talisman (see above).

If I push possibilities to their limit, I could even argue that the presence among the inscriptions of two characteristically Jewish names (out of thirty altogether), like a certain "Samoe, priest and wise teacher (*sophodidaskalos*),"[103] does not necessarily bear any significance for the nature of the building as a whole. Jewish names appear in the pagan contexts elsewhere, like those in an ephebe list from a gymnasium in Cyrene in the early first century C.E.[104] It would not be particularly strange if some Jews (albeit, in the eyes of some rabbis, bad ones)[105] decided to show public support for a pagan shrine erected in honour of the Jewish God, just as some Jews nowadays will attend Christian services, making mental reservations during elements of the liturgy incompatible with Jewish theology—and just as some pagans in ancient times made offerings in synagogues (see above).

It will be recalled that my aim in discussing the Sardis building was only to push the possible explanation of the evidence to the limit of reasonableness—to see what might have been, and not to suggest what is more plausible. To balance the picture, and to avoid misleading readers, I should make it clear that the hypothesis I have just outlined is no more probable than the traditional suggestion that the building was a synagogue, and that some factors are difficult to explain on this view just as they are if the traditional view is taken.

So, for example, if the building was used by pagan polytheists, the emphasis by many donors on their enjoyment of the citizenship of Sardis[106] is strange since it might be thought an attribute local

---

[102] Seager, "The Synagogue and the Jewish Community: The Building," 171.

[103] G. M. A. Hanfmann and J.B. Bloom, "Samoe, Priest and Teacher of Wisdom" *Eretz-Israel* 19 (1987) 10*–14*.

[104] G. Lüderitz, *Corpus jüdischer Zeugnisse aus der Cyrenaika*, Beihefte zum Tübinger Atlas des vorderen Orients, Reihe B. nr. 53 (Weisbaden: Dr. Ludwıg Reichert, 1983) no. 7; cf. T. Rajak, "Jews and Christians as Groups in a Pagan World" in *"To See Ourselves as Others See Us:" Christians, Jews, "Others" in Late Antiquity*, eds. J. Neusner and E. S. Frerichs (Chico: Scholars Press, 1985) 247–261.

[105] Cf. *y. Megillah* 1.13, 72b (ed. Krotoschin).

[106] Robert, *Nouvelles inscriptions de Sardes*, 55–56.

pagans could take for granted. Again, the apparently deliberate hiding of the image of other deities when an ancient stone on which images of Cybele and Artemis were carved was re-used in the floor of the forecourt would be an odd thing for polytheists to do.[107] If the latter behaviour took place in the fifth century, it could be argued that it marked a change of use of the building from pagan shrine to Jewish synagogue (below), along perhaps with the (undatable) decapitation of the eagles that flanked the marble table,[108] but I do not wish to press the issue, since I hope that in any case the methodological points I wish to make are sufficiently clear: the Sardis building, with its distinctive iconography and large number of donor inscriptions, *might* in the third and fourth century C.E. have housed a Jewish synagogue, in which case the Judaism of those who worshipped there may have been of a distinctive type, but it also *might* have housed a cult of non-Jews who revered the Jewish God without any intention of entering the fold of Judaism.

Explicitly Jewish identification in the epigraphical and archeological material from the late-Roman Mediterranean diaspora is much rarer than one would like. So, for instance, of the eighty-five inscriptions from the diaspora included in Lifshitz's collection of donors and founders in synagogues,[109] only twenty-four contain any clearly Jewish reference, such as "Jew," "synagogue," or "Hebrew," although the surmise that they were indeed set up by Jews is much stronger in some cases that (sic) in others.

In the light of all this, it is worth asking what, if historians totally lacked the benefit of evidence from literary texts, they would deduce about Judaism from archeology and inscriptions. I doubt if they would ever discover that Judaism was distinguished from most other ancient religions by being a system, or a number of systems, with a complex mythology based on the covenant and revelation on Mount Sinai. It would be clear that there were indeed religious groups who identified themselves as Jews and set up communal buildings and hierarchies,[110] but I suspect that few scholars would guess the significance of this fact: if they operated by analogy, I suspect that they would (probably quite wrongly) interpret hierarchical titles as evidence

---

[107] Seager, "The Synagogue and the Jewish Community: The Building," 176.
[108] Ibid., 170.
[109] Lifshitz, *Donateurs et fondateurs dans les synagogues juives.*
[110] Schürer, *The History of the Jewish People in the Age of Jesus Christ,* 87–107.

of grades of initiation like those in Mithraism, so that "Father of the synagogue" could be seen as parallel to the Mithraic *pater*.[111]

Not much else could be deduced about Judaism from the vast majority of Jewish sites and inscriptions.[112] The nature of Jewish religious beliefs would surely be totally obscure from the iconography of *menoroth*, lions, incense shovels, birds, *lulavim*, and so on.[113] I doubt if we would even be able to recognize *lulavim* (palm branches) for what they are, or to distinguish the significant elements of the iconography (*menoroth*, *lulavim*) from the (probably) purely decorative (lions and birds); only with literary knowledge can such distinctions be made, and even then the significance of incense shovels remains obscure.

None of the archeological and epigraphic evidence gives any hint of the really distinctive traits of Judaism as it appears in late-antique Jewish and Christian sources: the centrality of a written scripture, and its proclamation and explanation in public assemblies. To deduce that, we would need more inscriptions affirming the status of liturgical readers, which are curiously rare. Nothing in the iconography would give a clue to the main Jewish identity markers as we know them from elsewhere: shabbat, kashrut (dietary laws), and circumcision.

Inevitably, then, all interpretation of such archeological and epigraphic material carries with it a great burden of assumptions derived from the literary evidence which survives from antiquity through the Christian Church and rabbinic Judaism. The hope that archeological evidence can act as an objective, untainted corrective to those literary traditions is therefore in many cases over-optimistic.

EPILOGUE: THE END OF UNCERTAINTY

Even for the most skeptical historian, the radical uncertainty I have been advocating in the study of Mediterranean Judaism will no longer seem even marginally plausible by the medieval period. By (say) the

---

[111] Cf. Vermaseren, *Mithras, the Secret God*; Schürer, *The History of the Jewish People in the Age of Jesus Christ*, 101, n. 51.

[112] The great exception is the synagogue at Dura-Europos, with its remarkable frescoes, to which there is not parallel elsewhere (J. Gutmann, *The Dura-Europas Synagogue; a Re-evaluation* [Chambersburg, PA: American Academy of Religion and the Society of Biblical Literature, 1973]).

[113] Cf. Levine, *The Synagogue in Late Antiquity*.

tenth century c.e. no one would seriously suggest that Jewish-type evidence is likely to have derived from pagan God-worshippers, nor that non-rabbinic Judaism was widespread in the region, apart from among those Jews like the Karaites who self-consciously broke away from the rabbinic mainstream. It is worth asking from what date, and for what reason, this increased certainty in the interpretation of Jewish-type material becomes overwhelmingly plausible. I suggest, tentatively, a fairly precise date: the late fourth century c.e. If that date is correct, it will have been brought about by a specific agent, the Roman state, and, as often in Jewish history, change will have come about because of actions not by Jews, but by outsiders—in this case, the militantly Christian emperors of Rome and Constantinople from the time of Theodosius the Great.

All Roman emperors were Christian from the conversion of Constantine in 312 c.e., with only a very brief interlude under Julian the Apostate in 361–363 c.e., but the earliest Christian emperors, whatever their personal predilections, made no attempt to impose their faith upon their subjects. In the late 380s c.e. this liberal stance was to change quite dramatically. Theodosius the Great, impelled by personal conscience and zealous Christian clerics, began the systematic closure of pagan temples.[114] By the end of the century most temples in the main cities of the Roman empire were either deserted of converted into churches, and paganism, though not eradicated, was confined to the countryside.[115]

Thus by the fifth century it is very unlikely that a large public building in a major city would be a pagan shrine, even to the Jewish God, and whatever the Sardis building was in its earlier stages, it is most likely that by the fifth century the Jewish motifs found on the mosaic floors do indeed show it to have been a synagogue. The attitude of Theodosius and his successors to the erection, repair and preservation of synagogues was not exactly favourable, but it was much more ambivalent than their thoroughgoing hostility to pagan temples.[116]

---

[114] N. Q. King, *The Emperor Theodosius and the Establishment of Christianity* (Philadelphia: Westminster, 1960).

[115] J. Geffcken, *The Last Days of Greco-Roman Paganism* (Amsterdam and Oxford: North-Holland, 1978).

[116] B. S. Bachrach, "The Jewish community of the Later Roman Empire as seen in the Codex Theodosianus" in *"To See Ourselves as Others See Us:" Christians, Jews, "Others" in Late Antiquity*, 399–421.

Furthermore, if in the fifth century the building was a synagogue, it is likely that by that time the Jews who worshipped there had come under the influence of the rabbis of the land of Israel. There is evidence in the Roman legal codes that from the 380s until at least the 420s the Jewish *nasi* (patriarch) in Palestine was accorded by the Roman state power and authority over the Jews throughout the empire. By this period, Roman emperors took for granted the backing of the Roman state for the patriarch's collection of funds from the diaspora.[117] They assumed that he had the right to excommunicate deviants from Jewish communities,[118] which presumably implied the right to define what is deviant. Finally, and of most significance for the Sardis building, they took for granted his power to found and dismantle synagogues throughout the empire.[119] The patriarch by no means represented all rabbis, since the talmudic sources reveal conflict between individual *nesiim* and individual rabbis over questions of authority and halacha during many generations,[120] but he did at least come from within the same type of Judaism that the rabbis espoused.[121] After all, the foundation document of rabbinic Judaism, the Mishnah, had been codified by R. Judah ha-Nasi, patriarch at the end of the second century C.E. and the beginning of the third, and it was descent from him that gave later patriarchs their authority.

It is possible, then, to end on a reassuring note. Whatever the nature of the building in Sardis in which gentile God-worshippers dedicated their mosaic inscriptions in the mid-fourth century or earlier, it seems likely that the individual called "Samoe, priest and wise teacher," whose name was inserted into the floor of the hall in the late fifth century[122] was a rabbinic Jew,[123] and that the building which

---

[117] Cf. *Codex Theodosianus* 16.8.17.

[118] Ibid., 16.8.8.

[119] Cf. ibid., 16.8.22.

[120] L. I. Levine, *The Rabbinic Class of Roman Palestine in Late Antiquity* (Jerusalem and New York: Yad Izhak ben Zvi and Jewish Theological Seminary, 1989).

[121] Cf. I. Gafni, "'Staff and Legislator'—On New Types of Leadership in the Talmudic Era in Palestine and Babylonia" in *Priesthood and Monarchy* (In Hebrew) eds. I. Gafni and G. Motzkin (Jerusalem: Merkaz Shazar, 1987) 79–92.

[122] Hanfmann and Bloom, "Samoe, Priest and Teacher of Wisdom."

[123] Trebilco (*Jewish Communities in Asia Minor*, 50) argued that the fact that Samoe was not called a rabbi in the inscription may be evidence that he (and Jews in Sardis in general) was not under rabbinic influence, but I am not persuaded by this argument from silence.

he honoured was a synagogue. There is, after all, something that can be asserted about Jews and Judaism in the Mediterranean diaspora in the late-Roman period.

POSTSCRIPT

I am grateful to the editors of this volume and to the Mediterranean Institute of the University of Malta for the opportunity to republish here this article, which originally appeared in *Journal of Mediterranean Studies* in 1994. The central thesis of the article, that students of the religious history of late antiquity need to allow for the possibility that Jewish iconography on archaeological remains may reflect the activities not of Jews but of gentile worshippers of the Jewish God, has been cast in a new light by more recent studies. As a result, I think that the hypothesis presented so tentatively in the early 1990's can reasonably be presented now with slightly more confidence, although I must stress that my purpose in elaborating the hypothesis is still only to stimulate consideration of what might be possible rather than to describe what was certainly the case.

In this brief discussion of relevant scholarship since 1994, two major advances in the presentation of the primary epigraphic evidence take pride of place. First is the full publication of the inscriptions from the Sardis 'synagogue'.[124] The helpful commentaries on the dossiers, completed in 1994, reflect the state of the debate in the early 1990s. Second is the brilliant reconsideration of the Aphrodisias 'Godfearers' stele by Angelos Chaniotis,[125] in which he proposes a date in the second half of the fourth century or in the fifth century for the texts on both the inscribed faces.

This redating of the Aphrodisias texts, from the early third century to the mid fourth at earliest, coincides with a trend to redate on archaeological grounds the alteration of the Sardis gymnasium basilica into a religious building and the period of its use for that purpose:[126]

---

[124] J. H. Kroll, "The Greek insriptions of the Sardis Synagogue," *HTR* 94.1 (2001) 1–127; Frank Moore Cross, "The Hebrew Inscriptions from Sardis," *HTR* 95.1 (2002).

[125] A. Chaniotis, "The Jews of Aphrodisias: New Evidence and Old Problems," *Scripta Classica Israelica* 22 (2002).

[126] H. Botermann, "Die Synagoge von Sardes," *Zeitschrift für Neutestamentliche Wissenschaft* 81 (1990); M. Bonz, "Differing Approaches to Religious Benefaction: the Late Third-Century Acquisition of the Sardis Synagogue," *HTR* 86.2 (1993) 139.

the debate continues, but it is fair to say that all reinvestigation of the archaeological record has so far pushed the date of the building's use well away from the second century date originally favoured into the fourth century or later.

Other studies have mapped out a plausible historical context for the interpenetration of religious iconography, ideas and memberships, in which neutral religious phrases and ambiguous images were prudently favoured by public figures in the way they presented themselves to their fellow citizens and to the state.[127] Jas Elsner has emphasised the use by both Jews and Christians of a common iconography shared also with their pagan contemporaries, stressing that the differences between religious groups will generally have lain less in the images they employed than in the meanings they gave to those images.[128] Some scholars have even claimed that religious boundaries were so fluid that Judaism and Christianity were indistinguishable as separate religions until the fourth century,[129] a rather extreme view which itself may not sufficiently distinguish between ancient attitudes to group identity and the different issue of the problems faced by modern scholars in assigning a text or artefact to one such group or another.[130] What now seems generally agreed is the significance of the fourth century, after the edict of toleration of Christianity in 313 C.E., as a tolerant religious arena, in which it was possible for an individual both to cross religious divides and to seek wider ecumenical acceptability by adoption of ambiguous language.[131]

Of particular importance for study of the use of Jewish symbols has been the remarkable investigation by Stephen Mitchell of the cult of *theos hypsistos* ('the highest god').[132] Mitchell suggests that the abundant epigraphic material referring to this god from all over the east-

---

[127] For example, see R. R. R. Smith, "The Statue Monument of Oecumenius: An New Portrait of a Late Antique Governor From Aphrodisias," *Journal of Roman Studies* 92 (2002).

[128] J. Elsner, "Archaeologies and Agendas: Reflections on Late Antique Jewish Art and Early Christian Art," *Journal of Roman Studies* 93 (2003).

[129] Daniel Boyarin, *Dying for God: Martyrdom and the Making of Christianity and Judaism* (Standford: Ca: Stanford University Press, 1999).

[130] Martin Goodman, "Modelling the 'Parting of the Ways,'" in *The Ways that Never Parted: Jews and Christians in Late Antiquity and Early Middle Ages*, eds. A. H. Becker and A. Y. Reed (Tübingen: J. C. B. Mohr, 2003) 119–29.

[131] Cf. Chaniotis, "The Jews of Aphrodisias," 218, 224–5, 231–2.

[132] "The Cult of Theos Hypsistos between Pagans, Jews and Christians," in *Pagan Monotheism in Late Antiquity*, eds. P. Athanassiadi and M. Frede (Oxford: Clarendon Press; New York: Oxford University Press, 1999).

ern Mediterranean world in the Roman imperial period should be attributed to a specific pagan cult, which he characterizes as an aspect of pagan monotheism. Not all have been persuaded that 'highest god' should always be understood as designating the divinity worshipped rather than as an adjective applied to another god,[133] but even a modified form of Mitchell's thesis would render it plausible both that Jews could easily identify their God with the divinity worshipped by such pagans (cf. Ps. Aristeas 16) and (importantly for the present study) that such pagans could identify their 'highest god' with the God of the Jews. The former possibility I have explored at some length in a discussion of the image of the sun god in the synagogue mosaics in late-Roman Palestine.[134] The latter possibility would fit well with the suggestion in the current study about the role of the godfearers in the 'synagogue' in late-Roman Sardis.

---

[133] Cf., for example, Chaniotis, "The Jews of Aphrodisias," 224, n. 49.

[134] Martin Goodman, "The Jewish Image of God in Late Antiquity," in *Jewish Culture and Society Under the Christian Roman Empire*, eds. Richard Kalmin and Seth Schwartz (Leuven: Peeters, 2003).

BETWEEN ROME AND MESOPOTAMIA:
JOSEPHUS IN SASANIAN PERSIA

Did the rabbis of the Talmud read Josephus? Did books written in Rome during the late first-century c.e. reach Persian-controlled Mesopotamia and find a receptive audience there? In our efforts to describe the Jewish experience in antiquity and its place within the larger, non-Jewish world, do cultural ties between Rome and Mesopotamia deserve consideration alongside those between Athens (or Rome) and Jerusalem?

This paper is based on comparison between rabbinic and Josephan traditions about the Sadducees.[1] We will attempt to show that traditions in the Bavli tend to be hostile toward the Sadducees, while traditions in Palestinian compilations tend to reflect a more neutral attitude.[2] We will also demonstrate that since it is a fundamental tenet of rabbinic thought that the rabbis possessed traditions, which were authoritative despite their independence from scripture, the introduction into Babylonia of traditions which portray the Sadducees as accepting only scripture and rejecting traditions external to the Bible[3] motivated these hostile Babylonian portrayals. The source of

---

* Jewish Theological Seminary.

[1] As is well known, the printed texts of the Talmud often read "Sadducees," but examination of the manuscripts and medieval *testimonia* reveals that the correct reading is *minim*, "heretics." We have relied on the work of Günther Stemberger, *Jewish Contemporaries of Jesus: Pharisees, Sadducees, Essenes* (Minneapolis: Fortress Press, 1995) 38–66; and Yaakov Zussman, "Heker Toldot ha-Halakhah u-Megillat Midbar Yehudah: Hirhurim Talmudi'im le-Or Megillat 'Mikzat Ma'asei ha-Torah,'" *Tarbiz* 59 (1990) 44–45 (n. 147), 46, 48–49 (n. 166), 50 (n. 168), 51–52 (n. 171), and 53–55 (n. 176), for identification of the cases in which the correct reading is "Sadducees."

[2] See also Zussman, "Heker Toldot ha-Halakhah," 50–51, n. 168. Compare Anthony Saldarini, *Pharisees and Sadducees in Palestinian Society* (Edinburgh: T & T Clark, 1989) 231–35. See also pages 298–308, there, especially the bibliography cited on 298, n. 1.

[3] Jean Le Moyne, *Les Sadduceens* (Paris: Librairie Lecoffree, 1972) 357–79; and Zussman, "Heker Toldot ha-Halakhah," 57, n. 185.

the Bavli's portrayal of the Sadducees as a group, which accepts only scripture,[4] we will argue, is Rome, in the form of the writings either of (a) Josephus, or (b) traditions drawn upon independently by both Josephus and the rabbis.[5] Both the harsh criticisms of the Sadducees and their portrayal as rejecting extra-biblical traditions can be shown to have been incorporated into the Bavli at approximately the same time, and apparently by the same individuals or the same group of people, supporting our claim that a close relationship exists between these two phenomena.

This incorporation into the Bavli of Josephus' description of the Sadducees was part of a much larger phenomenon of the transmission of diverse Jewish traditions, both rabbinic and non-rabbinic, from Rome to Mesopotamia beginning in the mid-fourth century C.E. Further study is necessary to determine whether or not other literatures and cultural artifacts, both Jewish and non-Jewish, exhibit a similar eastward movement at approximately the same time, and also why this movement took place precisely in this direction at precisely this time.

Throughout this discussion, statements are referred to as Babylonian when they are preserved in the Babylonian Talmud (or Bavli), while statements preserved in Palestinian compilations are referred to as Palestinian. In one important case, however, chronological and geographical markers will allow us to approximate when a portrayal of the Sadducees made its way into Babylonian rabbinic circles, and to describe the subtle shifts in this portrayal throughout the rabbinic period. In other words, sometimes the layered nature of Talmudic

---

[4] It bears emphasizing that my claim is not that the Sadducees actually were literalists, accepting only teachings they found "explicitly" in the Bible, but rather that the Sadducees are sometimes portrayed in this fashion in Josephus and in the Bavli. See the discussion below.

[5] See Appendix One, below, where we argue that it makes no difference for our thesis whether the source is Josephus himself, or traditions drawn upon independently by Josephus and the rabbis. Regarding the connection between Josephus and several traditions in the Bavli, see Shaye J. D. Cohen, "Parallel Historical Traditions in Josephus and Rabbinic Literature," in *Proceedings of the Ninth World Congress of Jewish Studies* (Jerusalem: World Union of Jewish Studies, Division B. Vol. 1., 1986) 7–14; Stemberger, *Jewish Contemporaries of Jesus*, 106–9; Richard Kalmin, "Jewish Sources of the Second Temple Period in Rabbinic Compilations of Late Antiquity," in *The Talmud Yerushalmi and Graeco-Roman Culture*, ed. Peter Schäfer (Tübingen: Mohr, 2003) 36–44; and idem, "Kings, Priests, and Sages in Rabbinic Literature of Late Antiquity," in *Netiot le-David: David Weiss Halivni Jubilee Volume*, ed. Ephraim Halivni, et al. (Jerusalem: Orhot, 2003) 75–79.

discourse permits us to write the history of an idea or an institution, however, sometimes the process of editorial homogenization erases all or most evidence of such developments, which is precisely what we would expect to find in a literature as vast and variegated as that of the Babylonian Talmud.[6]

RABBINIC TRADITIONS ABOUT THE SADDUCEES

Support for our claim regarding the Bavli's unique tendency to denigrate the Sadducees[7] is found in b. Yoma 4a, which contains the following, presumably Tannaitic text:

(A)   (Hebrew) Aaron separated himself for seven days and he served [as high priest] for one day, and Moses sent to him all seven days in order to instruct him regarding the [sacrificial] service. And even in future generations the high priest separates himself for seven days and serves for one day, and two disciples of the sages from among the disciples of Moses—

---

[6] See also Richard Kalmin, *Sages, Stories, Authors, and Editors in Rabbinic Babylonia* (Atlanta: Scholars Press, 1994) 2–15 and passim; and Christine E. Hayes, *Between the Babylonian and Palestinian Talmuds: Accounting for Halakhic Difference in Selected Sugyot from Tractate Avodah Zarah* (New York: Oxford University Press, 1997) 8–15 and passim.

[7] In addition to the passages surveyed in detail below, compare b. Eruvin 68b and m. Eruvin 6:2. According to m. Eruvin 6:2 (a Palestinian tradition), Sadducees are legally differentiated from non-Jews with regard to the laws of carrying within a courtyard on the Sabbath. According to the tradition in the Bavli, in contrast, the majority view of the Tannaim on this subject is that Sadducees have the status of non-Jews. See also Le Moyne, *Les Sadduceens*, 117–18. Compare also b. Sukkah 48b-49a and the parallels in y. Sukkah 4:8 (54d) and y. Yoma 1:5 (39a). See also t. Sukkah 3:16; Raymond Harari, *Rabbinic Perceptions of the Boethusians* (PhD Dissertation, New York University, 1995) 145–64; and Appendix Two, below, for discussion of variation in rabbinic sources between Sadducees and Boethusians. In addition, unnamed sages in m. Sanhedrin 7:2 assert that the execution described by R. Elazar ben Zadok was carried out by a court that did not know the law, and Rav Yosef, a Babylonian Amora, claims in b. Sanhedrin 52b that this court "was a court of Sadducees." Rav Yosef does not say that the Sadducees carried out the sentence based on their own legal opinions, which differed from those of the sages or the Pharisees, but that they were inexpert. Surprisingly, no traditions in Palestinian compilations accuse Sadducees of being inexpert or ignorant. Mark 12:24, incidentally, asserts that the Sadducees "know neither the scriptures nor the power of God." Finally, see b. Baba Batra 115b, where Rav asserts that "Anyone, even a prince of Israel, who says that a daughter is to inherit with the daughter of a son, must not be obeyed, for such [a ruling] is only the practice of the Sadducees." See also Rashbam, s.v. *Amar Rav Huna amar Rav*, "*Kol*. . . ." Rav's statement, which implies that an opinion is disqualified simply because it is Sadducean, no matter how great the authority which accepts and propounds it, is unparalleled in Palestinian compilations.

(B)   (Aramaic)—to exclude Sadducees—

(C)   (Hebrew) send to him all seven days in order to instruct him regarding the [sacrificial] service.

Section (B) above, an obvious Aramaic interpolation into an earlier Hebrew tradition, interprets the curious phrase, "two disciples of the sages from among the disciples of Moses,"[8] to exclude Sadducees. By asserting that Sadducees are not "disciples of Moses," the author of this interpolation reveals extreme antipathy toward them. Elsewhere in rabbinic literature, the claim that a group[9] denies Moses as its rabbi serves to situate them not only outside the rabbinic movement but also outside of the Jewish people. This brief interpolation is per- haps the most extreme expression of disapproval of the Sadducees found in any ancient rabbinic text.[10]

  b. Yoma 19b also records a negative portrayal of the Sadducees which goes beyond what we encounter in Palestinian compilations:

(A)   Mishnah: We [the priests] adjure you [the high priest] in [the name of] He who dwells in this house [the Temple] that you will not change anything we told you [i.e., that you will perform the rit- ual exactly as we instructed you]. [The high priest] separates him- self and cries and they separate themselves and cry.[11]

(B)   Talmud: [The high priest] separates himself and cries, because they suspected him of being a Sadducee. And they separate them- selves and cry, for R. Yehoshua ben Levi said, "Whoever suspects those who are worthy suffers bodily harm."

The high priest weeps because he is "suspected" of being a Sadducee, which to provoke such consternation must be a serious charge. As

---

[8] To my knowledge, this expression is without parallel elsewhere in rabbinic literature.

[9] Or an individual.

[10] See *Dikdukei Soferim*, ed. Rafael Rabbinowicz (1868–1897; Reprint. Jerusalem: Ma'ayan ha-Hokhmah, 1960) n. *zayin*, who records one manuscript which lacks the phrase, "to exclude the Sadducees" in the body of the text, and has it only in the margin. Shamma Friedman, "Al Derekh Heker ha-Sugya," in *Perek ha-Ishah Rabbah ba-Bavli* (Jerusalem: Jewish Theological Seminary, 1978) 30, has noted that manu- script variation is often indicative of a later editorial or a post-Talmudic addition to a text. In addition, several manuscripts have the Aramaic phrase responding to the question, also in Aramaic, "What is this?" If the interpolation were post-Talmudic, then it would fall outside the purview of this study.

[11] M. Yoma 1:5.

utilized here by the Talmud's anonymous editors, furthermore, R. Yehoshua ben Levi's statement implies that if the high priest is a Sadducee he is not worthy. The priests weep out of concern that they are suspicious of someone who has done nothing wrong. The fact that he may be a Sadducee makes the risk worth taking.

In another brief but telling comment, b. Eruvin 68b contains a purportedly tannaitic tradition which quotes Rabban Gamliel referring to a Sadducee as an "abomination." This statement is parallel to m. Eruvin 6:2, a Palestinian source, and Rabban Gamliel's comment there lacks the pejorative epithet.

Along these same lines, b. Baba Batra 115b–116a depicts the Sadducees in bitter conflict with sages, and describes them in harshly negative terms unprecedented in traditions found in Palestinian compilations.[12] The story is as follows:[13]

(A) Said Rav Huna said Rav, "Anyone, even a prince of Israel, who says that a daughter is to inherit with the daughter of a son, must not be obeyed, for such [a ruling] is only the practice of the Sadducees.

(B) As it was taught [in a tannaitic statement]

(C) [Aramaic]: On the 24th of Tevet we returned to our [own] law.

(D) [Hebrew]: For the Sadducees maintained [that] a daughter inherited with the daughter of the son. Rabban Yohanan ben Zakkai joined issue with them. He said to them, "Fools! From where do you derive this?" Not one of them answered, except for an old man who babbled at him,[14] saying, "If the daughter of his son, who comes [to inherit] by virtue of his son's right, is heir to him, how much more so his daughter who derives her right from himself?" [Rabban

---

[12] This narrative is derived from and modeled after a story in b. Menahot 65a–b, which features a controversy between Rabban Yohanan ben Zakkai and a Boethusian, and contains many of the same motifs. Stemberger, *Jewish Contemporaries of Jesus*, 63, also claims that the story in Baba Batra borrowed motifs from Menahot, but he does not explain why. See Appendix Three, below.

[13] The following translation, with modifications, is based on that of Israel W. Slotki, *Baba Bathra* (London: The Soncino Press, 1935) 475–76.

[14] Marcus Jastrow, *A Dictionary of the Targumim, Talmud Babli, Yerushalmi, and Midrashic Literature* (1886–1903; Reprint. New York: The Judaica Press, 1971) 1156. Compare Jacob Levy, *Neuhebräisches und Chaldäisches Wörterbuch über die Talmudim und Midraschim*, vol. 4 (2nd edition, revised by Lazarus Goldschmidt. Berlin: Benjamin Harz, 1924) 28.

Yohanan ben Zakkai] applied to him the verse, "'These are the sons of Seir the Horite, the inhabitants of the land: Lotan and Shobal and Zibeon and Anah' (Gen 36:20), and [lower down] it is written, 'And these are the children of Zibeon: Aiah and Anah' (Gen 36:24). [But this] teaches that Zibeon had intercourse with his mother and fathered Anah."

(E)   Is it not possible that there were two [called] Anah? Rabbah said, ". . . Scripture says, 'This is Anah,' [implying] the same Anah that was [mentioned] before."

(F)   [The Sadducee] said to [Rabban Yohanan ben Zakkai], "Rabbi, do you dismiss me with such [a feeble reply]?" [Rabban Yohanan ben Zakkai] said to [the Sadducee], "Fool! Is not our perfect Torah as good as your worthless talk? A son's daughter [has a right of inheritance] because her claim is valid where there are brothers, but can the same be said of the [deceased's] daughter whose right [of inheritance] is impaired where there are brothers?" Thus they were defeated. And that day was declared a festive day.

According to this narrative, the Sadducees are "fools," such that no one among them is able to respond to Rabban Yohanan ben Zakkai's challenge, except for an "old man"[15] who "babbles" at the rabbi and who is himself a "fool." Moreover, the "perfect Torah" of the rabbis is in stark contrast to the "worthless talk" of the Sadducees. Only when the Sadducee explicitly acknowledges Rabban Yohanan ben Zakkai's superiority, referring to him as "Rabbi," does Rabban Yohanan ben Zakkai reveal to him the true reason for the sages' opinion. Only after his submission is the Sadducee, though still a "fool" and still the purveyor of "worthless talk," worthy of knowing the true scriptural proof.

Significantly, this halakhic dispute is recorded in two Palestinian compilations, and in neither of the parallels is there the slightest hint of contempt for or criticism of the Sadducees or their opinion.[16]

In addition, b. Berakhot 29a is more critical of the Sadducees

---

[15] The term translated here as "old man" often has the meaning "elder" in rabbinic literature. In that sense the term is an expression of respect. In this context, the translation "old man" makes better sense.

[16] See y. Baba Batra 8:1 (16a). See also t. Yadayim 2:20 (Boethusians vs. Pharisees), and the discussion below.

than is a parallel discussion in Pesikta de-Rav Kahana, a Palestinian compilation.[17] The Bavli's discussion is as follows:

(A) Said Abaye, "We have a tradition that a good person does not become bad."

(B) No? But behold it is written, "When a righteous person turns away from his righteousness and does evil" (Ezek 18:24).

(C) That [scriptural verse] refers to someone who was originally wicked, but someone who was originally righteous, no [they do not become wicked].

(D) We taught [in a Tannaitic tradition],[18] "Do not trust yourself until the day of your death, for Yohanan the High Priest served in the office of High Priest for 80 years and in the end he became a Sadducee."

(E) Said Abaye, "[King] Yannai and Yohanan [the High Priest] are one [and the same person]."

(F) Rava said, "[King] Yannai and Yohanan [the High Priest] are different people."

(G) [King] Yannai was originally wicked and Yohanan [the High Priest] was originally righteous.[19]

According to parts (F) and (G) of this discussion, Yohanan the High Priest was originally "righteous" but later in life he became wicked, a transformation proven by the fact that he became a Sadducee.

Part (D) is closely paralleled in a Palestinian compilation, Pesikta de-Rav Kahana,[20] where the comment is found in the context of a discussion of the evil inclination. In its context in the Pesikta, the

---

[17] The following quotation is part of a lengthy discussion in b. Berakhot 28b–29a. The material quoted here probably originated independently of the larger discussion and was placed in its present context by later editors. For my present purposes, the larger context is irrelevant and is therefore omitted from this discussion.

[18] The term *tenan* generally introduces the quotation of a mishnah. The first half of the statement ("Do not trust yourself until the day of your death") is, in fact, found verbatim in m. Avot 2:4, while the second half is found in Pesikta de-Rav Kahana (see below), a post-tannaitic midrashic compilation. The Bavli, apparently, intends to designate both halves as Tannaitic in origin.

[19] For reasons that need not detain us here, part (G) is an anonymous addition to the statement attributed to Rava.

[20] Pesikta de-Rav Kahana 11, ed. Bernard Mandelbaum (New York: Jewish Theological Seminary, 1962) 176.

statement, "They said about Yohanan the High Priest that he served
in [the office of] the high priesthood for 80 years and in the end
became a Sadducee," implies that there is something anomalous
about Yohanan becoming a Sadducee after so many years of faithful service to God, and the anomaly is evidence of the power of the
evil inclination.

It is only when we turn to Abaye's statement in the Bavli [part
(E)], that we find a significant difference between the Bavli's and the
Pesikta's attitudes toward the Sadducees. Abaye declares that Yohanan
the High Priest is none other than the Hasmonean king, Yannai,
the subject of numerous stories in the Bavli which describe his depravity. As I have demonstrated elsewhere, Babylonian rabbis routinely
depict the Hasmoneans in a bad light, with King Yannai usually
made to play the role of the evil Hasmonean monarch.[21] It is likely
that Abaye has at least some of this background in mind when he
identifies King Yannai and Yohanan the High Priest.[22] By identifying these two figures, Abaye asserts that the act of becoming a
Sadducee transformed Yohanan into the evil Hasmonean king par
excellence, the wicked murderer of rabbis and the perpetrator of a
variety of other colorful monstrosities.

Turning now to an examination of the scanty evidence of negative attitudes toward the Sadducees in Palestinian compilations, we
find a substantially different picture.[23] In y. Eruvin 1:1 (18c) we find
the following:

> [The rabbis] said to [R. Meir], "If so, let the enemies of R. Yohanan
> be like a Sadducee vis-a-vis the occupants of the courtyard and let the
> occupants of the courtyard be forbidden [to carry within the courtyard].

The Yerushalmi here employs a circumlocution ("let the enemies of
R. Yohanan be like a Sadducee"), adding the phrase "the enemies

---

[21] Richard Kalmin, *The Sage in Jewish Society of Late Antiquity* (London: Routledge
Press, 1999) 61–67.

[22] See Appendix Four, below.

[23] I omit discussion of the account of the origin of the Sadducees and Boethusians
in Avot de-R. Natan Version B Chapter 10 and Version A Chapter 5, ed. Solomon
Schechter (1887; Reprint, with an introduction by Menahem Kister; New York:
Jewish Theological Seminary, 1997) 26. Avot de-R. Natan was probably redacted
later than the period surveyed in this study. While it probably contains some (much?)
earlier material, it is difficult to determine whether or not any particular statement
is early. The relevance of this tradition to the present study is therefore highly questionable. For the same reason, I also omit from the discussion traditions in Megillat
Ta'anit.

of'" to the text to avoid the suggestion that R. Yohanan himself was like a Sadducee. The statement implies nothing whatsoever about R. Yohanan's ethical character, his obedience to the sages, or his observance of halakhah, but the thought of associating R. Yohanan and Sadducees was so disturbing that the phrase "the enemies of" was added to the text so that anyone reading or repeating it would associate R. Yohanan's enemies, rather than R. Yohanan, with the hated Sadducees. The phrase is not an integral part of the discussion, however, and it may have been added by very late, post-Talmudic copyists, since other than this one easily detachable comment the Yerushalmi nowhere expresses disapproval of the Sadducees.

A second negative statement, in Sifrei Bemidbar 112,[24] may also be a later addition to the text. We read there: "'For he despised the word of the Lord'" (Num 15:31), this is a Sadducee. 'And he broke his commandments'" (Num 15:31), this is an Epikoros." Clearly this tradition is harshly critical of Sadducees. Once again, however, it is uncertain whether or not the negative attitude is an integral part of the text, since the passage cited above is missing from two versions of the Sifrei.[25] This tradition may have been added long after the Sifrei's final editing, when the term "Sadducee" was routinely substituted for the term *min* (heretic), and negative judgments about heretics were routinely associated with Sadducees.[26]

---

[24] Sifrei Bemidbar 112, ed. Haim Shaul Horowitz (1917; Reprint. Jerusalem: Wahrmann Books, 1966) 121.

[25] See also Shaye J. D. Cohen, "The Significance of Yavneh: Pharisees, Rabbis, and the End of Jewish Sectarianism," *Hebrew Union College Annual* 55 (1984) 39, n. 30.

[26] See also Pesikta de-Rav Kahana 11, ed. Mandelbaum, 176, discussed above in connection with b. Berakhot 29a. T. Hagigah 3:35 may also be relevant: "A table that became impure, it is immersed at the appropriate time (*bi-zemano*), even on the Sabbath. It happened that they immersed the menorah [used in the Temple] on a holiday (*yom tov*) and the Sadducees said, 'Come and see the Pharisees who immerse the moon (*meor ha-levanah*).'" Perhaps this story is critical of the Sadducees for ridiculing the Pharisees, but if so the criticism is quite muted. The Sadducees are not punished for their behavior, nor is it even explicit in the story that they are halakhically incorrect. See m. Hagigah 3:8; Saul Lieberman, *Tosefta ki-Feshutah* vol. 5 (New York: Jewish Theological Seminary, 1962) 1336; and Stemberger, *Jewish Contemporaries*, 51. See also Zussman, "Heker Toldot ha-Halakhah," 65–68, according to whom the Sadducees are not ridiculing the Pharisees. According to several portrayals in Palestinian and Babylonian sources, the Sadducees restrict their opposition to the theoretical realm, confining themselves to halakhic opinions contrary to those of the sages. With the exception of the occasional zealot, these stories claim, Sadducees are harmless, although the exceptional Sadducee who defies the sages in practice is in several instances a high priest, and is thus in a position to inflict significant damage to the community since he plays a key role in the sacrificial

Both quantitatively and qualitatively, therefore, traditions in Palestinian compilations are less harshly critical of and hostile to the Sadducees than are traditions in the Bavli.[27] Significantly, whenever we found parallels between Palestinian and Babylonian sources, the latter were always more hostile toward the Sadducees than were the Palestinian parallels. This phenomenon calls out for explanation, although our conclusions must remain tentative due to the paucity of relevant data.

How might we explain these curious facts? We cannot argue that the larger number of negative traditions is simply a function of the larger number of relevant traditions of any sort, since Sadducees are mentioned no less frequently in Palestinian compilations than in the Bavli.[28] Furthermore, according to this explanation the greater hostility of Babylonian traditions remains unaccounted for.

cult. These occasional zealots, however, are swiftly punished with death at the hands of heaven, and the danger they pose is therefore localized and contained. See t. Parah 3:8; t. Niddah 5:3; b. Yoma 19b; and b. Niddah 33b. See also t. Yoma 1:8 and y. Yoma 1:5 (39a–b) (par. y. Sukkah 4:8 [54d]) (involving Boethusians). We find the same motif in Josephus, Antiquities 18.15 and 18.17. Compare Stemberger, *Jewish Contemporaries*, 63. One of these stories, t. Parah 3:8, is truncated, and parts of it are difficult to understand. It appears to contain the motif, familiar to us from other stories, of the father of the high priest accepting his son's death as punishment for his acting in accordance with Saducean opinion. This story lacks, however, a clear statement of the obedience of Sadducees in general to the halakhic opinions of the sages.

[27] Babylonian traditions: 9–10 out of a total of 19 (b. Berakhot 29a; b. Eruvin 68b [twice; see above, n. 8]; b. Yoma 4a and b. Yoma 19b; b. Sukkah 48b–49a; b. Baba Batra 115b–116a [twice]; b. Sanhedrin 52b [see above, n. 8]); and possibly b. Kiddushin 66a. Palestinian traditions: 1–4 out of a total of 18–19 (Pesikta de-Rav Kahana 11 and possibly t. Hagigah 3:35 [see above, n. 38]; Sifrei Bemidbar 112; and y. Eruvin 1:1 [18c]). Phrased in statistical terms, 47–53% of the Babylonian traditions about Sadducees are critical, as opposed to only 5–22% of the Palestinian traditions. See also Stemberger, *Jewish Contemporaries*, 46–66; and Joseph M. Baumgarten, "The Pharisaic-Saducean Controversies About Purity and the Qumran Texts," *JJS* (1980) 165–69.

[28] As noted above, we find 18–19 traditions in Palestinian compilations and 19 in the Bavli. The 18–19 Palestinian traditions are found in m. Eruvin 6:2; m. Makkot 1:6; m. Parah 3:7; m. Niddah 4:2; m. Yadayim 4:6; m. Yadayim 4:7 (twice); t. Hagigah 3:35; t. Parah 3:7–8; t. Niddah 5:2–3; Sifra Aharei Mot Perek 3:11; Sifrei Bemidbar 112 (ed. Horowitz, 121); Sifrei Devarim 190, ed. Louis Finkelstein (1939; Reprint. New York: Jewish Theological Seminary, 1969) 231; Midrash Tannaim to Deuteronomy 19:18, ed. David Zvi Hoffman (1908–1909; Reprint Jerusalem, 1984) 117 (the text of this tradition, however, has probably been influenced by that of the parallel in the Bavli); y. Eruvin 1:1 (18c); y. Yoma 1:5 (39a–b); y. Sukkah 4:8 (54d) (and parallel); y. Baba Batra 8:1 (16a); Pesikta de-Rav Kahana 11 (ed. Mandelbaum, 176); and possibly y. Sukkah 4:8 (58d) (and parallel). See also y. Sanhedrin 6:2 (23b). The 19 traditions in the Bavli are found in b. Berakhot

We also cannot account for the difference purely on the basis of genre, explaining that the Bavli is richer in narratives than are Palestinian compilations, and narratives are more apt to depict conflict and hatred between the protagonists. This explanation fails, since only one or two of the Babylonian traditions examined above criticizes the Sadducees in the context of a narrative which has no close parallel in a Palestinian compilation.[29] In addition, as noted above there are elaborate narratives about the Sadducees in both Babylonian and Palestinian compilations, but it is primarily in the Bavli that we find harsh criticisms of the Sadducees. While in general the greater narrativity of the Bavli is an indisputable fact, it does not account for the greater negativity of the Bavli's traditions about the Sadducees.

How else might we account for these phenomena?[30] In an earlier study, I examined rabbinic traditions about the Hasmoneans and

---

29a; b. Yoma 4a, 19b (twice), and 53a; b. Sukkah 48b–49a; b. Hagigah 16b (and parallel); b. Baba Batra 115b-116a (twice); b. Sanhedrin 33b, 52b, and 90b; b. Horayot 4a and 4b; b. Menahot 65a; and b. Niddah 33b–34a (3 times). In compiling the above figures, we count exact parallel traditions within a single compilation as one. We count as one cases in which the Sadducees are mentioned more than once in a single discussion, unless they are mentioned by more than one tradition within the discussion. For example, we count as two cases in which Sadducees are mentioned once in a single Baraita and then again in an Amoraic statement based on the Baraita. We also count as two cases in which the Sadducees are mentioned in two Amoraic statements. We count as one cases in which Sadducees are mentioned more than once in the Mishnah or Tosefta but the two usages occur within a single tradition; if they occur within separate traditions, we count them as two. To determine whether or not more than one tradition is involved, we do not rely on the traditional numbering system, since these divisions are later impositions onto the text and are often not consistent from one manuscript to the next. Instead, we attempt to determine whether or not a particular tradition or set of opinions would be quoted in the Talmud as a single tradition or as multiple traditions. It is certainly possible that we have incorrectly categorized and counted some traditions, but this fact does not have a significant impact on our findings since the errors will tend to cancel one another out. That is, if according to our criteria we mistakenly inflate the number of cases in which Sadducees are mentioned in the Bavli, we will very likely do the same for the Yerushalmi, since we employ the same criteria for both compilations.

[29] The exceptions are b. Baba Batra 115b-116a and possibly b. Kiddushin 66a. Compare m. Eruvin 6:2 with b. Eruvin 68b; and y. Sukkah 4:8 (54d) (and parallel) with b. Sukkah 48b–49a. See the analyses of these traditions above.

[30] Cohen, "The Significance of Yavneh," 39–40, points out that "the amoraim of Babylonia, begin to see themselves more clearly as the descendants of the Pharisees." See also Martin Jaffee, *Torah in the Mouth* (New York: Oxford University Press, 2001) 52–60. Might this explain in part why the Bavli dislikes Sadducees, the traditional enemies of the Pharisees, who Babylonian Amoraim came to view as their progenitors? This explanation, however, accomplishes nothing, since to answer one question ("Why is the Bavli anti-Sadducee?") raises another, equally

found that Babylonian traditions tend to be critical of Hasmoneans while Palestinian traditions tend to be neutral or even positive toward them, similar to the distinction noted here.[31] I concluded that Babylonian rabbis used these unflattering stories and statements to criticize Babylonian contemporaries who claimed Hasmonean descent.[32] Perhaps, therefore, Babylonian rabbis were competing against contemporary Jews who referred to themselves as Sadducees or who exhibited Sadducean traits.[33]

Who or what might such a group or such individuals have been like? What might have marked one as a Sadducee in third- to seventh-century Babylonia? Several traditions in the Bavli, as well as Josephus, characterize Sadducees as a group which accepts only scripture and rejects the traditions of the Pharisees or the sages.[34] In this guise they bear a striking resemblance to Karaites,[35] who originated

---

difficult question ("Why do Babylonian rabbis identify with Pharisees?"). Perhaps it would be preferable to argue that the Bavli's dislike of the Sadducees induced them to have greater sympathy for Pharisees, the Sadducees' opponents.

[31] I say "similar" because Palestinian traditions about Sadducees tend to be neutral, but not positive.

[32] Kalmin, *The Sage in Jewish Society*, 61–67 and 135–38.

[33] Or to what they considered to be Sadducean traits. See the discussion below. See also Martin Goodman, "A Note on Josephus, the Pharisees and Ancestral Traditions," *JJS* 50.2 (1999) 17–18; and Albert I. Baumgarten, "The Pharisaic Paradosis," *HTR* 80.1 (1987) 64–65 and 70.

[34] Regarding Josephus' description of the Sadducees, see Antiquities 13.297 and 408; and 17.41. See also the discussion below.

[35] Ben Zion Wacholder, *The Dawn of Qumran: The Sectarian Torah and the Teacher of Righteousness* (Cincinnati: Hebrew Union College Press, 1983) 141–69 and 264–70; and Yaakov Elman, "The World of the 'Sabboraim:' Cultural Aspects of Post-Redactional Additions to the Bavli," a paper delivered at a conference on "Creation and Composition: The Contribution of the Bavli Redactors (Stammaim) to the Aggada," hosted by New York University, February, 2003, argue for the existence of proto-Karaite groups in Babylonia during these centuries. For further discussion of possible connections (or the lack thereof) between Karaites and earlier Jewish groups, see, for example, Naphtali Wieder, *The Judean Scrolls and Karaism* (London: East and West Library, 1962) 253–57; Yoram Erder, "Eimatai Hehel ha-Mifgash shel ha-Kar'ut im Sifrut Apokrifit ha-Kerovah le-Sifrut ha-Megilot ha-Genuzot?"; idem, "Divrei Teshuvah," and Haggai ben Shammai, "He'arot Metodiot le-Heker ha-Yahas bein Kara'im le-Vein Kitot Yehudiot Kedumot (be-Heksher ha-Islami ve-ha-Erez-Yisraeli)," *Katedra* 42 (1987) 54–68 and 85–86; and 69–84 respectively; Zussman, "Heker Toldot ha-Halakhah," 45, n. 147 and 59, n. 187; and Robert Brody, *The Geonim of Babylonia and the Shaping of Medieval Culture* (New Haven: Yale University Press, 1998) 85–95. Regarding the possibility of the continued existence in Palestine of Sadducees after the destruction of the Temple, perhaps for centuries, see Martin Goodman, "Sadducees and Essenes After 70 CE," in *Crossing the Boundaries; Essays in Biblical Interpretation in Honour of Michael D. Gouldner*, ed. Stanley E. Porter, et al. (Leiden: Brill, 1994) 347–56.

in Persia and only subsequently moved to Israel.[36] Early Karaites were often referred to by their medieval rabbanite contemporaries and opponents as Sadducees, in part because one of the fundamental tenets of Karaism is the denial of the rabbinic tradition and the claim to be reliant on the authority of the Bible alone.[37] While the Karaite movement "coalesced only about the end of the ninth or beginning of the tenth century,"[38] it is theoretically possible that Karaite tendencies percolated in the Babylonian Jewish community for centuries prior to Karaism's crystallization as a movement. Perhaps third- to seventh-century Babylonian rabbis were aware of some proto-Karaite groups or individuals in Jewish society, and perhaps they polemicized against them or took literary vengeance on them by telling stories which portrayed ancient Sadducean characters as villains.

Several factors, however, militate against this explanation. First, in my earlier study of the Hasmoneans I found evidence that Babylonian rabbis competed with contemporary Jews who claimed Hasmonean descent. One story, for example, features a character who opposes a prominent Babylonian rabbi while claiming Hasmonean descent.[39] I found no evidence, however, of Babylonian Jews of the third to seventh centuries claiming Sadducean descent, or of Babylonian rabbis responding to Sadducee-like groups as a continued presence during the rabbis' own era. We have no evidence before the ninth or tenth centuries of actual groups or individuals in Babylonia who were referred to as Sadducees or who exhibited Sadducean tendencies. The advent of the Karaite movement in ninth or tenth century Persia still leaves a gap of at least two centuries between the Talmudic and the post-Talmudic evidence. And the Karaite movement began in and around Baghdad at the center of the Arab empire, far from the Babylonian rabbinic centers of Talmudic and early gaonic times. The findings of the present study, therefore, appear to call for a different explanation than that offered in my earlier work. Finally, it is strange, although not impossible, that the rabbis would attack proto-Karaites only by tampering with stories about first century (or earlier) Sadducees. Babylonian rabbis were not at all shy

---

[36] See Erder, "Eimatai," 54–68; and Brody, *The Geonim of Babylonia*, 85 and 88–89.
[37] Erder, "Eimatai," 57.
[38] Brody, *The Geonim of Babylonia*, 88.
[39] B. Kiddushin 70a–b.

about criticizing their opponents directly, for example by means of stories depicting the misdeeds of their contemporaries.[40]

We avoid these problems if we adopt an explanation based on two closely related literary phenomena: the incorporation into the Bavli of Josephus or Josephus-like traditions,[41] and the influx into Babylonia of traditions from the west, that is from Jews in the Roman Empire, beginning in the fourth Babylonian Amoraic generation (mid-fourth century C.E.).[42] To be specific, I will attempt to show that the introduction of Josephus or Josephus-like traditions into mid-fourth century Babylonia motivated the Bavli's tendency to portray the Sadducees in negative terms. Josephus, or the Josephus-like traditions mentioned above, had relatively little impact on Palestinian compilations (as is shown by the simple fact that parallels between Josephus and traditions in Palestinian compilations are rare), which explains the tendency of traditions in Palestinian documents to depict the Sadducees in neutral fashion. As noted in the introduction, above, in this one instance Roman Jewish culture appears to have had a greater impact on rabbinic Mesopotamia than on rabbinic Palestine. Scholars are more accustomed to viewing Palestine within the orbit of the ancient Greek and Roman worlds much more so than seeing Jewish Babylonia in this fashion.

As noted above, this conclusion does not preclude the possibility that Babylonian rabbis were also reacting to the existence of proto-Karaites in their midst. In fact, the presence of such groups or individuals would help explain why Babylonian rabbis were receptive to Josephus or Josephus-like traditions and incorporated them into their developing compilation. It remains the case, however, that no positive evidence has yet been found for the existence of such groups

---

[40] One exception appears to have been the exilarch, whom they seem to have criticized only indirectly, via criticisms of the exilarch's servants, or his "household." The exilarch, however, was a politically powerful individual who had police power and would have been capable of inflicting great harm on the rabbis. Presumably proto-Karaites (if they existed) would not have been.

[41] The term "Josephus-like traditions" is intended to leave open the possibility that in several instances the Bavli and Josephus drew narratives from an earlier compilation no longer extant.

[42] This is not to suggest that traditions from the west did not reach Babylonia prior to this time. The acceptance of the Mishnah by the earliest Babylonian Amoraim shows clearly that they did. It is simply to maintain that the mid-fourth century marked the beginning of a particularly extensive influx of western traditions into Babylonia.

or individuals in Sasanian Babylonia, and the arguments raised above against this possibility establish it as rather unlikely, although not impossible.

THE PORTRAYAL OF SADDUCEES AS A GROUP
THAT ACCEPTS ONLY SCRIPTURE

What is the basis for the claim that Josephus or Josephus-like traditions motivated the Bavli's negative portrayals of Sadducees? The answer is that we find in the Bavli descriptions and portrayals of the Sadducees strikingly similar to those found in Josephus, and unlike anything found in Palestinian compilations. Moreover, it is easy to see why people portrayed with such characteristics would be anathema to the rabbis, and the negative portrayals of Sadducees and the portrayals of them as a group which accepts only scripture are known to the same Babylonian rabbis, attested beginning in the mid-fourth century C.E.

In b. Horayot 4a, for example, we find the following:

(A) Said Rav Yehudah said Shmuel, "A court [which issues an incorrect opinion, causing the community to sin inadvertently] is not obligated [to bring a sacrifice] until it rules on a matter with which the Sadducees disagree. But if it is a matter with which the Sadducees agree, the court is exempt [from bringing a sacrifice].

(B) What is the reason?

(C) It is a matter of "Go and read in [the children's] schoolhouse [*zil karei bei rav*]."

According to this brief discussion, and according to a strikingly similar but independent discussion in b. Sanhedrin 33b,[43] the expression

---

[43] A closely related tradition is preserved in b. Sanhedrin 33b. We read there:

(A) Mishnah: [In the case of] monetary matters, they bring back [the accused] both for [possible] exoneration [following conviction] and for [possible] conviction [following exoneration]. [In the case of] a capital crime, they bring back [the accused] for [possible] exoneration [following conviction] but not for [possible] conviction [following exoneration].

(B) Talmud: Said R. Hiyya bar Abba said R. Yohanan, "Provided that [the court] erred regarding a matter with which the Sadducees disagreed, "a matter with which the Sadducees agree" is synonymous with scripture, since scripture is what is "read in [the children's] schoolhouse."[44] The term *bei rav* often refers to a school for children, and the usage here of the term *karei*, "read," to denote what goes on there supports this understanding, since every curriculum of children's study mentioned in classical rabbinic literature specifies scripture as the one and only thing which children learned to read.[45] According to this discussion, the Sadducees accepted scripture but rejected rabbinic learning *in toto*.

We have yet to determine, however, approximately when this conception of the Sadducees is first attested in Babylonia. As noted above, it is important to decide this question because it is crucial for making our case that Josephus or Josephus-like traditions motivated the Bavli's negative portrayals of the Sadducees. And linking the two phenomena in this fashion allows us to measure more precisely in one specific instance the impact of Josephus, or Josephus-like traditions, on the rabbis of Babylonia. For no longer do these traditions from Rome merely manifest themselves in the portrayal by a few traditions in the Bavli of the Sadducees as accepting only scripture; they also display themselves in the richly negative por-

---

(C)   but regarding a matter with which the Sadducees agreed,

(C1)   it is a matter of "Go and read in [the children's] schoolhouse [*zil karei bei rav*]."

This brief discussion, like the discussion on b. Horayot 4a (see above), asserts that Sadducees accept scripture but reject rabbinic tradition. And like the previous discussion, the concluding sections [(C) and (C1)] probably derive from the anonymous editors rather than from the early Amoraim (B). Once again, at issue is a change from Hebrew to Aramaic, with only the Aramaic part of the discussion asserting that the Sadducees accepted only the Bible and rejected rabbinic tradition. Confining ourselves to the Hebrew part (B) alone, the early to mid-third century Palestinian Amoraim, like Shmuel and Rav Yehudah above, perhaps use the expression, "a matter with which the Sadducees agree," to indicate the basic minimum requirements or beliefs shared by all Jews, even Sadducees. Once again, there is no reason to assume that this coincides with what is explicit in scripture.

Incidentally, part (C) is also in Hebrew, but it does not stand by itself, without the Aramaic part (C1). If (C1) is a later addition to the statement, therefore, as I believe it is, then part (C) is also a later addition.

[44] See David Goodblatt, *Rabbinic Instruction in Sasanian Babylonia* (Leiden: Brill, 1975) 108–9.

[45] See Catherine Hezser, *Jewish Literacy in Roman Palestine* (Tübingen: Mohr, 2001) 68–72, 75–84, and passim. As David Halivni pointed out in a paper delivered at a conference on "Creation and Composition: The Contribution of the Bavli Redactors (Stammaim) to the Aggada," hosted by New York University, February, 2003, there are several references in the Bavli to "books of aggadah," but they are never said to have been studied by children.

trayals of Sadducees found only in the Bavli and unattested elsewhere in rabbinic literature of antiquity. As noted in the introduction, above, chronology is crucial in establishing this link, since we will find that both phenomena, both the Bavli's negative portrayals of the Sadducees and its portrayal of them as accepting only scripture, are attested for the first time in Babylonia by rabbis who flourished during the mid-fourth century C.E.

Based on the attribution of the statement examined above to Shmuel, it would appear that the earliest attestation in the Bavli of the portrayal of Sadducees as accepting only scripture is from the beginning of the Amoraic period, in the first half of the third century C.E. Closer examination, however, reveals that only part (C) of the statement attests to this portrayal, and part (C) most likely derives from the Bavli's anonymous editors rather than from the early Amora.

What is the evidence for this claim? Part (A) of the discussion is in Hebrew and parts (B) and (C) are in Aramaic, and as Shamma Friedman has shown, a change of language often indicates a change of speaker.[46] It is likely, therefore, that the statement by Shmuel as quoted by Rav Yehudah originally[47] consisted of part (A) alone. Supporting this conclusion is the strangeness, which is by no means the impossibility, of a single individual making a statement (A) in Hebrew and then asking "What is the reason?" in Aramaic, with the latter question based on his own statement.[48]

I belabor this point because it is only according to part (C) that the Sadducees are clearly conceived of as accepting only scripture and as rejecting rabbinic tradition. If we confine ourselves to part (A) alone, i.e., to the original core of the statement,[49] then a strict division between scripture and rabbinic tradition need not be implied. Rather, the early third century C.E. Babylonian Amoraim (Shmuel

---

[46] Friedman, "Al Derekh Heker ha-Sugya," 25–26.

[47] By the term "originally," I mean the most "original" form of his statement that we are at present capable of reconstructing. It is possible, of course, that the statement looked different in earlier stages of development, but these are at present inaccessible to us.

[48] Perhaps the expression, "Go and read in [the children's] schoolhouse" is a proverb, and it is common to find popular proverbs rendered in Aramaic in rabbinic sources. This consideration may partly explain the change in language from Hebrew to Aramaic. This consideration still leaves unexplained the fact that part (B), which is certainly not part of the proverb, is also in Aramaic. It also leaves unaccounted for a statement by Rav Sheshet on b. Horayot 4b, to be examined in detail below.

[49] See above, n. 47.

and Rav Yehudah) may be saying that if a court issues a ruling that even the Sadducees accept, it may be assumed that the ruling is common knowledge and/or practice,[50] agreed upon by all, since the issues upon which the Sadducees and the sages agreed represent the bare minimum that every Jew, even a Sadducee, could be assumed to share in common. And if a matter is common knowledge or practice, the court is not obligated to bring a sacrifice since they have not caused the community to sin. In other words, it may be a matter of indifference to the early Amoraim, with respect to the issue of determining the court's liability to bring a sacrifice, whether or not a particular law or practice is present in the Bible. The important variable may be whether or not the law or practice in question is a matter of common knowledge or agreed upon by every Jew, independent of its provenance.

According to our conclusions above, therefore, it is the anonymous authors of part (C) who are the first to assert that the Sadducees accept only scripture and reject rabbinic tradition. It would appear that this notion entered the Talmud some time between the early third century (when Shmuel flourished) and the early seventh century (after the Muslim conquest of Babylonia, when the Talmud as a recognizable book was almost certainly complete). Since it is the growing consensus of modern scholars that the anonymous portions of the Talmud are among its latest layers, it is likely that this anonymous commentary was added to the Talmud some time during the latter part of this period.

A statement in b. Horayot 4b provides perhaps the strongest support for our claim regarding the early Amoraic conception of the Sadducees. That is, during the early Amoraic period, in other words prior to the mid-fourth century, the Sadducees were not portrayed in Babylonia as a group which accepted only scripture. This portrayal is not attested until the mid-fourth century, which we will see below is the time when the negative portrayals of Sadducees are first attested in the Bavli.

We read in b. Horayot 4b:

> Said Rav Sheshet, and so [it was] taught [in] the house of R. Yishmael, "Why did they say, '[If the court] rules concerning a matter with which the Sadducees agree, [the members of the court] are exempt

---

[50] See Goodman, "A Note on Josephus," 17–20.

[from bringing a sacrifice]?' Because [the community] should have learned [what the proper ruling is] and they did not learn."[51]

This statement is entirely in Hebrew, and is apparently Amoraic from start to finish. Rav Sheshet is a late third-, early fourth-century Babylonian Amora, and Hanokh Albeck has demonstrated that the term Tanna de-vei R. Yishmael has the status of an Amoraic statement.[52] Unlike the statement examined previously,[53] where it was necessary to hypothesize the existence of an earlier Amoraic core to which was added anonymous commentary, here we have an unadorned Amoraic statement and it conforms to our claim above regarding the Amoraic versus the anonymous editorial parts of the statements. As we argued above, this Amoraic statement does not explicitly credit Sadducees with the rejection of rabbinic tradition and with the acceptance of scripture alone. As noted above, there is no reason to assume that the expression "a matter with which the Sadducees agree" refers to scripture. The phrase apparently refers to the fundamentals of Jewish law, whatever their source or mode of derivation.

We must once again be wary of drawing far-reaching conclusions on the basis of a small number of cases. Rav Sheshet's statement, however, supports our claim above that the Aramaic section of the statement in b. Horayot 4a[54] is an anonymous editorial addition to a statement by an Amora. The Amoraim (at least the early Amoraim; see the discussion below) do not define "what the Sadducees agree with" as acceptance by the Sadducees of scripture and scripture alone.

Analysis of another set of traditions may enable us to fix with greater precision when, prior to the anonymous editors, the conception of the Sadducees as accepting only scripture made its first appearance in the Bavli. The ensuing discussion argues that this took place during or shortly after the mid-fourth century, in the form of two statements attributed to Abaye, a fourth-generation Babylonian Amora. As noted above, this conclusion is essential to our argument because we will find that the rabbis who present the Sadducees as

---

[51] R. Hananel quotes the reading of the printed edition, but reports an alternative reading: "[If the court] rules concerning a matter in the Torah, [the members of the court] are exempt." According to this reading, this statement is not relevant to our inquiry since it does not mention the Sadducees.

[52] Hanokh Albeck, *Mavo la-Talmudim* (Tel Aviv: Devir, 1969) 39–43.

[53] Actually, the two statements. See above, n. 46.

[54] As well as that on b. Sanhedrin 33b.

accepting only scripture are the same rabbis who cite traditions which depict the Sadducees negatively, supporting our claim that the two phenomena are linked. It is therefore likely that not only the few rabbinic traditions that explicitly characterize the Sadducees as accepting only scripture betray the influence of Josephan or Josephus-like traditions; the traditions in the Bavli that are sharply negative toward the Sadducees do so as well. Dating these two phenomena to the mid-fourth century c.e. allows us, therefore, to add to the growing body of evidence pointing precisely toward this time as the beginning of a prolonged period of cultural exchange, apparently one-way, between Rome and Mesopotamia. It supports our characterization of this period as one of Babylonian receptivity to Jewish traditions deriving from Rome and the Roman Empire, adding depth and perspective to our understanding of Jewish culture in late antiquity.

It is important to note that the conclusion that the conception of the Sadducees as accepting only scripture reached Babylonia in the mid-fourth century depends on accepting the attribution of two statements to Abaye as indicative at least of the approximate period during which the statements were made.[55] The fact that earlier Amoraic traditions attest to one conception of the Sadducees, and later traditions, both anonymous and Amoraic, attest to another, supports this methodology, a point we will develop below.

The first of Abaye's two statements is part of a discussion in b. Berakhot 29a, examined preliminarily above:

(A)   We taught [in a Tannaitic tradition]: Do not trust yourself until the day of your death, for Yohanan the High Priest served in the office of the high priesthood for 80 years and in the end he became a Sadducee.

(B)   Said Abaye, "[King] Yannai and Yohanan [the High Priest] are one [and the same person]."

At first blush Abaye's statement is strange. What induces him to equate King Yannai and Yohanan the High Priest, given the obvious fact that they have different names and are portrayed so differently throughout rabbinic literature?

For reasons to be spelled out in detail below, it is likely that a

---

[55] See also Appendix Four, below.

lengthy narrative, quoted by Abaye in b. Kiddushin 66a, helps answer this question.[56] We read there:

> Abaye said, "What is the basis for [my opinion]? It is taught [in a Tannaitic teaching]: Yannai the king went to Kohlit in the desert and conquered 60 cities. When he returned, he rejoiced greatly and called to all of the sages of Israel. [He] said to them, 'Our ancestors ate mallows when they built the Temple, so too we shall eat mallows in memory of our ancestors.' They placed mallows on golden tables and ate. And there was an elder there, a scoffing, evil, worthless man named Elazar ben Poerah. And Elazar ben Poerah said to Yannai the king, 'Yannai the king, the hearts of the Pharisees are against you.' [Yannai] said to him, 'What shall I do?' [Elazar] said to him, 'Make them swear an oath by the frontlet between your eye.' [Yannai] made them swear an oath by the frontlet between his eyes. There was an elder there and Yehudah ben Gedidiah was his name. And Yehudah ben Gedidiah said to Yannai the king, 'Yannai the king, the crown of kingship is enough for you, leave the crown of priesthood to the seed of Aaron.' For people had said, 'His mother had been taken captive in Modi'im.' The matter was investigated but not confirmed, and the sages departed in anger. And Elazar ben Poerah said to Yannai the king, 'Yannai the king, such is the law for a commoner in Israel. For you who are king and high priest should such be the law?' [Yannai said to him], 'What shall I do?' [Elazar said to Yannai], 'If you listen to my advice, trample them.' [Yannai said to Elazar], 'And what will become of the Torah?' [Elazar said to Yannai], 'It is bound up and lying[57] in a corner. Whoever wants to learn it, let him come and learn.'"
>
> Said Rav Nahman bar Yizhak, "Immediately heresy was cast into him," for [Yannai] should have said, "It is well [with regard to] the written Torah. What about the oral Torah?'" "Immediately the evil sprouted forth as a result of Elazar ben Poerah [and as a result of

---

[56] For further discussion of this story and its relationship to the account in Josephus (see below), see, for example, M. J. Geller, "Alexander Jannaeus and the Pharisee Rift," *JJS* 30 (1979) 202–11; Lee I. Levine, "Ha-Ma'avak ha-Politi bein ha-Perushim li-Zedukim bi-Tekufat ha-Bayit ha-Sheni," in *Perakim be-Toldot Yerushalayim bi-Yemei Bayit Sheni: Sefer Zikaron le-Avraham Shalit* (Jerusalem: Yad Yizhak Ben-Zvi, 1981) 70–73; Albert I. Baumgarten, "Rabbinic Literature as a Source for the History of Jewish Sectarianism in the Second Temple Period," *Dead Sea Discoveries* 2 (1995) 36–52, and the references cited on 36, n. 81, there; Jaffee, *Torah in the Mouth*, 53–55; and Kalmin, "Kings, Priests, and Sages," 72–79.

[57] I am not convinced by the arguments of Ephraim E. Urbach, "Ha-Derashah ki-Yesod ha-Halakhah u-Va'ayat ha-Soferim," *Tarbiz* 27, Nos. 2–3 (1958) 181; and idem, *Ha-Halakhah: Mekoroteha ve-Hitpathutah* (Givatayim, Israel: Yad la-Talmud, 1984) 181, n. 52, in favor of the reading "written and lying," i.e., written and officially published in an archive. Urbach's claim depends upon emendation of the text (removal of the words, "in a corner") and upon acceptance of a reading of the story attested only in some versions of a 16th-century collection, *Aggadot ha-Talmud.*

Yehudah ben Gedidiah],[58] and all of the sages were killed, and the world was desolate until Shimon ben Shetach came and restored the Torah as of old."

This narrative makes no explicit mention of Sadducees, but it closely parallels an account in Josephus, which identifies the opponents of the Pharisees as Sadducees.[59] It will be helpful to quote the relevant passage from Josephus:

> As for Hyrcanus, the envy of the Jews was aroused against him by his own successes and those of his sons; particularly hostile to him were the Pharisees, who are one of the Jewish schools, as we have related above. And so great is their influence with the masses that even when they speak against a king or high priest, they immediately gain credence. Hyrcanus too was a disciple of theirs, and was greatly loved by them.
>
> And once he invited them to a feast and entertained them hospitably, and when he saw that they were having a very good time, he began by saying that they knew he wished to be righteous and in everything he did tried to please God and them—for the Pharisees profess such beliefs; at the same time he begged them, if they observed him doing anything wrong or straying from the right path, to lead him back to it and correct him. But they testified to his being altogether virtuous, and he was delighted with their praise. However, one of the guests, named Eleazar, who had an evil nature and took pleasure in dissension, said, "Since you have asked to be told the truth, if you wish to be righteous, give up the high-priesthood and be content with governing the people." And when Hyrcanus asked him for what reason he should give up the high-priesthood, he replied, "Because we have heard from our elders that your mother was a captive in the reign of Antiochus Epiphanes." But the story was false, and Hyrcanus was furious with the man, while all the Pharisees were very indignant. Then a certain Jonathan, one of Hyrcanus' close friends, belonging to the school of the Sadducees, who hold opinions opposed to those of the Pharisees, said that it had been with the general approval of all the Pharisees that Eleazar had made his slanderous statement; and this, he added, would be clear to Hyrcanus if he inquired of them what punishment he deserved—for, he said, he would be convinced that the slanderous statement had not been made with their approval if they fixed a penalty commensurate with the crime—, and they replied that

---

[58] The printed text lacks the phrase "and Yehudah ben Gedidyah," but it is found in mss. Munich 95, Oxford 842, and Vatican 111.

[59] Josephus, *Jewish Antiquities 13.288–300*. For earlier discussion of this passage, see, for example, Steve Mason, *Flavius Josephus on the Pharisees: A Composition-Critical Study* (Boston: Brill Academic Publishers, Inc., 2001) 215–45.

Eleazar deserved stripes and chains; for they did not think it right to sentence a man to death for calumny, and anyway the Pharisees are naturally lenient in the matter of punishments. At this Hyrcanus became very angry and began to believe that the fellow had slandered him with their approval. And Jonathan in particular inflamed his anger, and so worked upon him that he brought him to join the Sadducean party and desert the Pharisees, and to abrogate the regulations which they had established for the people, and punish those who observed them. Out of this, of course, grew the hatred of the masses for him and his sons, but of this we shall speak hereafter.

For the present I wish merely to explain that the Pharisees had passed on to the people certain regulations handed down by former generations and not recorded in the Laws of Moses, for which reason they are rejected by the Sadducean group, who hold that only those regulations should be considered valid which were written down, and those which had been handed down by former generations need not be observed.

And concerning these matters the two parties came to have controversies and serious differences, the Sadducees having the confidence of the wealthy alone but no following among the populace, while the Pharisees have the support of the masses. But of these two schools and of the Essenes a detailed account has been given in the second book of my *Judaica*.

And so Hyrcanus quieted the outbreak, and lived happily thereafter; and when he died after administering the government excellently for thirty-one years, he left five sons. Now he was accounted by God worthy of three of the greatest privileges, the rule of the nation, the office of high priest, and the gift of prophecy; for the Deity was with him and enabled him to foresee and foretell the future; so, for example, he foretold of his two elder sons that they would not remain masters of the state. And the story of their downfall is worth relating, to show how far they were from having their father's good fortune.

As noted above, Abaye, the author of the strange statement, identifying Yannai and Yohanan the High Priest in b. Berakhot 29a, quotes the story about Yannai's conflict with the Pharisees in b. Kiddushin 66a. As also noted above, the story in Kiddushin motivates, at least in part, Abaye's peculiar statement in Berakhot, since the story can easily be read (and in fact is read by Rav Nahman bar Yizhak, Abaye's younger contemporary; see below) as depicting King Yannai's adoption of a heresy which bears a striking resemblance to Josephus' description of a fundamental tenet of Sadduceeism,[60] as

---

[60] I refer to Josephus' observation in the lengthy passage quoted above that "The Pharisees had passed on to the people certain regulations handed down by former

well as to a belief attributed to the Sadducees by the Bavli's anonymous editors in b. Horayot 4a and b. Sanhedrin 33b (see above).
While the Kiddushin story nowhere mentions the term "Sadducee,"
Abaye in Berakhot easily could have inferred that Yannai became
a Sadducee according to Kiddushin had he known Josephus or a
Josephus-like source, or had he known or shared the anonymous editorial description of them in Horayot and Sanhedrin. Furthermore,
the role of Yannai in Kiddushin is played by John Hyrcanus (= the
rabbis' Yohanan the High Priest) in Josephus, and by Yohanan the
High Priest in Berakhot.[61]

In other words, Abaye in Berakhot asserts that Yohanan the High
Priest, who became a Sadducee after 80 years of service as high
priest, is the same as Yannai in Kiddushin, who consistently follows
the advice of Elazar ben Poerah. And Elazar ben Poerah clearly
shows himself to be a Sadducee as described by Josephus and the
anonymous editors of the Bavli when he has the following exchange
with King Yannai:

> [Elazar said to Yannai], 'If you listen to my advice, trample them"
> [i.e., have all of the sages killed].
>   [Yannai said to Elazar], "And what will become of the Torah?"
> [Elazar said to Yannai], "It is bound up and lying in a corner. Whoever
> wants to learn it, let him come and learn." ... Immediately the evil
> sprouted forth as a result of Elazar ben Poerah [and as a result of
> Yehudah ben Gedidiah], and all of the sages were killed. ...

Since this story portrays Yannai as totally dependent on Elazar ben
Poerah and as following all of his advice, it is not much of a leap
to conclude that Yannai comes to accept Elazar's claim that all of
the Torah is contained in scripture, and killing the sages does not
diminish or endanger the Torah in the slightest. When Abaye asserts
in Berakhot that Yohanan the High Priest and King Yannai are one
and the same, he is in effect saying that the belief shared by Yannai
and Elazar according to this plausible reading of Kiddushin is a
tenet of Sadduceeism. Abaye's two statements taken together yield
the earliest rabbinic expression of the notion that the Sadducees
accept scripture alone, and reject rabbinic tradition.

---

generations and not recorded in the laws of Moses, for which reason they are
rejected by the Sadducean group, who hold that only those regulations should be
considered valid which were written down, and those which had been handed down
by former generations need not be observed." See the discussion below.
   [61] See also Josephus, *Antiquities* 13.372–376.

It is possible, of course, that the attributions to Abaye of the statements in Berakhot and Kiddushin are pseudepigraphical, in which case we have no evidence regarding mid-fourth century Babylonian Amoraic conceptions of Sadducees. It strains credulity, however, to claim that Abaye's statements do not derive from a single individual, or at least from a single school or group. For if they are pseudepigraphical, and/or they derive from different schools, then we render incoherent the claim in b. Berakhot 29a that "[King] Yannai and Yohanan [the High Priest] are one [and the same person]." It is understandable why a single person or group would make this statement in combination with the statement on b. Kiddushin 66a. We need posit only (as we posited above) that the person or group who identified Yannai and Yohanan the High Priest in b. Berakhot 29a also knew the story in b. Kiddushin 66a, which features Yannai the king, and knew as well that the story describes the king's conversion to Sadduceeism, as is clear from Josephus' version of the story and as is deducible from the anonymous Babylonian texts discussed above.

If the attributions are pseudepigraphical, then the same pseudepigraphers knew all of this information, and for some unknown reason attributed all of it to Abaye, and also attributed it to Abaye's younger contemporary, Rav Nahman bar Yizhak (see below). These same pseudepigraphers, presumably, attributed a different conception of the Sadducees to pre-fourth generation Amoraim, creating the illusion of chronological development (why, we cannot say), and arranged as well for conceptions about the Sadducees in anonymous editorial additions to conform to those of the later Amoraim, striving as they were for chronological verisimilitude.

It is much more likely, as noted above, that the attributions in this case are trustworthy, or at least are indicative of the approximate time period when the statements were made. It is important to emphasize that this is not an argument in favor of trusting ancient rabbinic attributions in general; it is simply to say that in the cases under consideration here it makes sense to do so. Our conclusions certainly increase the likelihood that other rabbinic attributions are reliable, but we have no idea how many, nor can we be confident that this is the case (or is not the case!) regarding any statement in the absence of concrete proof.

Be that as it may, if we accept on the basis of his statement in b. Berakhot 29a that Abaye believes the story in b. Kiddushin 66a is about Sadducees, and also accept the attribution to Abaye of the quotation of the story in b. Kiddushin 66a, we have proof that some time between Rav Sheshet and Abaye, between the third and fourth Babylonian Amoraic generations, i.e., some time during the mid-fourth century C.E., the Josephan characterization of the Sadducees as a group which accepted only scripture and rejected rabbinic traditions became known to and accepted by at least one Babylonian rabbi.

This conclusion is strengthened by the fact that Rav Nahman bar Yizhak, also a mid-fourth century Babylonian Amora, comments on the story in b. Kiddushin 66a and apparently shares Abaye's characterization of the Sadducees. Rav Nahman bar Yizhak's comment and the immediate context are worth examining in greater detail:

> And Elazar ben Poerah said to Yannai the king, "Yannai the king, such is the law for a commoner in Israel. For you who are king and high priest should such be the law?" [Yannai said to him], "What shall I do?" [Elazar said to Yannai], "If you listen to my advice, trample them." [Yannai said to Elazar], "And what will become of the Torah?" [Elazar said to Yannai],
>
> "It is bound up and lying in a corner. Whoever wants to learn it, let him come and learn." Said Rav Nahman bar Yizhak, "Immediately heresy was cast into him," for [Yannai] should have said, "It is well [with regard to] the written Torah. What about the oral Torah?"

In this crucial section of the story, Yannai worries about the fate of the Torah should the sages be disposed of, implying that he at least entertains the possibility that the sages are custodians or teachers of the Torah, and perhaps that their wisdom, independent of scripture, has the status of Torah. When Elazar ben Poerah says, "It is bound up and lying in a corner," he asserts that the Torah consists of scripture alone, and the loss of the sages will not affect it in the slightest.

To more fully understand the significance of Rav Nahman bar Yizhak's comment, it is important to note that his statement is divisible into two parts. The first part is in Hebrew and is apparently Amoraic, and the second part is in Aramaic and is apparently later, anonymous commentary based on the earlier Amoraic core.[62] The Hebrew core of the statement consists of the phrase: "Immediately heresy was cast into him," and most likely the "him" referred to is

---

[62] See above, n. 47.

Yannai, who allows the sages to be murdered because he is convinced by Elazar ben Poerah's argument. According to Rav Nahman bar Yizhak, therefore, Yannai accepts Elazar ben Poerah's claim that "the Torah" and "scripture" are synonymous, thereby accepting the Sadducean heresy as described by Josephus and as reflected in the statements of Abaye and the Bavli's anonymous editors. The fact that both Abaye and Rav Nahman bar Yizhak share this conception, but earlier Amoraim share a subtly but demonstrably different idea, allows us to approximate when the Josephan portrayal of the Sadducees reached or at least found acceptance in rabbinic Babylonia. This took place after the time of Rav Sheshet and during or shortly after the fourth generation of Babylonian Amoraim, approximately midway through the fourth century C.E.

What do we make of the Aramaic continuation ("He should have said, 'It is well [with regard to] the written Torah. What about the oral Torah?'"), which we argued above was most likely an anonymous addition to Rav Nahman bar Yizhak's statement? According to this anonymous addition, Yannai's heresy was his denial of the oral Torah, his refusal to consider as Torah anything but the written scroll.

This characterization of Yannai's heresy is similar but not identical to the characterization of Sadducean doctrine which we attributed above to the fourth-generation Amoraim and the anonymous editors of b. Horayot 4a.[63] The anonymous editors grafted onto Rav Nahman bar Yizhak's statement concern for the distinction between the oral and the written Torah. For Rav Nahman bar Yizhak, the salient part of Yannai's heresy was his denial of the proposition that the sages' learning was Torah; for the author of the anonymous addition it was Yannai's denial that the Torah was divisible into two parts, distinguishable above all by their mode of transmission.[64]

---

[63] And b. Sanhedrin 33b. See the discussion above.

[64] With regard to the question of the date of the advent of this conception, see Peter Schäfer, *Studien zur Geschichte und Theologie des Rabbinischen Judentums* (Leiden: Brill, 1978) 153–97; and Stemberger, *Jewish Contemporaries of Jesus*, 94, n. 108. See also Jaffee, *Torah in the Mouth*, 10 and *passim*, who argues that for centuries there existed a distinction in practice between texts transmitted orally and in writing, without the crystallization of the concept of the Oral Torah versus the Written Torah. It is not out of the question that the same conceptual difference distinguishes the statement of Rav Nahman bar Yizhak and the later addition by the anonymous editors.

Interestingly, modern scholars differ over the question of whether
or not the Sadducees portrayed by Josephus reject non-scriptural
traditions because these traditions are oral or because they are not
part of the Bible. The modern scholarly debate revolves around
opposing interpretations of Josephus' description of the Sadducees in
the lengthy account cited above, as follows:

> The Pharisees had passed on to the people certain regulations handed
> down by former generations and not recorded in the Laws of Moses,
> for which reason they are rejected by the Sadducean group, who hold
> that only those regulations should be considered valid which were writ-
> ten down, and these which had been handed down by former gener-
> ations need not be observed.

This modern scholarly debate may have an ancient analogue in the
different emphases of Rav Nahman bar Yizhak, and the anonymous
commentators who added to his statement. Some modern scholars,
in other words, have interpreted Josephus' Sadducees as accepting
the written Torah and rejecting Pharisaic oral tradition, and it is
not out of the question that the anonymous commentators who added
to Rav Nahman bar Yizhak's statement in b. Kiddushin 66a interpreted Josephus, or Josephus' source, in precisely this fashion. Along
these same lines, it is possible that Rav Nahman bar Yizhak minus
the anonymous addition to his statement interpreted Josephus to be
saying that the Sadducees reject the Pharisees' traditions because
they are non-scriptural and not because they are oral.

To date, the most comprehensive analysis of this controversial passage from Josephus is that of Steve Mason, who explains it in accordance with the interpretation of Abaye and Rav Nahman bar Yizhak.
Mason translates the passage as follows:

> [T]he Pharisees passed on to the people certain ordinances from a
> succession of fathers, which are not written down in the laws of Moses.
> For this reason the party of the Sadducees dismisses these ordinances,
> averring that one need only recognize the written ordinances, whereas
> those from the tradition of the fathers need not be observed.[65]

Mason claims that this passage

> says nothing whatsoever about the question whether the Pharisees actu-
> ally transmitted their teachings orally or in writing. . . . Josephus has
> nothing to say about the matter. His point is that the Pharisaic ordi-

---

[65] Mason, *Flavius Josephus on the Pharisees*, 217.

nances were not part of the written Law of Moses and that for this reason they were rejected by the Sadducees.[66]

Why mid-fourth century Babylonian rabbis were especially receptive to western traditions is not completely clear, although institutional developments may be at least partially responsible. There is evidence that the fourth Amoraic generation in Babylonia played a particularly prominent role in the editing of the Talmud,[67] a role which may have been facilitated by the increased complexity of the rabbis' academic institutions,[68] which facilitated direct contact between leading rabbis and the collection of Jewish traditions, both rabbinic and non-rabbinic (e.g., Josephus, the Fasting Scroll, and Ben Sira), from diverse sources and localities in the Roman Empire and throughout rabbinic Babylonia. Perhaps Palestinian rabbinic compilations tended not to incorporate such material during the fourth century C.E., i.e., non-rabbinic traditions as well as rabbinic traditions from localities such as Babylonia, because Palestinian rabbinic institutions were less well developed, and were therefore less conducive to the collection and compilation of traditions from diverse localities and diverse corpora, both rabbinic and non-rabbinic.

CONCLUSION

What does this mean for our argument here? It will be recalled that we started our discussion with the observation that statements and

---

[66] Ibid., 243. See also pages 230–45, there. For further discussion of this passage, see Jacob Neusner, *Rabbinic Traditions About the Pharisees Before 70*, vol. 3 (1971; Reprint. Atlanta: Scholars Press, 1999) 163–65; Ellis Rivkin, *A Hidden Revolution* (Nashville: Abington Press, 1978) 41–42 and passim; Baumgarten, "The Pharisaic Paradosis," 64–65, 69, and 72, n. 33; Jaffee, *Torah in the Mouth*, 50–52; Stemberger, *Jewish Contemporaries of Jesus*, 93–95; Goodman, "A Note on Josephus," 17–20, and the literature cited on 18, n. 3, there; and Daniel Boyarin, "The Diadoche of the Rabbis; Or, Judah the Patriarch at Yavneh," in *Jewish Culture and Society Under the Christian Roman Empire*, ed. Richard Kalmin and Seth Schwartz (Leuven: Peeters Publishing, 2003) 297, n. 318. Compare Urbach, "Ha-Derashah ki-Yesod ha-Halakhah," 181; Joseph M. Baumgarten, "The Unwritten Law in the Pre-Rabbinic Period," *JJS* 3 (1972) 7–29; and Saldarini, *Pharisees and Sadducees*, 308 (but see 117, there).

[67] See Yizhak Halevy, *Dorot ha-Rishonim*, vol. 2 (1897–1939; Reprint. Berlin: Benjamin Harz, 1923) 473 and 480–500 (see the review of Halevy in Julius Kaplan, *The Redaction of the Babylonian Talmud* (1933; Reprint; Jerusalem: Makor, 1973), 19–25; and Kalmin, *Sages, Stories, Authors, and Editors*, 69–73.

[68] See, for example, Goodblatt, *Rabbinic Instruction*, 166–69 and 185–87; and Gafni, *Yehudei Bavel*, 190, 210–13, and 223–26.

stories in the Bavli tend to be more harshly negative toward the
Sadducees than statements and stories in Palestinian compilations.
We were uncertain why this should be, however, since we found no
indication that any Babylonian Jews referred to themselves as Sadducees
or exhibited Sadducean traits, such that the Babylonian rabbis would
be polemicizing against them by telling nasty stories about their
ancient namesakes or counterparts, as we found to be the case in
an earlier study of rabbinic traditions about the Hasmoneans.

The traditions analyzed above suggest that the introduction into
Babylonia of the writings of Josephus, or of traditions used by
Josephus,[69] during the mid-fourth century may provide a key to solv-
ing this puzzle. For as noted above, apparently during the fourth
Amoraic generation the Josephan characterization of the Sadducees
achieved currency in Babylonia. Abaye and Rav Nahman bar Yizhak,
both mid-fourth century Amoraim, know the story in b. Kiddushin
66a which depicts a pernicious heresy, which we know Abaye considered to be Sadducean on the basis of his statement in b. Berakhot
29a. The heresy to which Abaye attests is strikingly similar to Josephus'
depiction of the Sadducees in his version of the same story.

Whether the Babylonians received this portrayal from Josephus
himself or from a source similar to Josephus is at present a moot
point. Also unclear is why Babylonians should have been receptive
to such a portrayal, unless its presence in an ancient source is explanation enough. This portrayal, namely of the Sadducees as accepting only the Bible and rejecting the traditions of the sages (or the
Pharisees),[70] induced Babylonian rabbis to alter the image of the
Sadducees in the texts they inherited from Palestine, or, to be more
precise, to bring out the theme of the Sadducees' wickedness, only
a minor theme in Palestinian texts, and make it more prominent in
their retelling of the stories.[71]

Josephus wrote in Rome, which like Palestine was "west" vis-a-vis
Babylonia, and appears to have first written his books in Aramaic,
in which form they could have been accessible to the rabbis. The
phenomenon of selections from Josephus or from a source like Josephus
reaching Babylonia in the mid-fourth Amoraic century C.E., or becom-

---

[69] See Appendix One, below.
[70] See the discussion of b. Kiddushin 66a, above.
[71] Josephus also depicts the Sadducees negatively in War 2.166 and Antiquities
20.199.

ing incorporated into the developing Bavli only at this time, is part and parcel of a larger phenomenon, namely the influx of western learning into Babylonia, and/or the much greater receptivity on the part of Babylonian rabbis to western learning, beginning in the mid-fourth century and continuing largely unabated until the final editing of the Talmud.[72] By the term "western" I include the learning of Palestinian rabbis, and Josephus or Josephus' source, both of which influence Babylonian rabbis particularly beginning in the fourth Amoraic generation.[73]

Our ability to separate the anonymous editorial from the Amoraic sections of the Talmud was critical to this study, as was our ability to divide the talmudic discussion into chronological layers. Armed with these methodological tools, we attempted to shed light on the cultural connections between Rome and Mesopotamia, connections which are poorly documented and even more poorly understood compared to those between Palestine and Babylonia, and which are too often eclipsed by modern scholarly preoccupation with the more obvious ties between Athens (or Rome) and Jerusalem.

Appendix One: Josephus or Josephus' Sources

I have maintained the distinction throughout between "Josephus" and "Josephus' source," since it is not entirely clear whether the rabbis of the Bavli received these traditions directly from Josephus, or whether Josephus and the rabbis drew upon a common fund of traditions. This issue confronts scholars of rabbinic literature, and in fact of any ancient literature, in a variety of different ways. When a tradition preserved in the Tosefta, an early compilation of rabbinic traditions, is also preserved in the Bavli, although with significant changes, did the tradition exist in an Ur-form prior to both the Tosefta and the Bavli, from where it was taken up and modified to a greater or lesser extent by both later compilations, or did the

---

[72] See Zvi Moshe Dor, *Torat Erez Yisrael be-Bavel* (Tel Aviv: Devir, 1971); Kalmin, *Sages, Stories, Authors, and Editors*, 127–40; and *The Sage in Jewish Society*, 46–48 and passim; and Christine E. Hayes, *Gentile Impurities and Jewish Identities: Intermarriage and Conversion from the Bible to the Talmud* (New York: Oxford University Press, 2002) 190–91.

[73] Josephus apparently gained access to this source between his composition of The Jewish War and Antiquities. That Josephus gained access to this source during this time is indicated by the fact that the narratives most closely paralleled in Josephus and the Bavli are absent from The Jewish War and are present in Antiquities. Furthermore, these narratives tend to be easily detachable from their contexts in Josephus and in the Bavli, with no loss of and often an obvious gain to the coherence of the discussion remains. See Cohen, "Parallel Historical Traditions," 13–14; and Kalmin, "Kings, Priests, and Sages," 72–79.

Bavli take the tradition directly from the Tosefta, such that all or most of the differences between the two traditions are the work of Babylonian editors?

This question is extremely difficult to answer in most cases, but one important consideration with regard to the relationship between Josephus and the Bavli suggests that we are dealing with an Ur-text incorporated into two later compilations. I refer to the fact that in a large proportion of the cases in which Josephus and the Bavli share traditions, the tradition in question is missing from Josephus' earlier work, *The Jewish War*, and is found only in his later work, *Antiquities*, where its connection to Josephus' larger discussion is extremely tenuous.[74] It is peculiar that the Babylonian rabbis should exhibit a preference for Josephan materials that fit only loosely into Josephus' larger discussion and which he discovered between the composition of his earlier and later works. More likely, both Josephus and the rabbis are drawing on a common body of traditions which they altered, and/or which had undergone development during the 100 to 400 years between the time Josephus incorporated them into his work and the time the Babylonian rabbis incorporated them into the developing Talmud.

For our primary purposes, however, it makes no difference whether the rabbis' source for these traditions is Josephus or some Ur-compilation we no longer have. For as noted above, Josephus encountered these traditions between the time he wrote *The Jewish War* and *Antiquities*, when he resided in Rome. Whether Babylonian rabbis found these traditions in Josephus or in Josephus' source, therefore, we are dealing with Jewish traditions deriving from Rome, at least at a certain stage of their development.[75]

APPENDIX TWO: *SADDUCEES AND BOETHUSIANS*[76]

The above discussion focused on stories and statements about the Sadducees in rabbinic literature. No such discussion, however, can ignore the rabbinic depiction of the Boethusians,[77] since several scholars have shown that rabbinic portrayals of these two groups are sometimes indistinguishable, and parallel traditions in different compilations sometimes disagree about whether a particular narrative features Sadducees or Boethusians.[78]

---

[74] See, for example, Cohen, "Parallel Historical Traditions," 13–14; and Kalmin, "Kings, Priests, and Sages," 72–77.

[75] In an earlier work I argued that a tradition shared by Josephus and the rabbis bears traces of partial modification by both Josephus and the rabbis. See Kalmin, "Kings, Priests, and Sages," 72–79.

[76] Scholars disagree about the significance and derivation of this name. According to one view adopted by several scholars, the correct reading of this name in rabbinic texts is "Beit Sin." See, for example, Saul Lieberman, *Tosefta ki-Feshutah*, vol. 4 (New York: Jewish Theological Seminary, 1962) 870–71. We use the conventional spelling "Boethusians," however, to avoid unnecessary confusion. The issue of the original spelling and pronunciation of the name has no bearing on our findings.

[77] For earlier discussions of the Boethusians, see, for example, M. D. Herr, "Mi Hayu ha-Baytosin?" *Proceedings of the Seventh World Congress of Jewish Studies: Studies in the Talmud, Halacha and Midrash* (Jerusalem: World Union of Jewish Studies, 1981) 1–20, and the literature cited there.

[78] See especially y. Yoma 1:5 (39a), where an opinion is attributed first to the Boethusians and subsequently to the Sadducees. Scholars have noted that the Tosefta prefers the term "Boethusians" to "Sadducees," using the term "Sadducee" in only one case, and referring to Boethusians even when parallel traditions use the term

Although as noted above we should be cautious about drawing far-reaching conclusions based on a small corpus of traditions, it appears that attention paid to the
level and type of criticism directed at these groups in rabbinic sources yields one
answer to the long-standing question of how or even whether the ancient rabbis
distinguished between them.[79]

To be specific, our research revealed that the rabbis did draw such a distinction,
in cases where parallel versions in the various compilations agree that a story is
about Boethusians. For in contrast to most Palestinian stories about Sadducees, in
the small number of cases in which the reading "Boethusian" is stable from compilation to compilation, Palestinian stories depict them guilty of serious legal and
ethical offenses.

In such cases, (a) the Boethusians are implicated *en bloc* in despicable schemes to
sabotage the sages' attempts to observe the halakhah; and (b) common people ally
themselves with the sages, helping them foil the Boethusians' schemes.[80] In contrast,
several traditions in the Bavli and in Palestinian compilations depict the Sadducees
as obedient to or fearful of the sages, with the exception of a single zealot who
defies them and is swiftly and justly killed by heaven as a result.[81] In addition, no
stories depict the common people as the sages' allies against the wicked Sadducees.

A story about the Boethusians in t. Rosh Hashanah 1:15 will illustrate several of
these points:[82]

> At first they accepted testimony [regarding the new moon] from every man.
> One time the Boethusians hired two witnesses to come and cause the sages to
> err, since the Boethusians think that Shavuot should always fall after the
> Sabbath. One witness came, gave his testimony, and left, and the second [wit-
> ness] came and said, "I was ascending Ma'aleh Adumim and I saw [the moon]
> crouching between two rocks. Its head resembled a calf's, its ears resembled
> a kid's, its horns resembled a gazelle's. I saw it and was startled and I fell
> backwards and behold, 200 zuz were tied to my belt."
>
> [The sages] said to him, "The coins are yours as a gift and those who hired
> you shall come and be lashed. Why did you get mixed up in this business?"
> He said to them, "Because I heard that the Boethusians wanted to come and
> cause the sages to err. I said, 'It is good that I go and inform the sages.'"
> The Boethusians hire false witnesses and attempt to cause Israel to sanctify the
> new moon at the wrong time. Clearly this story depicts Boethusians as guilty
> of an extremely serious transgression.

A parallel to the above narrative, in y. Rosh Hashanah 2:1 (57d), tells basically the
same story. The Yerushalmi's version is based on m. Rosh Hashanah 2:1:

"Sadducee." This phenomenon has yet to be explained satisfactorily. See also Jean
Le Moyne, *Les Sadducéens*, 101–2; and Zussman, "Heker Toldot ha-Halakhah," 51–52,
n. 171, and 52–53.

[79] See also Zussman, "Heker Toldot ha-Halakhah," 48–49, nn. 166–67, who
observes that the portrayal of Sadducees in rabbinic texts differs from the portrayal
of Boethusians in that the former, in contrast to the latter, are never mentioned in
connection with calendrical matters or the dates of holidays.

[80] See Josephus, Antiquities 13.298, who describes the Pharisees as having "the
masses as their ally." See also Antiquities 13.401 and 18.17.

[81] See above, n. 26.

[82] For further discussion of these texts, see Harari, *Rabbinic Perceptions of the
Boethusians*, 235–53.

(A)   Mishnah: At first they accepted testimony [regarding the] new moon from every man. After the heretics (*minim*) sinned, they ordained that they should only accept [testimony] from [people they] recognized.

(B)   Yerushalmi: It happened that the Boethusians hired two false witnesses to testify that the new moon had been sanctified. One of them came and gave his testimony and left. The other came and said, "I was ascending Ma'aleh Adumim and I saw [the moon] crouching between two rocks. Its head resembled a calf's and its ears resembled a kid's. I saw it and was startled and sprang backward, and behold 200 zuz were tied to my belt."

They said to him, "Behold the 200 zuz are yours as a gift, and those who sent you shall come and be lashed. Why did you get mixed up in all of this?" He said to them, "I saw that they wanted to cause the sages to err. I said, 'It will be good if I go and inform the sages.'"

In both Palestinian versions of this story, the Boethusians are guilty of extremely serious offenses and no distinction is drawn between "good Boethusians" and "bad Boethusians." The same is true of the Bavli's version, likewise based on m. Rosh Hashanah 2:1:

Our rabbis taught [in a Baraita]: How did the Boethusians sin? One time the Boethusians wanted to cause the sages to err. They hired two people with 400 zuz, one of ours [i.e., a member of the sages' party] and one of theirs [i.e., a member of the Boethusian party]. Theirs testified and left. They said to [ours], "Say how you saw the moon." He said to them, "I was ascending Ma'aleh Adumim and I saw [the moon] crouching between two rocks. Its head resembled a calf's and its ears resembled a kid's, its horns resembled a gazelle's, and its tail wasbetween its legs. I looked at it and was startled and fell backward. And if you don't believe me, here are 200 zuz that were wrapped in my neckerchief."

They said to him, "What caused you to get mixed up in this?" He said to them, "I heard that the Boethusians wanted to cause the sages to err. I said, 'I will go and inform them lest unworthy people come and cause the sages to err.'" They said to him, "The 200 zuz are yours as a gift, and he who hired you will be stretched on the pillar." At that time they ordained that testimony is only accepted from [people that one] recognizes.

The portrayal of Boethusians, therefore, is quite stable from one compilation to the next. The Boethusians portrayed in these texts bear little or no resemblance to rabbinic portrayals of Sadducees, which supports our claim that the rabbis sometimes distinguished clearly between the two groups.

Another relevant case is found in t. Sukkah 3:1. We read there:

[The requirement of] the lulav overrides the Sabbath at the beginning [of the holiday, and [that of] the willow [overrides the Sabbath] at the end [of the holiday]. It happened that the Boethusians pressed large rocks over [the willows] on the eve of the Sabbath. The common people (*amei ha-aretz*) saw them and came and dragged [the willows] out[83] from underneath the rocks on the Sabbath, since the Boethusians do not agree that [the ceremony of] beating the willow overrides the Sabbath.

A parallel to this tradition in b. Sukkah 43b shows that once again the reading, "Boethusians," is stable from one compilation to the next, and once again the depic-

---

[83] The reading of the printed text, *gadrum*, "fenced," should be emended to *garerum*, "dragged." See Jastrow, *Dictionary*, 272.

tion of Boethusians is clearly distinguishable from that of the Sadducees. In this case as well the Boethusians attempt to sabotage the sages' observance of the law; there is no distinction between "good Boethusians" and "bad Boethusians;" and non-rabbis come to the sages' aid and foil the Boethusians' plot.

The paucity of sources makes firm conclusions impossible at present, but it would appear that we find preserved in rabbinic texts narratives about two distinct groups referred to by distinct names and depicted in diverse ways, which, however, have merged significantly during the course of transmission.[84] One example of this amalgamation bears examining in detail, since the variation in terminology may be attributable to the fact that the story depicts neither a "typical" Boethusian nor a "typical" Sadducean as we described them above. I refer to the following story in t. Sukkah 3:16:

> It already happened that a Boethusian poured the [water] libation onto his feet and all of the people pelted him with their citrons. The horn of the altar was damaged and the [sacrificial] service was nullified on that very day, until they brought a clump of salt and put it on [the horn of the altar] in order that the altar not appear to be damaged, for every altar that lacks a horn, a ramp, and a base is unfit.[85]

This story is paralleled in b. Sukkah 49a. For our present purposes, the only notable distinction between the two versions is that the Bavli's version features a Sadducee instead of a Boethusian.[86] This story depicts an individual sinner acting in defiance of the sages (characteristic of stories about Sadducees), the sinner surviving his act of defiance of the sages (characteristic of stories about Boethusians), and the common people acting in opposition to the non-rabbinic protagonist (also characteristic of stories about Boethusians). This story, therefore, does not consistently follow either the Boethusian or the Sadducean story patterns described above, and it is perhaps for this reason that the story's terminology is not consistent in all of the parallels.

APPENDIX THREE

B. Baba Batra 115b–116a's derivative character vis-a-vis b. Menahot 65a–b is evident from both the reason the Sadducee provides for his opinion and Rabban Yohanan ben Zakkai's supposedly mocking application of a biblical verse to the Sadducee. The problem with both of these motifs in Baba Batra is that there is nothing at all objectionable or foolish, from a rabbinic perspective, about the Sadducee's proof, and yet Rabban Yohanan ben Zakkai responds, as in Menahot, by insulting the Sadducees' foolishness and "worthless talk." The Sadducee bases himself on a *kol ve-homer*,[87] an *a fortiori* argument: "If the daughter of one's son inher-

---

[84] See, for example, m. Yadayim 4:6–7 compared to t. Yadayim 2:20. In the former case, Sadducees "cry out" against the Pharisees; in the latter, Boethusians "cry out" against them.

[85] See also y. Sukkah 4:8 (51d) (and parallel), where this story is alluded to and quoted in part. We are not told there whether the Yerushalmi's version of the story reads "Boethusian" or "Sadducean."

[86] It also bears mentioning that according to Josephus, Antiquities 13.372, the villain of the story is Alexander Jannaeus, a Hasmonean king.

[87] The conventional transliteration of this term is *kal ve-homer*. See, however, Hermann L. Strack and Günther Stemberger, *Introduction to the Talmud and Midrash* (Minneapolis: Fortress Press, 1992) 21.

its [property] on the strength of the son's [claim], is it not all the more so that
one's daughter [inherits], since her claim derives directly from the father?" Comparable
arguments are found throughout rabbinic literature; from a rabbinic perspective this
is a perfectly fine argument, an assessment supported by the fact that precisely the
same halakhic argument is used by the Sadducees elsewhere in Palestinian literature,[88] and nowhere else do the Sadducees' interlocutors ridicule them or express
even a hint of contempt.

In addition, the derivative nature of the Baba Batra narrative is indicated by the
fact that the discussion based on the Sadducee's argument has nothing to do with
that argument. In response to the Sadducee, Rabban Yohanan ben Zakkai ostensibly quotes contradictory verses from Genesis 36, one of which describes Ana as
the brother of Tzivon and another of which describes Ana as Tzivon's father; neither this nor the Amoraic responses that follow have anything to do with the
halakhic dispute at hand: whether or not a daughter inherits along with sons. In
contrast, in the Menahot narrative Rabban Yohanan ben Zakkai answers the
Sadducee on the latter's own terms, by means of an argument which directly contradicts the Sadducee's and which bases itself on what is from a rabbinic point of
view the Sadducee's faulty logic (see below). Finally, the discussion based on the
Sadducee's argument contains a series of Amoraic responses, clear indication that
we are dealing with a later interpolation into an originally Tannaitic narrative.[89]

In contrast, the rabbinic audience of the story in b. Menahot 65a–b would readily assent to the story's characterization of the Boethusian's teaching as "worthless
talk," given his outrageous claim that the date of Shavuot was determined by Moses
rather than God ("Moses our rabbi loved Israel and knew that Shavuot lasts only
one day. He therefore ordained that it come after Shabbat so that Israel would
celebrate for two days"). According to the Boethusian, an important feature of the
Jewish calendar is of human rather than divine origin, an absurd, heretical notion
from a rabbinic perspective.

The Boethusian's feeble attempt at a response leads Rabban Yohanan ben Zakkai
to respond in kind with a deliberately feeble argument of his own. The rabbi answers
the Boethusian with an argument which replicates the latter's foolish claim that
Moses rather than God is in control of Israel's destiny: ". . . And if Moses our rabbi
loved Israel, why did he detain them in the desert for 40 years?"

The story in Baba Batra, therefore, is a later editorial reworking (just how late
is not clear) of an earlier story (just how early is also not clear), but it remains the
case that the editors who reworked the story saw fit to retain from the model narrative strikingly negative portrayals and evaluations of the Sadducees, yielding a
story which expresses a level of contempt for the Sadducees which is unparalleled
in Palestinian compilations.

APPENDIX FOUR

[Kind] Yannai and Yohanan [The High Priest] Are One [And the Same
Person]

The ensuing discussion depends on acceptance of the reliability of the attribution
of the statement to Abaye, or at least the feasibility of assigning the statement to
the approximate time and place when Abaye is known to have flourished (the mid-
fourth century C.E. in Babylonia). I am well aware that this position is controver-

---

[88] See the references cited above, n. 16.
[89] See the Tannaitic parallel in t. Yadayimn 2:20.

sial and must be defended, but I discussed above my reasons for venturing onto this methodological limb.

As noted above, it is likely that Abaye, a relatively late Amora who is mentioned on virtually every other page of the Talmud, is acquainted at least partially with the well-documented Babylonian tendency to treat Yannai as a villain. b. Kiddushin 66a, where Abaye quotes a story about King Yannai, supports this claim. This story probably motivates in part Abaye's curious identification of Yohanan the High Priest and Yannai the king, despite their different names and different depictions throughout the Bavli. The story in Kiddushin, furthermore, closely parallels Josephus' account of the decision of John Hyrcanus (= Yohanan the High Priest in rabbinic literature) to leave the Pharisaic party and become a Sadducee. While b. Kiddushin 66a, therefore, never uses the term "Sadducee" (Josephus' version does, however), Abaye in b. Berakhot 29a probably has this story in mind. As we shall observe below, in more than one context the Bavli's later, anonymous editors identify as Sadducean precisely the position which Yannai ultimately accepts in Kiddushin, namely that "the sages" (hakhamim, the usual rabbinic term for "rabbis") can be dispensed with without any diminution of Torah. In other words, Abaye knows and explicitly comments on the brief statement in b. Berakhot 29a that Yohanan the High Priest became a Sadducee late in life; he also knows and quotes the story in b. Kiddushin 66a, which describes King Yannai's adoption of the Sadducean heresy. And it is possible, although not certain, that Abaye is familiar with Josephus' version of the story (or a Josephus-like version; see below), which states explicitly that John Hyrcanus became a Sadducee later in his life.

It will be helpful to remind ourselves what is at stake in concluding that Abaye is acquainted with the Bavli's dominant portrayal of Yannai. If Abaye knows this portrayal, then he views Yannai as extremely wicked, so when he asserts in b. Berakhot 29a that "Yannai and Yohanan are one [and the same person]," we know that Abaye considers Yohanan's conversion to Sadduceeism to have been symptomatic of his depravity. It is likely, therefore, that Abaye's statement further supports our claim regarding the tendency of Babylonian sources to criticize the Sadducees.

It is conceivable, although unlikely, that Abaye does not view the Sadducees quite as negatively as I claimed above, since it is theoretically possible that his knowledge of Yannai is based solely on the narrative which he quotes in b. Kiddushin 66a. As I have noted elsewhere, Yannai in this story is by no means a hero, but he is depicted as passive and totally dependent on his wicked adviser, Elazar ben Poerah.[90] Yannai according to this story brings about the death of the rabbis and the near eradication of their Torah, but the story informs us that "the evil sprouted forth because of Elazar ben Poerah and Yehudah ben Gedidyah." That is, Yannai according to this account is hardly praiseworthy, but he is more the hapless agent of an unscrupulous villain than actively evil himself. It is conceivable, although unlikely, that Abaye does not share the Bavli's dominant view regarding Yannai, in which case the Pesikta and the Bavli are perhaps not very different in their evaluation of Sadducees after all.

I consider this possibility unlikely because there is additional evidence that Abaye was acquainted with a more negative view of Yannai, such that when he identifies Yohanan and Yannai in Berakhot, he probably has in mind Yannai the murderous heretic rather than Yannai the passive simpleton.

---

[90] With the exception of the opening scene, which, however, probably derives from a different source than the rest of the story. See Kalmin, "Kings, Priests, and Sages," 79.

What is the proof of this claim? Rav Nahman bar Yizhak claims in Kiddushin 66a that "Immediately heresy [*epikorsut*] was cast into [Yannai],"[91] according to which Yannai accepted Elazar ben Poerah's claim that Torah would not be adversely affected by the demise of the sages, because "it is bound up and placed in the corner; whoever wants to learn can come and learn." We had more to say about Rav Nahman bar Yizhak's statement above; in this context it suffices to note its depiction of Yannai as more than the passive puppet of an evil mastermind. The fact that Rav Nahman bar Yizhak goes beyond the story and describes Yannai as a heretic (thereby implying more initiative on Yannai's part than is strictly warranted by the story) suggests that he knows at least something of Yannai's portrayal elsewhere in the Talmud, which increases the likelihood that Abaye, Rav Nahman bar Yizhak's older Babylonian contemporary, also knows something of this portrayal.[92] Abaye in b. Berakhot 29a most likely views Yohanan the Sadducee as Yannai the murderous miscreant; part of the discussion in b. Berakhot 29a, therefore, goes beyond the Pesikta in its negative assessment of the Sadducees.

---

[91] See above for a fuller discussion of this story.

[92] The Munich manuscript, incidentally, attributes the statement to "Abaye, and some say Rav Nahman bar Yizhak." Obviously if the reading "Abaye" is correct, the support for my claim is even stronger.

INDEX

SUPPLEMENTS

TO THE

JOURNAL FOR THE STUDY OF JUDAISM

49. LIETAERT PEERBOLTE, L.J. *The Antecedents of Antichrist.* A Traditio-Historical Study of the Earliest Christian Views on Eschatological Opponents. 1996. ISBN 90 04 10455 0

50. YARBRO COLLINS, A. *Cosmology and Eschatology in Jewish and Christian Apocalypticism.* 1996. ISBN 90 04 10587 5

51. MENN, E. *Judah and Tamar (Genesis 38) in Ancient Jewish Exegesis.* Studies in Literary Form and Hermeneutics. 1997. ISBN 90 04 10630 8

52. NEUSNER, J. *Jerusalem and Athens.* The Congruity of Talmudic and Classical Philosophy. 1996. ISBN 90 04 10698 7

54. COLLINS, J.J. *Seers, Sibyls & Sages in Hellenistic-Roman Judaism.* 1997. ISBN 90 04 10752 5

55. BAUMGARTEN, A.I. *The Flourishing of Jewish Sects in the Maccabean Era: An Interpretation.* 1997. ISBN 90 04 10751 7

56. SCOTT, J.M. (ed.). *Exile: Old Testament, Jewish, and Christian Conceptions.* 1997. ISBN 90 04 10676 6

57. HENTEN, J-.W. VAN. *The Maccabean Martyrs as Saviours of the Jewish People.* A Study of 2 and 4 Maccabees. 1997. ISBN 90 04 10976 5

58. FELDMAN, L.H. *Studies in Josephus' Rewritten Bible.* 1998. ISBN 90 04 10839 4

59. MORRAY-JONES, C.R.A. *A Transparent Illusion.* The Dangerous Vision of Water in Hekhalot Mysticism: A Source-Critical and Tradition-Historical Inquiry. 2002. ISBN 90 04 11337 1

60. HALPERN-AMARU, B. *The Empowerment of Women in the* Book of Jubilees. 1999. ISBN 90 04 11414 9

61. HENZE, M. *The Madness of King Nebuchadnezzar.* The Ancient Near Eastern Origins and Early History of Interpretation of Daniel 4. 1999. ISBN 90 04 11421 1

62. VANDERKAM, J.C. *From Revelation to Canon.* Studies in the Hebrew Bible and Second Tempel Literature. 2000. ISBN 90 04 11557 9

63. NEWMAN, C.C., J.R. DAVILA & G.S. LEWIS (eds.). *The Jewish Roots of Christological Monotheism.* Papers from the St. Andrews Conference on the Historical Origins of the Worship of Jesus. 1999. ISBN 90 04 11361 4

64. LIESEN, J.W.M. *Full of Praise.* An Exegetical Study of Sir 39,12-35. 1999. ISBN 90 04 11359 2

65. BEDFORD, P.R. *Temple Restoration in Early Achaemenid Judah.* 2000. ISBN 90 04 11509 9

66. RUITEN, J.T.A.G.M. VAN. *Primaeval History Interpreted.* The Rewriting of Genesis 1-11 in the book of Jubilees. 2000. ISBN 90 04 11658 3

67. HOFMANN, N.J. *Die Assumptio Mosis.* Studien zur Rezeption massgültiger Überlieferung. 2000. ISBN 90 04 11938 8

68. HACHLILI, R. *The Menorah, the Ancient Seven-armed Candelabrum.* Origin, Form and Significance. 2001. ISBN 90 04 12017 3

69. VELTRI, G. *Gegenwart der Tradition.* Studien zur jüdischen Literatur und Kulturgeschichte. 2002. ISBN 90 04 11686 9

70. DAVILA, J.R. *Descenders to the Chariot.* The People behind the Hekhalot Literature. 2001. ISBN 90 04 11541 2

71. PORTER, S.E. & J.C.R. DE ROO (eds.). *The Concept of the Covenant in the Second Temple Period.* 2003. ISBN 90 04 11609 5

72. SCOTT, J.M. (ed.). *Restoration.* Old Testament, Jewish, and Christian Perspectives. 2001. ISBN 90 04 11580 3

73. TORIJANO, P.A. *Solomon the Esoteric King.* From King to Magus, Development of a Tradition. 2002. ISBN 90 04 11941 8

74. KUGEL, J.L. *Shem in the Tents of Japhet.* Essays on the Encounter of Judaism and Hellenism. 2002. ISBN 90 04 12514 0

75. COLAUTTI, F.M. *Passover in the Works of Josephus.* 2002. ISBN 90 04 12372 5

76. BERTHELOT, K. *Philanthrôpia judaica.* Le débat autour de la "misanthropie" des lois juives dans l'Antiquité. 2003. ISBN 90 04 12886 7

77. NAJMAN, H. *Seconding Sinai.* The Development of Mosaic Discourse in Second Temple Judaism. 2003. ISBN 90 04 11542 0

78. MULDER, O. *Simon the High Priest in Sirach 50.* An Exegetical Study of the Significance of Simon the High Priest as Climax to the Praise of the Fathers in Ben Sira's Concept of the History of Israel. 2003. ISBN 90 04 12316 4

79. BURKES, S.L. *God, Self, and Death.* The Shape of Religious Transformation in the Second Temple Period. 2003. ISBN 90 04 12954 5

80. NEUSNER, J. & A.J. AVERY-PECK (eds.). *George W.E. Nickelsburg in Perspective.* An Ongoing Dialogue of Learning (2 vols.). 2003. ISBN 90 04 12987 1 (set)

81. COBLENTZ BAUTCH, K. *A Study of the Geography of 1 Enoch 17-19.* "No One Has Seen What I Have Seen". 2003. ISBN 90 04 13103 5

82. GARCÍA MARTÍNEZ, F., & G.P. LUTTIKHUIZEN. *Jerusalem, Alexandria, Rome.* Studies in Ancient Cultural Interaction in Honour of A. Hilhorst. 2003. ISBN 90 04 13584 7

83. NAJMAN, H. & J.H. NEWMAN (eds.). *The Idea of Biblical Interpretation.* Essays in Honor of James L. Kugel. 2004. ISBN 90 04 13630 4

84. ATKINSON, K. *I Cried to the Lord*. A Study of the Psalms of Solomon's Historical Background and Social Setting. 2004. ISBN 90 04 13614 2

85. AVERY-PECK, A.J., D. HARRINGTON & J. NEUSNER. *When Judaism and Christianity Began*. Essays in Memory of Anthony J. Saldarini. 2004. ISBN 90 04 13659 2 (Set), ISBN 90 04 13660 6 (Volume I), ISBN 90 04 13661 4 (Volume II)

86. DRAWNEL, H. *An Aramaic Wisdom Text from Qumran*. A New Interpretation of the Levi Document. 2004. ISBN 90 04 13753 X. *In Preparation*

87. BERTHELOT, K. *L'«humanité de l'autre homme» dans la pensée juive ancienne*. 2004. ISBN 90 04 13797 1

88. BONS, E. (ed.) *«Car c'est l'amour qui me plaît, non le sacrifice ...»*. Recherches sur Osée 6:6 et son interprétation juive et chrétienne. 2004. ISBN 90 04 13677 0

89. CHAZON, E.G., D. SATRAN & R. CLEMENTS. (eds.) *Things Revealed*. Studies in Honor of Michael E. Stone. 2004. ISBN 90 04 13885 4. *In Preparation*

91. SCOTT, J.M. *On Earth as in Heaven*. The Restoration of Sacred Time and Sacred Space in the Book of Jubilees. 2005. ISBN 90 04 13796 3

92. RICHARDSON, P. *Building Jewish in the Roman East*. 2005. ISBN 90 04 14131 6.

93. BATSCH, C. *La guerre et les rites de guerre dans le judaïsme du deuxième Temple*. 2005. ISBN 90 04 13897 8.

94. HACHLILI, R. *Jewish Funerary Customs, Practices and Rites in the Second Temple Period*. 2005. ISBN 90 04 12373 3.

95. BAKHOS, C. *Ancient Judaism in its Hellenistic Context*. 2005. ISBN 90 04 13871 4

ISSN 1384-2161